YOUR GUIDE TO
Survey Research Using the SAS® System

Archer R. Gravely

Comments or Questions?

The authors assume complete responsibility for the technical accuracy of the content of this book. If you have any questions about the material in this book, please write to the authors at this address:

SAS Institute Inc.
Books by Users
Attn: Archer R. Gravely
SAS Campus Drive
Cary, NC 27513

If you prefer, you can send e-mail to sasbbu@sas.com with "comments for Archer R. Gravely" as the subject line, or you can fax the Books by Users program at (919) 677-4444.

The correct bibliographic citation for this manual is as follows: Gravely, Archer R., *Your Guide to Survey Research Using the SAS® System*, Cary, NC: SAS Institute Inc., 1998. 304 pp.

Your Guide to Survey Research Using the SAS® System

Copyright © 1998 by SAS Institute Inc., Cary, NC, USA.

ISBN 1-58025-146-3

1st printing, February 1998

Table of Contents

Acknowledgments

The foundations for this book emerged from a series of professional development workshops sponsored by the Association for Institutional Research (1990 to 1997). I would like to thank a number of people who have contributed to this work.

I owe a special note of thanks to two of my University of North Carolina at Asheville colleagues. Ken Wilson taught this nonprogrammer how to do the more advanced DATA step programming that is included in this book. I am very appreciative of Tom Cochran and UNC Asheville for providing me with a Macintosh Power-Book computer, which gave me the flexibility to work away from the office. I would also like to express my thanks to UNC Asheville for allowing me to use institutional survey data for the numerous examples in the book.

All of the folks at SAS Institute have been extremely helpful and a joy to work with. My editors, Hanna Schoenrock, Aaron Bittner, and Caroline Brickley have been a constant source of cheerful guidance in helping me to complete this work. Wanda Verreault was most helpful in developing procedures for integrating SAS/GRAPH output into Microsoft Word. I would also like to thank Candy Farrell, Nancy Mitchell, Gray Lewis, and Jeannie Keating Pope for their work in producing, designing, and marketing the book.

This book has greatly benefited from the suggestions and comments of a number of reviewers. I would like to thank the following SAS Institute reviewers for their contributions based on an expert knowledge of SAS procedures and statistics: Kristin Rahn, Brent Cohen, Jack Berry, Kathy Kiraly, and Bob Lucas. The following outside reviewers also provided useful criticisms and suggestions from the perspective of professional survey practice: Tom Bohannon (Baylor University), Keith Brown (UNC-General Administration), Robert Hill (UNC-General Administration), Denise Gardner (N.C. State University), David Cartwright (East Carolina University), and Kitty Klein (N.C. State University).

Last, and most important, I would like to thank my family: Sandra, Jessica, and Will, for their patience and understanding of the demands that this book has placed on my time over the last year.

Using This Book

This book uses the following type style conventions:

CAPITAL LETTERS

>   are used for literal elements of the SAS language such as procedure and statement names, as well as for the names of data sets and variables.

`nonproportional lowercase letters`

>   are used for SAS example programs and statements and for the values of character variables.

italics

>   is used for arguments or for user-supplied values such as *variable-name*. It is also used for emphasis in the text.

Finally, SAS statements or procedure steps that are featured in the text are highlighted (shaded) to make them easy to see in the sample programs.

Using the SAS® System to Apply General Principles of Efficient Survey Research

Chapter 1

Introduction

As one of the more widely used general-purpose software products, the SAS System is the ideal tool to use in survey research applications. This book is designed for survey research practitioners who have some experience with basic SAS DATA step programming. Although these advanced beginners and intermediate-level SAS users are the primary audience for this book, experienced researchers and SAS programmers should also find helpful information on reporting survey results in tables and graphs that exemplify the principles of graphical excellence. The sophistication of the material ranges from basic to advanced, but we have always tried to respect the needs of new users.

The beauty of the SAS System is that it enables an intermediate-level user, who developed skill through on-the-job training or nonformal instruction, to perform complex data analyses, data/file manipulation, and report-writing tasks in less time than the formally trained computer science graduate would require using basic languages. Readers will be shown how to use SAS to manage a personalized survey research process, report the results in customized tables and graphs, and perform data and file manipulation tasks that are common to all survey research applications. The major contribution of this book is the integration of information culled from numerous SAS Institute publications, classic survey methodology, principles of graphical excellence, and many years of survey research experience into a single source targeted to the needs of the survey research practitioner. Some of the major topics addressed are

- Selecting random samples

- Generating ID numbers

- Storing samples in ASCII or in SAS data sets

- Merging files to combine institutional records with survey data

- Generating personalized letters and envelopes

- Tracking respondents and conducting follow-up mailings

- Performing basic statistical analyses

- Reporting results in custom-designed tables and graphs.

To illustrate the use of SAS in the survey process, we will show examples of survey questions, SAS code, and resulting output. In a few cases, the SAS code shown may not be the most elegant or efficient, as our intention is to enable researchers with basic to intermediate-level SAS skills to accomplish sophisticated survey computing tasks without programmer support. Given the importance of decisions often made on the basis of survey research findings, we think that it is critical for users to have the confidence in their work that is inspired by an intuitive understanding of the SAS code used to conduct the survey process and to report the findings. In today's computing and business environment, these objectives are far more important than programming efficiency and the use of CPU time.

Resources/Manuals

As a comprehensive, flexible system, SAS can meet the computing needs of both novices and advanced users in providing solutions to virtually any research application such as:

- Data analysis

- Report writing

- Graphics

- Data manipulation

- File manipulation

- Data entry.

The power and flexibility of the SAS System is reflected in extensive documentation that is often intimidating to beginners. Listed below are useful SAS resources as well as resources written outside the Institute that cover conducting and reporting survey research.

- *Introduction to Market Research Using the SAS System*

- *SAS Language: Reference, Version 6, First Edition*

- *SAS Procedures Guide, Version 6, Third Edition*

- *SAS Language and Procedures: Usage 2, Version 6, First Edition*

- *SAS/STAT User's Guide, Version 6, Fourth Edition, Volume 1* and *2*

- *SAS/GRAPH Software: Reference, Version 6, First Edition, Volume 1* and *2*

- *SAS Guide to TABULATE Processing, Second Edition*

- *SAS/STAT Software: Changes and Enhancements through Release 6.12*

- SAS Technical Support on the World Wide Web: http://www.sas.com/service/techsup/intro.html

- *SAS Users Group International on the Internet and on Usenet*[1]

- *Mail and Telephone Surveys: The Total Design Method,* by Don A. Dillman, John Wiley & Sons, 1978.

- *How to Conduct Your Own Survey,* by Priscilla Salant and Don A. Dillman. John Wiley & Sons, 1994.

- The *Visual Display of Quantitative Information,* by Edward R. Tufte. Graphics Press, 1983.

- *Elementary Survey Sampling,* 2nd Edition, by Richard L. Scheaffer, William Mendenhall, and Lyman Ott. Duxbury Press, 1979.

General Principles of Efficient Survey Practice

Avoid asking respondents for information that is available through electronic records. It is surprising how much this rule is violated, probably because the investigators are not using SAS or they lack the necessary skills or computer support to manipulate data files. In many survey projects, the samples are either drawn from or can be electronically linked to organizational databases (e.g., student records, personnel files, car registration records, membership files, etc.) that contain a wealth of demographic information to assist in the analysis of research questions. It is important to note that mail and telephone surveys, because of cost, time, and reliability factors, are usually the least desirable method of data collection. A survey should only be undertaken if the data cannot be obtained from alternative sources. The advantages of not asking respondents to report information that can be

---

[1] See Appendix A for A Beginners Guide to SAS-L and Appendix B for additional SAS World Wide Web Resources.

obtained from other sources are three-fold: shorter survey forms and less cost; increased response rates; and more accurate or complete information. Respondents may also have a greater feeling of confidentiality if they are not asked to report personal characteristics such as grade point average, salary, age, race, sex, length of service, etc. If available in electronic form, this type of information can be merged with survey responses using ID numbers to create a combined file for analysis. An exception to this principle is found in surveys of sensitive topics (e.g., drug use, personnel/program assessment) where respondent identification numbers are not used to ensure respondents that their responses are not only confidential but anonymous.

Obtain high response rates by using a personalized survey design. The personalization of mail surveys (cover letters with individual names in upper- and lowercase, correct use of Mr. or Ms., etc.) will greatly enhance the professional appearance of the survey product and significantly increase response rates. SAS functions and procedures are designed to facilitate the computer tasks required to achieve a high degree of personalization in the survey process with a minimal amount of effort. Dillman's (1978) work[2] remains a classic primer on the use of personalization techniques, question formatting, cover design, and the tricks of the trade in obtaining high response rates.

Standardize procedures for conducting surveys. The use of standardized procedures and SAS programs in implementing a personalized mail survey and conducting follow-up mailings will enable clerical staff to administer the survey process with minimal supervision. Procedures for creating and editing name and address files, generating cover letters, envelopes, mailing labels, and keeping track of survey respondents can be standardized for numerous survey projects. For surveys repeated over time, the survey process and the reporting of findings can become routine and far less time-consuming than most one-time data collection and analysis projects. SAS macro language commands can be used to make numerous update revisions to filenames and to TITLE statements in longitudinal analyses based on different data sets for each reporting cycle.

Create camera-ready tables and graphs with SAS. By creating final tables and graphs directly with SAS, you save a tremendous amount of labor and greatly reduce the probability of typographical errors in reporting the survey findings. SAS/GRAPH software can produce color or gray scale graphs on almost any type of printer or graphic device. Custom-designed statistical tables can be created directly with SAS using PROC TABULATE and other procedures. SAS output can also be downloaded to word processing and spreadsheet programs on a

---

2 D. A. Dilllman, *Mail and Telephone Surveys: The Total Design Method* (New York: John Wiley & Sons, 1978).

microcomputer. We have found it to be much more efficient and rewarding to use the full capabilities of the SAS System to produce camera-ready output than to re-key SAS output into a word processor or graphics program.

Overview of SAS Procedures Used in Survey Research

The SAS System contains numerous procedures for manipulating, analyzing, and reporting data. These procedures are called procs, and it is important to note that SAS procs perform operations on variables *across* observations or records. SAS functions, which are discussed in the next section, perform operations on variables *within* a record. This section will present a brief description of procs that are useful in virtually all survey research applications. Readers not familiar with some of these procs will find time spent reviewing the details in the *SAS Procedures Guide* to be well spent.

PROC FREQ

PROC FREQ is probably the single most useful SAS procedure for reporting data. As the name implies, PROC FREQ generates frequency tables and cross-tabs. PROC FREQ can also be used to perform chi square tests of independence. A limitation of PROC FREQ is that it will produce lengthy output for multiple cross-tabulations. For example, income group by race by sex will produce a table (race by sex) and a separate page for each value of income group.

PROC SORT

PROC SORT is used to order observations according to the values of a specified variable(s). The sort order can be *ascending* or *descending*. PROC SORT is useful for arranging data prior to printing and is often used to order files according to an identification number prior to merging with another file. PROC SORT can also be used to eliminate records with duplicate values of a specified variable.

PROC PRINT

PROC PRINT is used to print a SAS data set. In survey applications, PROC PRINT is used to list names and addresses prior to generating personalized letters and envelopes. Additionally, PROC PRINT is often used as an edit procedure for printing observations that have unusually high/low or invalid values. Several SAS procedures create output data sets, and PROC PRINT must be used to view them.

PROC MEANS

PROC MEANS provides basic descriptive statistics (mean, N, standard deviation, kurtosis, etc.). PROC SORT and PROC MEANS (with a BY statement) can be used to analyze variables within subgroups, e.g., income by race and sex.

PROC UNIVARIATE

PROC UNIVARIATE is similar to PROC MEANS but provides a more comprehensive set of descriptive statistics. It is important to note that PROC UNIVARIATE is one of the few SAS procedures that will generate the median[3] statistic. PROC UNIVARIATE will also provide normality plots and perform a test of normality for the sample distribution of the data. Similar to PROC FREQ, PROC UNIVARIATE will produce lengthy output when numerous variables are specified or subgroup analyses are requested.

PROC SUMMARY

PROC SUMMARY is very useful for producing descriptive statistics (sum, N, means, standard deviation) for analysis variables by one or more subgroups or classification variables in a condensed output. By default, PROC SUMMARY produces an output data set and *no* printed output. The PROC SUMMARY output file may be printed with PROC PRINT. PROC SUMMARY is very useful for complex data manipulations and for creating aggregated data sets for displaying data in graphical form.

PROC TABULATE

PROC TABULATE is designed to produce customized tables and is *ideally* suited for reporting the results of survey research. PROC TABULATE will generate descriptive statistics[4] (sum, N, mean, standard deviation), percentages, and calculate row and column totals. PROC TABULATE provides intermediate-level users with total control over column and row formatting. This powerful SAS procedure will enable nonprogrammers to generate customized camera-ready output.

PROC FORMAT

PROC FORMAT is one of the more powerful, but underused, procedures in the SAS System. It is primarily used to assign value labels in printed output to enhance the readability of a report. It can also be used to efficiently group variable values into a smaller number of categories. This type of data manipulation is usually done in the DATA step with IF, THEN, and ELSE statements, but it can actually be done more efficiently with PROC FORMAT.

PROC CORR

In addition to basic descriptive statistics, PROC CORR provides a correlation (Pearson Product Moment, Spearman, Kendall, Hoeffding) matrix and descriptive statistics for each numeric variable that is included in the analysis. PROC CORR will also compute a reliability index (Cronbach's Coefficient Alpha) for a specified set of psychometric scale items.

---

[3] Medians can also be generated by PROC FREQ (base SAS) and PROC CAPABILITY (SAS/QC).

[4] PROC TABULATE does not compute medians in Version 6 of the SAS System. The median statistic is available in the TABULATE procedure in Version 7.

PROC CHART/GCHART

PROC CHART and PROC GCHART generate vertical and horizontal histograms and pie charts. PROC CHART is part of the base SAS product and will not produce customized output of presentation quality. PROC GCHART is part of the SAS/GRAPH product and gives users full control over color, fonts, labeling, and choice of symbols and patterns.

PROC PLOT/GPLOT

PROC PLOT and PROC GPLOT create line and scatter plots. PROC PLOT is part of the base SAS product and will not produce customized output. Like PROC GCHART, PROC GPLOT is part of the SAS/GRAPH product and provides users with full control over color, fonts, labeling, and choice of symbols.

PROC CONTENTS

PROC CONTENTS is used to display the characteristics (variable names, data type, number of observations, variable length, date created, etc.) of a SAS data set. SAS can be used to read and save ASCII files or SAS data sets. SAS data sets are especially useful for research applications as they have the following advantages:

- Self-documenting

- No input statement for reading file

- Reduced processing time and disk storage requirements.

PROC RANK

PROC RANK is used for computing ranks for numeric variables. This procedure creates a new SAS data set. PROC RANK can also generate normal scores. PROC RANK can be used for nonparametric statistical analyses and as a tool for selecting random samples (see Chapter 2).

SAS Functions and Automatic Variables

SAS functions are preprogrammed routines for performing operations on variables *within* an observation. The procs that were reviewed in the previous section perform operations *across* observations. There are a number of SAS functions that are designed to manipulate character data and to perform mathematical operations that are essential to efficient survey research practice. The character manipulation functions (TRIM, CONCATENATE, SUBSTR) are often used to transform name and address variables to meet the data requirements for a personalized mail survey process. Examples of how these functions are used are presented in Chapter 3.

SAS automatic variables are created by the SAS System and can be used in the DATA step to control which observations are output. This section will describe the use of the IF FIRST.*varname* and IF LAST.*varname* as a method of eliminating observations with duplicate ID values.

CONCATENATE: Combine Variables

The CONCATENATION function is used to combine two or more character variables into a single character string as a new variable. The concatenation operator symbols || are used to concatenate variables. In the example below, NAME1 is a new variable that is created by concatenating FNAME and LNAME with a blank space between the two variables.

```
data address;
    input  @1 fname  $10   @12 lname  $20.;
    name1 = fname||lname;
    cards;
John Smith
;
```

Note: The value of NAME1 is `John   Smith` The TRIM function described in the following section will remove the extra spaces between the first and last name.

TRIM Function: Remove Trailing Blanks

TRIM is used to remove trailing blanks in a text string. Trailing blanks occur when a variable is defined as having a maximum of X characters, but a particular observation uses *less* than the X length or number of characters. SAS will pad the used length with blanks. To illustrate, in the preceding example, the variable FNAME is concatenated with LNAME and the resulting new NAME1 variable has six unneeded blank spaces between the two names. The unnecessary blanks are included in NAME1 because `John` is four characters long and the variable FNAME was defined in the INPUT statement to have a width of ten characters. The solution to the trailing blanks problem is the TRIM function.

```
name2 = trim(fname)||' '||trim(lname);
```

Note: The value of NAME2 is `John Smith`.

SUBSTR: Extract Part of a Variable

The SUBSTR function is used to extract a character variable into two or more separate elements. The SUBSTR function can also be used on numeric variables, but this is not recommended as the results can be unpredictable. To substring numeric variables, the best approach is to first use the PUT function (described later in this section) to convert a numeric variable to a character string and then to use SUBSTR. The form of the SUBSTR function is

```
newvar = substr(oldvar,x,y);
```

Where:

```
newvar = new variable to be created.


oldvar = previously defined variable.

x = starting position/character of OLDVAR to begin SUBSTR
    operation.

y = ending position/character of OLDVAR to end SUBSTR
    operation.
```

SUBSTR Example	
`yr_mo = '9701';`	
	Result
`year = substr(yr_mo,1,2);`	97
`month = substr(yr_mo,3,4);`	01

UPCASE/LOWCASE: Change Variable Casing

The SAS functions UPCASE and LOWCASE are used for reversing the case of character strings. The use of all uppercase text in survey communications is to be avoided as it gives the appearance of "junk mail." However, it is not uncommon for survey researchers to have to work with names and addresses that are stored in electronic data files as all uppercase characters. When researchers are presented with all uppercase name and address text, these functions are useful tools for personalizing survey cover letters and envelopes (see Chapter 5). The UPCASE and LOWCASE functions can be used with SUBSTR to selectively modify the case of a character string. Additionally, these functions can be used to standardize the case of character variables that have been stored inconsistently.

```
                     UPCASE/LOWCASE Examples

make = 'FORD';
model = 'taurus';
name = 'MCDONALD';
                                                                Result
make = LOWCASE(MAKE);                                           ford
model = UPCASE(MODEL);                                          TAURUS
substr(name,2,1) = lowcase(substr(name,2,1));                   McDONALD
substr(name,4,5) = lowcase(substr(name,4,5));                   McDonald
```

PUT: Convert Numeric Variables to Character

The PUT function converts numeric variables to character strings. Numeric variables should be converted to character strings before concatenation or substringing operations are performed. PUT can also be used to create a new variable that takes the values defined in a FORMAT statement. This is useful for sorting the values according to the format label rather than the variable value. The PUT function always results in a *character* string. Character-to-numeric conversions can be handled with the INPUT function as discussed in the next section.

The form of the PUT function is

    newvar = put(oldvar,format);

Where:

    newvar = new character variable.

    oldvar = existing numeric variable.

    format = width of character variable to be created
    (e.g., $3.).

In the following example, YEAR is initially defined as a numeric variable and is redefined as the character variable YR_CHAR.

```
    PUT Example

year = 98;
yr_char = put(year,$2);
```

INPUT: Convert Character Variables to Numeric

The INPUT function converts character to numeric variables. In working with permanent SAS data sets, you may need to perform numerical operations on variables that have been defined and saved with character formats. The form of the INPUT function is

newvar = INPUT(*oldvar*, *format*);

Where:

newvar = new numeric variable.

oldvar = existing character variable.

format = width and decimal specification of numeric variable to be created (e.g. , 3.0).

In the following example, TEMP is defined as a character variable and redefined as a numeric variable TEMP_N.

INPUT Example

```
temp = '98.6';
temp_n = input(temp,4.1);
```

SUM: Add Variable Values within an Observation

As the name suggests, the SUM function adds the values of two or more variables *within* an observation and stores them as a new variable. The SUM function is very useful in scoring questionnaire items and creating scale scores. This type of operation can also be done without the SUM function by using the SAS arithmetic operators (+ = / * -). The key difference between the two methods is in how they handle missing data. The SUM function will *ignore* missing data as it sums the remaining variables specified. Conversely, when the + operator encounters a missing value, the sum of the expression is set to missing. Note also that survey research projects nearly always have a considerable amount of missing data. Here is an example of how the SUM function is used to add the values for survey items within an observation:

```
scale1 = sum(q01,q02,q03,q04);
```

MEAN: Average Variables within an Observation

The MEAN function calculates the arithmetic average of a specified list of variables *within* an observation. (Recall from the previous section that PROC MEANS computes descriptive statistics *across* observations.) The same operation can also be performed for each observation using the SAS + and / operators. The advantage of the MEAN function is that it automatically determines the appropriate denominator and adjusts the denominator for missing values. This is a very useful feature for processing survey data and eliminates the tedious coding that would be needed to perform these functions using SAS arithmetic operators. An example of the MEAN function follows:

```
avg1 = mean(q01,q02,q03,q04);
```

RANUNI: Generate Random Numbers

Most mail and telephone surveys are based on random sampling procedures, and SAS has a number of powerful functions for generating random numbers. RANUNI is recommended as a good all-purpose random number generator. RANUNI must be supplied a seed value to generate random numbers. The seed can be a string of numbers, e.g., 12345 or the value 0. If a nonzero string is used, RANUNI can duplicate the same results in a later run if the source file has not changed. If the value 0 is used, the seed value is based on the clock time of your host computer and cannot be replicated in a later run. Here are two examples of using RANUNI for random sampling.

RANUNI Example	
`if ranuni(12345) <= .5;`	takes an approximate 50% random sample of observations that are read into a DATA step.
`x = ranuni(12345);`	creates a variable named X that contains a randomly generated number for each observation that can be manipulated to select a random sample of observations (see Chapter 2).

IF FIRST.*varname*/IF LAST.*varname*: Eliminate Duplicate Records

It is not uncommon to work with data sets that have multiple records with duplicate ID values. IF FIRST.*varname* or IF LAST.*varname* can be used to select a single ID value based on the order specified. IF FIRST.*varname* and IF LAST.*varname* are SAS automatic variables that are created when a BY statement is used in the DATA step. Before a BY statement can be used in the DATA step, the file must be presorted by the variable specified in the BY statement. In the example to follow, the highest SAT score is selected for students who have taken the test more than once. You could use the NODUP option on PROC SORT, but you would not necessarily get the highest SAT for each student. The NODUP option on PROC SORT is useful when it doesn't matter which duplicate record is selected.

IF FIRST.varname/If LAST.varname Example

```
data scores;
   input @1 id $3. @5 yr_mo $4. @10 sat 4. ;
   cards;
001  9704    970
001  9803   1100
002  9803    950
002  9704   1000
003  9803   1300
003  9704   1200
004  9704    850
004  9803    970
;
proc sort data = scores; by id sat;

data highest;
   set scores; by id;
if last.id;

proc print data = highest;
title 'Highest SAT Scores by ID';
```

```
                                13:40 Tuesday, June 18, 1998
     Highest SAT Scores by ID

       OBS    ID    YR_MO       SAT

        1    001    9803       1100
        2    002    9704       1000
        3    003    9803       1300
        4    004    9803        970
```

Note: IF FIRST.*varname* is used in exactly the same way as IF LAST.*varname* to remove duplicate observations. The only difference is in whether the first or last occurrence of a multiple ID value is output to the SAS data set created.

ROUND: Eliminate Extra Decimals

The ROUND function is used to eliminate unnecessary decimals when printing custom reports. Most SAS analysis procedures will produce output with eight decimal places. For most types of survey data, this level of precision is artificial and too detailed for a custom report. For ordinal and interval type data, we think it is good practice to report only one decimal place for means or percentages. The ROUND function allows you to specify the number of decimal places to retain with appropriate rounding. You can modify an existing variable and keep the same name or create a new variable. Here is an example of the ROUND function.

ROUND Example	
x = 4.14639	
	Result
x1 = round(x,1);	4
x1 = round(x,.1);	4.1
x1 = round(x,.01);	4.15
x1 = round(x,.0001);	4.1464

Chapter

2 Creating Survey Files

Introduction

Most survey research projects require a common set of data management tasks that can be handled extremely well by the SAS System. This chapter will illustrate how to use the SAS System to perform a variety of survey research data management and file-building tasks.

Determining Sample Size

One of the first steps in planning a survey project is to determine the sample size. This decision is usually a compromise between the desired maximum sampling error and resources available to conduct the survey. To determine the sample size, consider the following factors:

- Population size

- Desired sampling error

- Costs and budget for data collection

- Estimate of variance for key variables.

An estimate of the population variance can be obtained from previous research or estimated with a pilot study. If the key variable of interest is measured as a percentage or proportion, which is often the case in survey research, a proportion estimate of .5 can be used to calculate the sample size needed to obtain a specified sampling error. The use of $p = .5$ is a conservative approach as this value yields the maximum possible variance and hence a larger required sample size than would be needed for other p values. Two SAS programs are shown to assist in making the calculations needed to make survey sampling decisions.[1] The first program provides a procedure for calculating the *required* sample size for a specified error rate in the estimation of a proportion or percentage variable. The results of this program are shown in **Output 2-1**. The second program calculates the *sample error* for a given sample size, observed proportion (p), and population size (N) as shown in **Output 2-2**.

SAS Code to Determine Sample Size

```
options ls=80 nodate nonumber;

data compute;
************** Define Parameters ****************;
N = 2000;    ** Population Size              **;
p = .5;      ** Estimated Sample Proportion  **;
b = .05;     ** Bound on the Error of Estimation **;
****************************************************;
q = 1-p;
d = (b*b)/4;
sample = (N*p*q)/(((N-1)*d)+(p*q));

proc print data = compute label;
id N;
var p b sample;
label  N = 'Population Size'
       p = 'Estimated Proportion'
  sample = 'Sample Size Needed'
       b = 'Sampling Error';
title1 'Needed Sample Size';
run;
```

[1] The formulas used in these examples are documented in R. Scheaffer, W. Mendenhall, and L. Ott, *Elementary Survey Sampling*, 2nd Edition (North Scituate, Mass.: Duxbury Press, 1979), 46-48.

Output 2-1: Sample Size Calculations

```
                        Needed Sample Size

                                              Sample
         Population      Estimated    Sampling   Size
           Size          Proportion    Error    Needed
           2000            0.5         0.05    333.472
```

As shown in **Output 2-1**, for a population size of 2,000, a sample size of 334 is needed to have a maximum sampling error of .05 in estimating a proportion. It is important to note that, for mail surveys, the sample size will need to be *increased to allow for nonresponses*. In this example, the 334-sample-size figure is the number of *completed surveys* needed; if you mail to only 334 individuals, you will undoubtedly have a number of nonresponses and thus a sampling error greater than .05. Using Dillman's (1978) survey techniques, we can usually get a response rate of 60% to mail surveys. Therefore, using this example, we would select a random sample 334/.60 or 557 to allow for a 40% nonresponse and a yield of 334 completed surveys. A generalized statement of this adjustment[2] for nonresponse is as follows:

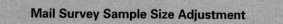

Mail Survey Sample Size Adjustment

Adjusted Sample Size = (Sample Size Needed/Estimated Response Rate)

It is often of interest to determine the amount of sampling error for a given sample size, observed proportion value, and population size. The SAS program to follow will compute the error when these parameters are defined in the DATA step as shown in the following program. The results are shown in **Output 2-2**.

---

[2] It is important to note that this sample size adjustment does not address the issue of nonresponse bias or the extent to which respondents to a mail survey differ systematically from nonrespondents.

SAS Code to Determine Sampling Error

```
options nodate nonumber ls=80;

data sample;
******* Define Parameters **********;
p = .15;        ** Sample Proportion **;
N = 3000;       ** Population Size    **;
sample = 100; ** Sample size         **;
***********************************;
error = 2*(sqrt(((p*(1-p))/(sample-1))*(N-sample)/N));
error = round(error,.01);

proc print data=sample;
id N;
var sample p error;
title1 'Bound on the Error of Estimation';
run;
```

Output 2-2: Sampling Error Calculations

```
                Bound on the Error of Estimation
          N      SAMPLE      P        ERROR
         3000     100      0.15       0.07
```

Simple Random Sampling

A simple random sample is the selection of a subset of observations from a population using a process where every observation has an equal probability of being selected. The random sampling example to follow is based on the RANUNI function. The method shown will provide an exact number of randomly selected observations. There are more sophisticated ways (i.e., fewer but more complicated commands) of using SAS to select random samples, but the method shown works well and is easily understood by beginner- and intermediate-level users.

Selecting a Simple Random Sample

SAS Code	Comments

`data simple;`
`input @1 ssn 9 @10 race $1.`
`x = ranuni(12345);`
	Initiate SAS DATA step
	INPUT statement - read variables
	Create new variable X with random values

`proc sort data = simple; by x;`	Sort file by random variable X

`data exact;`
`set simple; by x;`
`if _n_ <= 150;`
	Create new SAS data set
	Set SIMPLE by random X order
	_N_ is an internal SAS variable present in every SAS DATA set. This code tells SAS to execute the DATA step 150 times. Hence, we now have a random sample of exactly 150 cases

`drop x;`	Efficiency tip for eliminating unneeded variables

Stratified Random Sampling

A *stratified* random sample is taken when a population is segmented into two or more mutually exclusive subgroups or strata. You can think of a stratified sample as taking a simple random sample for each defined strata. A stratified random sample is usually used instead of a simple random sample for reasons of efficiency or reduced sampling error for a given sample size. A good, easy-to-understand, introductory text on basic sampling designs is found in Scheaffer, Mendenhall, and Ott (1979). The SAS code to select a stratified random sample is a logical extension of the code used to select a simple random sample. The following example is not elegant as a piece of programming work, but it will enable beginner- to intermediate-level SAS users to understand and have full confidence in the results of their SAS program[3]. This program selects a random sample stratified by race with the following distribution.

	Strata		
	B=Black	O=Other	W=White
Obs	80	50	80

---

[3] If CPU time is an issue, a more advanced technique for selecting a stratified random sample is described in SAS Institute Inc., *Introduction to Market Research Using the SAS System* (Cary, NC: SAS Institute Inc., 1994), 21-27.

Stratified Random Sampling

SAS Code	Comments
```data pop; input @1 ssn 9. @10 race $1. ; x = ranuni(12345); cards;```	Create and define POP data set Assign random number to new variable X
```proc sort data = pop; by race;```	Sort POP file by RACE
```proc rank data = pop; out = rankpop; by race; var x;```	PROC RANK assigns a rank value for each value of X (smallest to highest). The rank value replaces the original value of X. A separate analysis is performed for each value of RACE.
```data sample; set rankpop; if race = 'B' and x >80 then delete; else if race = 'O' and x > 50 then delete else if race = 'W' and x > 80 then delete;```	Final SAS data set has exact number of randomly selected observations for each racial category.

Generating Random Telephone Numbers

An excellent way to develop a sample for telephone surveys of the general population is to use SAS to create a file of random numbers that can be translated into phone numbers appropriate for the survey population geographical area. The random digit dialing (RDD) approach provides two major advantages: it provides a quick, easy, and inexpensive way of developing a sampling frame, and it eliminates the sampling bias of not having unlisted or new numbers when the sample is taken from published phone directories. The first step in using this technique is to identify the area codes and telephone prefixes in the geographical area that defines the survey population. Local telephone companies can provide this information and also identify blocks of phone numbers that are not in service or that are used for commercial purposes.

<table>
<tr><td colspan="2">TIP: Using Random Telephone Numbers</td></tr>
<tr><td colspan="2">Generate three or four times more random telephone numbers than the number of interviews you plan to complete. The RDD process will always generate a lot of numbers that are not in service or that are used by businesses. Having a lot of phone numbers ready at the start of the project helps in managing the work flow among interviewers. It's always good to avoid having interviewers exhaust their list of phone numbers and lose an evening of work while you run a fresh batch of numbers that do not match any of the original numbers.</td></tr>
</table>

Generating Random Digit Telephone Numbers

SAS Code	Comments
`options ls=80 nodate nonumber;`	Set width of output page to 80 columns, suppress date and page numbering
`data sample;` `length phone $8;`	Begin DATA step; create SAS data set Assigns width of 8 characters to new variable called PHONE
`do i = 1 to 25;`	Repeat the following operation 25 iterations. If you wanted 500 phone numbers you would substitute the value **500** for **25**.
`x1 = ranuni(0);`	Assign random number value to X1. (Note that RANUNI values are fractions with 4 decimals)
`x2 = x1*10000;`	Transform X1, which has 4 decimals, to a whole number
`last4 = put(x2,z4.);`	Store X2 as LAST4; the Z4. format retains a leading 0 from X2 in LAST4. Without using the Z4. format the leading 0 would be lost.
`phone='251-'||(last4);`	Create entire PHONE value by concatenating known prefix '251' with a '-' and the randomly generated LAST4 variable.
`output;`	Outputs observations to a SAS temporary data set named SAMPLE
`end;`	End of DO loop
`proc sort data = sample nodupkey;` `by last4;`	Sort the SAMPLE file by last four digits of PHONE. The NODUPKEY option eliminates duplicate LAST4 values that could appear in file.

`proc print data = sample;`
`var x1 x2 last4 phone;`
`title1 'Random Phone Numbers' ;`
	Prints SAMPLE file
	Specifies variables to be printed
	Heading for PROC PRINT output

Output 2-3: Generated Random Phone Numbers

```
                       Random Phone Numbers


        OBS      X1          X2       LAST4       PHONE

         1     0.02698     269.77     0270      251-0270
         2     0.06073     607.31     0607      251-0607
         3     0.06807     680.68     0681      251-0681
         4     0.07520     751.98     0752      251-0752
         5     0.10792    1079.22     1079      251-1079
         6     0.11775    1177.49     1177      251-1177
         7     0.19643    1964.30     1964      251-1964
         8     0.32091    3209.10     3209      251-3209
         9     0.33095    3309.54     3310      251-3310
        10     0.36387    3638.67     3639      251-3639
        11     0.40176    4017.60     4018      251-4018
        12     0.45614    4561.35     4561      251-4561
        13     0.49129    4912.87     4913      251-4913
        14     0.51078    5107.78     5108      251-5108
        15     0.53469    5346.85     5347      251-5347
        16     0.55026    5502.60     5503      251-5503
        17     0.56145    5614.46     5614      251-5614
        18     0.60960    6096.04     6096      251-6096
        19     0.72679    7267.88     7268      251-7268
        20     0.74475    7447.54     7448      251-7448
        21     0.86158    8615.80     8616      251-8616
        22     0.88653    8865.29     8865      251-8865
        23     0.90030    9002.96     9003      251-9003
        24     0.91256    9125.63     9126      251-9126
        25     0.94607    9460.75     9461      251-9461
```

Saving Files

SAS can read and save both ASCII files and SAS data sets. SAS data sets are a special type of file whose internal characteristics are known only to the SAS Institute. SAS data sets are ideally suited for research applications, but most users find it necessary to read and create ASCII files as well.

Creating ASCII Files

SAS reads ASCII data with an INPUT statement and can write an ASCII file with the PUT statement. The FILENAME statement is used to identify ASCII files that are read with the INPUT statement or saved with the PUT statement. The example to follow illustrates the process of reading an ASCII file and saving a subset of the original file in a new file.

STUDENT.DAT

Monterose, Sandra	JR	45	F	W
Cobbs, William	SO	20	M	W
Shields,Whitney	SR	23	F	W
Gravely, Will	JR	22	M	W
Butler, Roberta	FR	18	F	B
Sanchez, Juan	SO	21	M	H
Hall, Ruby	FR	18	F	W
Griffith, Judy	FR	18	F	W
Thomas, Frank	FR	19	M	B

TIP: Naming Variables

There are two strategies for naming variables used in survey projects. You can use names that have mnemonic qualities (e.g., WORKHRS, EMPLOY), or use survey form question numbers as variable names (e.g., Q01, A12, etc.). Our experience has shown that for one-time survey projects, it is easier to work with the data if you assign variable names to match the survey item numbers. As you analyze the data, it is much easier to look at a survey form to determine variable names than to remember if you called the Q10 variable HRSWRK, WORK, JOB, etc. The use of question numbers as variable names will also save you keystrokes and facilitate the use of the data by more than one analyst. However, if the survey project is repeated over time, then you should not use survey item numbers as variable names as you will undoubtedly add, delete, and modify survey questions over time. You would not want to work with a series of files that have the same variable names representing different variables. For surveys repeated over time, use variables names that have intrinsic meaning (HRSWRK) that can be stored with the same name if the survey form changes.

Reading and Writing ASCII Files

SAS Code	Comments
`filename data1 'student.dat';`	FILENAME identifies ASCII file used in program
`filename saveit 'fresh.dat';`	ASCII output file name
`data enroll;`	Initiate DATA step
`infile data1;`	INFILE is used to reference file listed in FILENAME statement (DATA1)

`input`
`  @01 name $17. @19 class $2. @22 age 2.`
`  @25 sex  $1. @27 race $1.;`
	SAS has many methods of defining variables. This example requires you to identify the column starting position and variable length and type.

`if class = 'FR';`	Select subset of observations
`keep name;`	Efficiency tip for deleting unneeded variables by identifying variables to be output to the data set ENROLL. Can also use DROP statement
`data _null_ ;`	Special SAS data set name that is used as an efficient way of creating an ASCII output file. _NULL_ cannot be used for subsequent SAS operations
`set enroll;`	Reads ENROLL to get observations
`file saveit;`	Writes observations to ASCII file identified in FILENAME statement with SAVEIT name (libref)
`put @1 name $17.;`	PUT is opposite of INPUT; it tells SAS where to store variables in output file

Creating Permanent SAS Data Sets

The use of SAS data sets provide a number of convenient features compared to reading and writing ASCII files. SAS data sets provide users with the following advantages:

- Data stored in SAS data sets are self-documenting; essential characteristics can be retrieved using PROC CONTENTS.

- Greater efficiency; less processing time is needed. Data can also be stored in a specified sort order. PROCs can be used directly on a SAS file without the use of a DATA step.

- Programs that read files with many variables are much shorter as INPUT statements are not used with SAS data sets. Multiple SAS files can be processed in a single DATA step.

- SAS data sets take less storage space on your operating system than ASCII files.

The following example is identical to the preceding ASCII example except that the final file is saved as a SAS data set. This example demonstrates how to read an ASCII file, save it as a SAS data set, and then read the same SAS data set. The self-documenting features of SAS data sets are shown in **Output 2-4.**

Creating and Accessing SAS Permanent Data Sets

SAS Code	Comments
`filename data1 'student.dat';`	FILENAME identifies ASCII file used in program
`libname saveit '[gravely]';`	LIBNAME is used to identify the directory name where a SAS file is stored. Note that FILENAME is used to read and write ASCII files
`data enroll;`	Initiate DATA step
`infile data1;`	INFILE is used to reference file listed in FILE NAME statement (DATA1)

`input @01 name $17. @18 class $2.`
`      @21 age  2.   @24 sex $1.`
`      @26 race $1. ;`
	SAS has many methods of defining variables. This example requires you to identify the column starting position and variable length and type.

`if class = 'FR';`	Select subset of observations
`data saveit.fresh;`	Creates permanent 2-level SAS file stored as [GRAVELY]FRESH.SSD. SAVEIT is a libref used to identify the directory specified in the LIBNAME statement. The .SSD[4] filetype extension is automatically created by SAS and indicates that the file is a special SAS data set.
`set enroll;`	Concatenates ENROLL into the permanent SAS data set defined in the previous command
`proc contents data = saveit.fresh;` `run;`	Generates a report to document the characteristics of a data set.

---

[4] Extension names for permanent SAS data sets vary by operating system.

Output 2-4: Results from PROC CONTENTS

```
                          CONTENTS PROCEDURE

Data Set Name: SAVEIT.FRESH               Observations:          4
Member Type:   DATA                       Variables:             5
Engine:        V608                       Indexes:               0
Created:       11:10 Saturday, September 14, 1996   Observation Length:   29
Last Modified: 11:10 Saturday, September 14, 1996   Deleted Observations:  0
Protection:                               Compressed:          YES
Data Set Type:                            Reuse Space:         YES
                                          Sorted:               NO
Label:

                -----Engine/Host Dependent Information-----

Data Set Page Size:        8192
Number of Data Set Pages:  1
File Format:               607
Filename:                  [GRAVELY]FRESH.SASEB$DATA
Host Format:               VAX
Disk Blocks Allocated:     20

            -----Alphabetic List of Variables and Attributes-----

                  #    Variable   Type    Len    Pos
                  -------------------------------------
                  3    AGE        Num      8     19
                  2    CLASS      Char     2     17
                  1    NAME       Char    17      0
                  5    RACE       Char     1     28
                  4    SEX        Char     1     27
```

Using SAS to Read and Write Spreadsheet Files

Spreadsheets (e.g., Excel, Lotus, etc.) are commonly used in almost every type of organization, and survey research practitioners often find it necessary to import spreadsheet files into a file that can be read by SAS and use SAS to export data to a spreadsheet file. Spreadsheets are also a convenient medium for sharing data with users who are not using SAS in a form that can be self-documenting (through the use of column headings and other explanatory text).

Importing Spreadsheet Data into SAS

As with most SAS applications, there are numerous ways of reading spreadsheet files with SAS. We will show one general-purpose technique that should meet the needs of most users. The following steps are usually required:

- Open the spreadsheet file and remove any special formatting definitions such as commas or dollar signs ($) using the software's global-change facility.

- Save another version of the spreadsheet file as a text file using a comma, tab, or other special character delimiter.

The text version of the original spreadsheet file is now ready to be read by SAS. On the INFILE statement you will need to specify the type of delimiter used to mark the beginning and end of each column. An easy way to do this is to save the spreadsheet file as a comma-delimited text file and use the DSD option on the INFILE statement. For example

```
INFILE filename DSD;
```

The DSD option assumes that the file is comma delimited and properly handles quotation marks that may have been inserted by the spreadsheet program when the text version of file was created. If the spreadsheet file was not delimited with commas, then you will need to use the DLM= option on the INFILE statement.

In this example, we will begin with a spreadsheet file as follows.

Original Spreadsheet File

Name	Make	Type	Year	Price
Jan Grimes	Nissan	Trk	96	$ 10,500
Dick Monterose	Oldsmobile	Car	95	$ 14,280
Janet Beason	Jeep	Trk	94	$ 11,800
Glenna Trull	Subaru	Car	97	$ 13,900
Ken Wilson	Toyota	Trk	93	$ 9,000

Open the spreadsheet file and perform the following steps:

1. Use the spreadsheet's global-change command to remove the $ and comma formatting for the Price column.

2. Save the file as a comma-delimited text file under a new name (REG in this example) to preserve the original spreadsheet.

Comma-delimited Text File

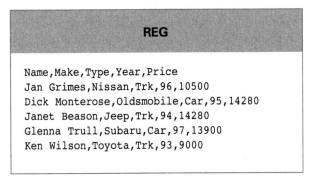

```
REG

Name,Make,Type,Year,Price
Jan Grimes,Nissan,Trk,96,10500
Dick Monterose,Oldsmobile,Car,95,14280
Janet Beason,Jeep,Trk,94,14280
Glenna Trull,Subaru,Car,97,13900
Ken Wilson,Toyota,Trk,93,9000
```

Reading Spreadsheet File with SAS

SAS Code	Comments
`filename reg 'hard drive:reg';` `options nodate nonumber;`	Specify location of spreadsheet file

`data cars;`
`length name $25 make $15 ;`
`infile reg dsd;`
	Assign lengths to character variables
	DSD option assumes file is comma delimited

`input name $ make $ type $ year $` `    ?? price ;`	?? option suppresses invalid data error messages for numeric variables
`if _n_ = 1 then delete;`	Eliminate spreadsheet column headings

`proc print;`
`format price dollar7.;`
`title1 'Car Registration Data Set';`
`run;`	

Output 2-5: Spreadsheet Example

```
                    Car Registration Data Set


   OBS         NAME         MAKE         TYPE     YEAR      PRICE

    1      Jan Grimes      Nissan        Trk       96      $10,500
    2      Dick Monterose  Oldsmobile    Car       95      $14,280
    3      Janet Beason    Jeep          Trk       94      $11,800
    4      Glenna Trull    Subaru        Car       97      $13,900
    5      Ken Wilson      Toyota        Trk       93       $9,000
```

Exporting Data from SAS to a Spreadsheet File

The process of exporting a SAS file to a spreadsheet is based on the same techniques described in the section "Creating ASCII Files." After an output ASCII file is specified, the PUT statement is used to write out specified variables separated by a user-defined delimiter. Delimiters can be tab codes, blanks, commas, or other characters. The SAS code to follow illustrates this process. It is based on the CARS data set used in the previous example. The following SAS program will store the NAME, MAKE, TYPE, YEAR, and PRICE variables in a comma-delimited text file named REG.EXCELL as shown in **Output 2-6**.

```
filename saveit 'reg.excell';
data _null_ ;
   set cars;
file saveit;
put name ',' make ',' type ',' year ',' price;
run;
```

Output 2-6: Comma-delimited Output File

```
Jan Grimes ,Nissan ,Trk ,96 ,10500
Dick Monterose ,Oldsmobile ,Car ,95 ,14280
Janet Beason ,Jeep ,Trk ,94 ,14280
Glenna Trull ,Subaru ,Car ,97 ,13900
Ken Wilson ,Toyota ,Trk ,93 ,9000
```

Most spreadsheet programs can import files such as that shown in **Output 2-6** if you simply open them and indicate what type of delimiter is used as a variable separator.

Additional Resources on Working with Spreadsheets

As previously mentioned, there are a number of techniques for using SAS to work with spreadsheet files. An excellent FAQ on this topic has been developed by Don Cram at the Stanford Graduate School of Business. This document is stored on the World Wide Web at the following URL:

Excel 2 SAS and Back Webpage
http://www-leland.stanford.edu/class/gsb/excel2sas.html#Q5.2EPI

Merging Files

In many research applications, it is often desirable to combine electronic information from two or more data files. It is always a good survey practice to shorten the length of the survey form by not asking respondents to report data elements that are available from other electronic sources. Questionnaire data can be augmented with information from other sources by performing file merge operations. In the following example, we have a survey file named VOTER.DAT that contains respondent presidential candidate choice (D=Dole, C=Clinton, P=Perot) for a sample of ten respondents. The second file contains voter registration information (party affiliation, race, age, sex) for 8,000 registered voters (REGISTER.DAT). Both files have a common ID number.

Questionnaire Data Files

VOTER.DAT	
ID	Choice
0017	D
0034	D
0012	D
0104	D
0321	C
3456	P
0090	C
0467	C
0781	P
5682	C

REGISTER.DAT				
ID	PARTY	AGE	Sex	Race
0001	D	59	F	B
0002	D	34	M	W
0003	R	29	M	W
0004	R	78	M	A
0005	D	18	F	W
0006	I	45	M	H
0007	D	22	M	H
0008	D	67	F	W
⋮				
8000	D	34	F	B

Merge Example: One-to-One Match Merge

To accomplish a one-to-one match merge, the two files must first be sorted by a common variable (ID in this example). The records for the two (or more) files are joined by using the MERGE statement in a separate DATA step that creates a new file. The results of the following example are shown in **Output 2-7**.

```
filename survey 'voter.dat';
filename pop 'register.dat';

data raw;
    infile survey;
    input @1 id 4. @5 choice $1.;

data votereg;
    infile pop;
    input @1 id 4. @6 party $1. @8 age 2. @11 sex $1.
        @13 race $1.;

proc sort data = raw;
    by id;
proc sort data = votereg;
    by id;

data combine;
    merge raw(in=a) votereg;
    by id;
if a = 1;

proc print data = combine;
title1
'Results of Merging Raw Survey File and Voter Registration File';
```

Output 2-7: Merge Example Results

```
    Results of Merging Raw Survey File and Voter Registration File

    OBS      ID     CHOICE    PARTY     AGE     SEX     RACE

      1      12       D         R        46      M       W
      2      17       D         D        43      F       B
      3      34       D         D        76      M       W
      4      90       C         D        19      F       A
      5     104       D         I        39      F       I
      6     321       C         I        53      F       W
      7     467       C         R        66      M       H
      8     781       P         R        19      F       W
      9    3456       P         D        22      M       B
     10    5682       C         D        20      M       A
```

If the two files to be merged contain common variables, the file listed on the *right* side of the merge statement will *overwrite* the values of the file listed on the left. The IN= data set option enables you to track the source file for merged records. In the first example, the sample data set contains 10 records for survey respondents and the second file contains 8,000 voter registration records. We want our new data set to contain all the sample respondent records, but we want to keep only those records from the voter registration file that match ID values of the first file. The IN= option creates a variable with a value of 1 or 0 to indicate if a designated file is the source of the record (1=**Yes**; 0=**No**). In the preceding example, we used IN = A to track observations that have a match with the data set RAW. The statement IF A = 1; outputs all observations from the data set RAW even if they do not have a match in the VOTEREG data set.

A common variation of the preceding example is to use the IN= data set option for all merge files. For example, you may want to keep only observations that match *both* merged files and delete all others. The following SAS program executes this type of merge:

```
data new;
    merge old(in=a)    update(in=b);   by id;
    if a=1 and b=1;
```

The effect of this code is to output those records from the data sets OLD and UPDATE to NEW that match on ID values. You could also use different combinations of A=1 or 0 and B=1 or 0 to achieve all possible result combinations.

Some Cautions About SAS Merge Operations

Merge operations can be tricky, and you should test your code to make sure that you are getting the desired results. Remember that it is always possible to have a logic error and *no* SAS code syntax error. Be especially careful when merging files with duplicate ID variables. Beginner- and intermediate-level SAS users may be advised to eliminate duplicate ID values where possible prior to performing file merge operations. SAS can also provide technically correct, but unanticipated, results when it is doing operations on variables that have missing values immediately after a MERGE statement. A simple solution to this complexity is to use another DATA step for these operations. In other words, use one DATA step to merge files; set the newly created merge file in a new DATA step; then perform IF/THEN/ELSE operations on variables that may have missing values.

Conducting Personalized Mail Surveys

Introduction

The personalization of mail surveys is one of the key elements required to obtain acceptable to high response rates. Although there are no formally acknowledged standards for defining "acceptable" response rates, Salant and Dillman (1994) suggest that mail surveys with a less than 60 to 70% response should have a "red flag" to indicate questionable validity[1]. The SAS System provides a powerful tool for achieving a high degree of personalization with *minimal* effort. Specifically, this chapter will illustrate the use of SAS to manage a variety of survey data management tasks.

Creating ID Numbers

The use of ID numbers in survey projects provides a mechanism for tracking respondent participation, identifying survey forms for correcting keypunch errors, and combining survey data with information from other electronic sources. Here are two methods of creating an ID number. The first uses the internal SAS automatic variable _N_ and the second uses the RETAIN statement.

---

[1] *Validity* in this context is the extent to which survey respondents differ from the population on one or more key variables. Sometimes this can be assessed by comparing respondents to non-respondents on variables known to be important to research question(s). If this type of information is not available, an abbreviated telephone survey of nonrespondents can be used to check for systematic differences between respondents and nonrespondents.

Method 1

```
data sample;
   set pop;
   id = _n_;
```

In this example, as each record from the POP data set is passed to the SAMPLE data set, SAS creates an internal or automatic variable _N_ that counts iterations of the DATA step. In this example, if we assume that SAMPLE has 500 observations, the first observation will have an _N_ value of 1 and the last observation will have an _N_ value of 500. The important thing to note when using the automatic _N_ variable is that a given observation's _N_ value can change if the file is sorted in a different order or if changes are made in the number of observations. By assigning a user-created variable (ID) to represent _N_ at a given point, you can maintain a consistent observation ID that will not change as a result of operations on the data set.

Method 2

A more elegant approach to creating ID numbers is to use the RETAIN statement. The following program creates a new ID variable and assigns a sequential number to each observation.

```
data sample;
   retain id 0;
   set pop;
   id + 1;
```

Name and Address Files

For mail surveys, it is useful to create a name and address file to manage the survey process. This file will serve the following functions:

- Serve as a data file for generating individualized form letters and envelopes.

- Keep track of respondents as they return a completed questionnaire.

- Identify nonrespondents who should not be sent a follow-up mailing (e.g., address information is invalid; person is deceased, etc.).

The name and address file makes it very easy to generate form letters for nonrespondents when you are conducting follow-up mailings. The following SAS program illustrates how to build a name and address file by merging a SAS data set (contains the survey sample) with an ASCII file of address information. This program also demonstrates the use of concatenation operators (| |), LENGTH statements, ARRAY and DO processing, and the SUBSTR function. The results of this program are shown in **Output 3-1**.

Creating Name and Address Files

SAS Code	Comments

```libname database '[gravely]';```
```filename address 'company.dat';```
```filename saveit 'address.dat';```
	Directory storing sample as a SAS data set
	Source of mailing address information
	Name and address file to be created

```data sample;``` ``` set database.survey;```	Read sample file Read file containing address information

```data mail;```
```length zip $10;```
``` infile address;```
```input```
```@001 ssn   09. @013 name $32.```
```@045 firname $20. @065 lasname $20.```
```@121 street1 $32. @153 street2 $32.```
```@185 city $20. @205 state $02.```
```@209 zip5 $05. @214 zip_ext $04.```
```@261 mi $01.```
``` ;```
	Modify length of ZIP

``` if zip_ext > ' ' then```
```   zip = zip5||'-'||zip_ext;```
``` else zip = zip5;```
	If ZIP code extension is present, then concatenate it on the end of the basic ZIP code

```proc sort data = sample;```
```   by ssn;```
```proc sort data = mail;```
``` by ssn;```	

Creating Name and Address Files (*continued*)

SAS Code	Comments

```data update;```
``` merge sample(in=a) mail;```
``` by ssn;```
```if a;```
```if sex = 'M' then title = 'Mr';```
```else if sex = 'F' then title = 'Ms';```
	Combine address file with sample file
	Keep all records in sample file
	Create title variable for use in form letter

```do p = 1 to 32;```
```if substr(street1,p,1) = '.' then```
```   substr(street1,p,1) = ' ';```
```if substr(street2,p,1) = '.' then```
```   substr(street2,p,1) = ' ';```
```if p < 21 and substr(city,p,1) = '.'```
``` then substr(city,p,1) = ' ';```
```end;```
	This DO loop checks every column
	in STREET1 and STREET2 for the presence
	of a period and if found changes it to a
	space to conform with postal regulations

```proc sort data = update;``` ``` by id;```	
```data _null_ ;``` ``` set update;```	Create name and address file

```file saveit recfm=f lrecl=83;```
```put```
```@02 id   z4. @06 title $2.```
```@09 firname $char20. @29 mi $1.```
```@31 lasname $char20.```
```@51 street1 $char32.```
	These options will vary according to
	operating system
	The Z4. format writes leading 0's for ID

```#2```	Each record is written on two lines. This makes it easier to edit from an 80-column screen
```@01 street2 $char32. @33 city $char20.``` ```@54 state $2. @57 zip $char10.;```	

Output 3-1: Name and Address File

```
0715Mr Jan          S Grimes      8 Glen Falls Rd
                      Bent Creek      NC 27377-9221
0716Mr William      J Monterose   144 Westwood Ave
                      Asheville       NC 28806
0717Mr Brian        G Adams       73 Queen St
                      Asheville       NC 28804
0718Mr James        R Boehm       3506 9th Avenue
                      Moline          IL 61265
0726Ms Jennifer     L Lee         17 Deep Creek Drive Unit K
                      Weaverville     NC 28787
0727Mr Bobby        R Sharpe Jr.  29 Pine Street PO Box 12
                      Ridgecrest      NC 28770
0729Ms Kyle         S Jones       205 River Drive
                      Easley          SC 29642
0730Mr Matthew      C Cochran     11 Highland Street
                      Asheville       NC 28801
0731Ms Rebecca      E Jones       305 Shamrock Dr.
                      Asheville       NC 28805
0735Mr Donald       R Smith       13 Rolling Hill Dr
                      Waynesville     NC 28786-2659
```

Note that each record is written on two lines and that the first column of the first line (before ID) is left blank. This space is used to manually input a flag to indicate that a completed survey has been received from a respondent. We use the following coding system to track respondents:

1 = Completed survey

2 = Bad address

9 = Remove from survey sample.[2]

---

[2] After the survey is underway, you may discover that some nonrespondents have been included in error, are deceased, or should be deleted from the survey sample for some other reason.

Survey Letter - Print Merge Operation

This section will supply a SAS program to read the address file and create a file that can be used by word-processing packages to create individualized survey letters with a print-merge operation. The file that is created is shown in **Ouput 3.2.**

In the following sample survey letter, we want to use SAS to store the NAME1 NAME2, STREET1, STREET2, CITY, STATE, and ZIP variables in a file that can be used by a word-processing package in a print-merge operation to create individualized form letters.

<<DATA letter.lis>>

September 24, 1996

<<name1>>
<<street1>>
<<if street2>><<street2>>
<<ENDIF>><<city>> <<state>> <<zip>>

Dear <<name2>> :

I am writing to ask you to take a few minutes to complete the enclosed **New Student Survey**. All new degree-seeking students are being asked to participate in this study. We use this information to better understand student characteristics and to conduct longitudinal studies of factors related to success in college. This survey provides one of the more important data sources in UNCA's overall evaluation and planning program.

The survey contains several items which may be sensitive or personal in nature. I would like to assure you that your responses will be treated as <u>confidential</u> information. The survey results will not be released so that any individual can be identified.

Please return the survey in the enclosed envelope. (If you live in one of the UNCA campus residence halls, please return the survey to us via campus mail.) Thank you for your assistance. If you have questions about the study, feel free to call me at 215-1966.

Sincerely,

Dr. Archer R. Gravely
Director

Creating a Letter File

SAS Code	Comments
| ```
filename addr   'address.dat';
``` | Name and address file |
| ```
filename output 'letter.lis';
``` | Output file for creating letters |
| ```
data address;
``` | Read address file |
| ```
length street1 $40 street2 $40 address $100;
``` | Assign lengths to new variables |
| ```
infile addr recfm=f lrecl=90;
input
``` | |
| ```
@1   flag        $1.
``` | Variable FLAG used to track respondents |
| ```
@02 id           $4. @06 title         $2.
@09 firname $char20.
@29 mi           $1. @31 lasname $char20.
@51 street1 $char32.
``` | |
| ```
#2
``` | Data for each observation stored on two |
| ```
@01 street2 $char32. @33 city     $char20.
@54 state        $2. @57 zip     $char10.

;
``` | records |
| ```
if flag in ('1','2','9') then delete;
``` | Do not create records for respondents who have not responded, have bad address, etc. |
| ```
name1 = title||'. '||trim(firname)||
``` | Create new name variable with concatenation |
| ```
        ' '||trim(lasname);
name2 = title||'. '||trim(lasname);
``` | |
| ```
street1 = trim(street1);
street2 = trim(street2);
``` | Eliminate unnecessary blanks with TRIM function |
| ```
city = '"'||trim(city)||','||'"';
address=trim(name1)||','||trim(name2)||','||
  trim(street1)||','||trim(street2)||','||
  trim(city)||','||trim(state)||','||trim(zip);
``` | |
| ```
proc sort data = address;
    by zip;
``` | |
| ```
data _null_ ;
set address;
file output recfm=v;
``` | Create output file |
| ```
if _n_ = 1 then put @1 'name1,name2,
``` | Create variable names recognized in form letter |
| ```
  street1,street2,city,state,zip';
``` | |
| ```
put @1 address;
``` | Store address information |
```

Output 3-2: Letter File

```
NAME1,NAME2,STREET1,STREET2,CITY,STATE,ZIP
Mr. Ryan McCall,Mr. McCall,6514 Brookstone Drive, ,"Stoney Creek,",NC,27377-9221
Ms. Berit Bjorklund,Ms. Bjorklund,943B St Mary's Street, ,"Raleigh,",NC,27605
Ms. Danielle Claycomb,Ms. Claycomb,1916 Thopshire Dr, ,"Raleigh,",NC,27615
Mr. David Finnan,Mr. Finnan,302 Hopewell Road #C, ,"Morganton,",NC,28655
Mr. Marc Ludvigsen,Mr. Ludvigsen,156 Monte Vista Road, ,"Statesville,",NC,28677
Ms. Sandi Roper,Ms. Roper,168 Pinecrest Drive, ,"Alexander,",NC,28701
Mr. Timothy Means,Mr. Means,222 Glenn Bridge Road B-16, ,"Arden,",NC,28704
Mr. John Elliott,Mr. Elliott,18 Willowcreek Lane, ,"Arden,",NC,28704
Ms. Deborah Sheppard,Ms. Sheppard,7 N Reece Drive, ,"Arden,",NC,28704
Mr. Spurgeon Gilbert,Mr. Gilbert,PO Box 960, ,"Arden,",NC,28704
Ms. Carole Cogburn,Ms. Cogburn,37 Morgan St, ,"Canton,",NC,28716
Ms. Monica Jernigan,Ms. Jernigan,PO Box 617 Ridge Road, ,"Dana,",NC,28724-0617
Ms. Joy Ciuro,Ms. Ciuro,23 Spring Mtn Rd, ,"Fairview,",NC,28730
Mr. Matthew Simmons,Mr. Simmons,111 Fairview Hills Dr ,"Fairview,",NC,28730- 9777
Mr. George Wagner III,Mr. Wagner III,160 Poplar Loop, ,"Flat Rock,",NC,28731
```

This file can be saved as a word-processing document and used in a print merge operation with a survey letter template to print individualized letters.

Creating Personalized Envelopes

To achieve maximum response rates for mail surveys, we advise against the use of stick-on mailing labels for survey envelopes. Based on Dillman's (1978) total design method for conducting surveys, it is very important for survey communications not to have a "junk mail" appearance. The printing of names and addresses directly on envelopes provides a much higher degree of personalization and professional appearance than is obtained by using mailing labels that are often applied slightly askew. The code to generate envelopes is similar to that used in the preceding example to create individualized form letters. The SAS program shown on the following page will create a file that can be read by a word processor to print and merge names, envelopes, or mailing labels. PROC FORMS will also create mailing labels. The file that is created is shown in **Output 3-3**.

Creating a File to Print Addresses on Envelopes

SAS Code	Comments
(SAS DATA step same as preceding example)	
`* ~ = soft return;`	Tilde character used to represent "soft return" for the word processor. The "~" character will be replaced by the actual soft-return character by the word processor's change command.

`if street2 = ' ' then do;`
`line01 = title||' '||trim(firname)||' '||`
`   trim(lasname)||'~';`
`line02 = trim(street1)||'~';`
`line03 = trim(city)||', '||state||' '||zip;`
`address='"'||trim(line01)||trim(line02)||`
`   trim(line03)||'"';`
`end;`
	Addresses with no STREET2 information will have three address lines
	Note use of "~" to mark place for later insertion of soft return by word processor.
	
	All three address lines concatenated as one variable

`else if street2 > ' ' then do;`
`line01 = title||'.'||' '||trim(firname)||' '||`
`   trim(lasname)||'~';`
`line02 = trim(street1)||'~';`
`line03 = trim(street2)||'~';`
`line04 = trim(city)||', '||state||' '||zip;`
`address='"'||trim(line01)||trim(line02)||`
`   trim(line03)||trim(line04)||'"';`
`end;`
	Addresses with nonblank STREET2 information will have four address lines
	
	All four address lines concatenated as one variable

`proc sort;` `by zip;`	Put file in ZIP code order
`data _null_ ;` `   set survey;`	Store ASCII file for use by word-processing package

`file output;`
`if _n_ = 1 then put @1 'address';`
 	
`put @1 address;`
	Write variable name for word processing on first line of file.
	Write address information

Output 3-3: Partial Envelope File

```
ADDRESS
"Mr Ryan McCall~6514 Brookstone Drive~Stoney Creek, NC 27377-9221"
"Ms Berit Bjorklund~943B St Mary's Street~Raleigh, NC 27605"
"Ms Danielle Claycomb~1916 Thopshire Dr~Raleigh, NC 27615"
"Mr David Finnan~302 Hopewell Road #C~Morganton, NC 28655"
"Ms Louise Cottrell~4515 Mt Olive Ch Rd~Morganton, NC 28655-7146"
"Mr Marc Ludvigsen~156 Monte Vista Road~Statesville, NC 28677"
"Ms Sandi Roper~168 Pinecrest Drive~Alexander, NC 28701"
"Mr Timothy Means~222 Glenn Bridge Road B-16~Arden, NC 28704"
"Mr John Elliott~18 Willowcreek Lane~Arden, NC 28704"
"Ms Deborah Sheppard~7 N Reece Drive~Arden, NC 28704"
```

TIP: Scheduling Mail Surveys

Schedule survey mailings on a Tuesday since there is less mail lost by the U.S. Postal Service on that day than any other day of the week. If you work in a large organization you will need to find out when the mail room actually gets your mail to the post office to plan your mailings.

Calculating Response Rates

The same address file that was used to generate letters and envelopes serves as a device for tracking respondent participation in the survey project. The address file is created so that the first column of the record for each observation is left blank. This field is used to manually input a flag variable to capture respondent participation status. Our practice is to update this field as incoming surveys are received in the mail. Note that it is not necessary to enter the questionnaire response data, but to simply record a "1" or some other value beside the appropriate ID number in the address file. The updating of this flag variable will enable quick calculation of the survey response rate at any point during the administration of the survey. This is often useful for estimating survey material needs and costs for follow-up mailings to nonrespondents. The use of the response flag also makes it easy to print letters, envelopes, and labels for only those individuals who have not returned a survey form. The following program illustrates the use of PROC FREQ to calculate the survey response rate and PROC FORMAT to provide value labels and to enhance the readability of the resulting report shown in **Output 3-4.**

SAS Code to Calculate Response Rate with PROC FREQ

```
filename nsdata 'address.dat';

proc format;
   value $return '1' = 'Yes'
                 '0' = 'No';

data survey;
infile nsdata recfm=f lrecl=90;
input
   @01 flag    $1.
   @02 id      $4. @06 title      $2. @09  firname $char20.
   @29 mi      $1. @31 lasname $char20. @51  street  $char32.
   #2
   @01 street2 $char32. @33 city   $char20. @54  state   $2.
   @57 zip     $char05. @63 phone   $char10.
;

if flag in('2','9') then delete;
if flag = '1' then return = '1';
else return = '0';

proc freq data = survey;
   tables return;
format return $return. ;
title1 'Response Rate to New Student Survey';
```

Output 3-4: Survey Response Rate

```
                   Response Rate to New Student Survey

                      15:40 Saturday, September 28, 1996

                                Cumulative  Cumulative
          RETURN  Frequency  Percent  Frequency   Percent
          -------------------------------------------------
          No           35      35.0        35       35.0
          Yes          65      65.0       100      100.0
```

TIP: Monitor Response Rate to Initial Mailing

To assist in survey planning and budgeting, it is important to be able to estimate the percentage of competed responses that result from the *first* mailing alone. This information is obtained by monitoring the response rate during the data-collection phase using techniques described in the previous section. Knowledge of the response rate will enable you to estimate material, printing, and postage costs with some confidence.

Labeling SAS® Output

Introduction

This chapter will describe how to use the SAS System to create titles, footnotes, and labels for both variable names and variable values. The use of these labeling features will greatly enhance the readability of SAS output. Variable *name* labels are created with the LABEL statement, and variable *value* labels are defined with PROC FORMAT. This chapter will also discuss the use of PROC FORMAT to collapse observations into subgroups.

Titles

TITLE statements provide an easy-to-use mechanism for writing headers to describe SAS output. SAS will allow up to ten title statements per procedure or PROC statement. If no TITLE statements are specified for a proc that generates printed output, the default title **"The SAS System"** will be printed. The form of the TITLE statement is

TITLE*n* *'character-string'*;

Where:

    n is a number 1-10.

TITLE statement examples follow:

```
title 'This is the First Title Line';

title01 'University of North Carolina at Asheville';
title02 'Office of Institutional Research';
title03 'Cumulative GPA by Class and Residence Hall';

title1 'North Carolina''s Public Liberal Arts College';
```

Note: Apostrophes are coded with two " symbols.

A blank title line can be generated by specifying TITLE*n* with no text. Use numbers if you have more than one TITLE statement (e.g., TITLE01 to TITLE10). Once a TITLE statement is specified it remains in effect for procedure output in the same job or interactive session until the TITLE statement is canceled. All preexisting TITLE statements can be canceled by specifying TITLE with no argument. Alternatively, previous TITLE statements can be selectively canceled by specifying TITLE with the appropriate number, e.g., TITLE05.

Footnotes

FOOTNOTE statements write text at the bottom of a page following procedure output. Up to ten footnotes can be specified for any proc. The rules for writing FOOTNOTE statements are the same as for TITLE statements. Here is a sample FOOTNOTE statement:

```
footnote1
'Data Source: NC Statistical Abstract of Higher Education';
```

Unlike the TITLE statement, an absent FOOTNOTE statement does not generate a default footnote.

TIP: Positioning FOOTNOTE Text

SAS will always position FOOTNOTE statements at the bottom of the page as defined by your PAGESIZE option setting. If you have a short amount of procedure output that takes up less than three-quarters of the output page, it is visually disconcerting to have footnotes placed on the very last line(s) of the page, far removed from the object that they annotate. To force footnote text to appear closer to the procedure output, reduce the PAGESIZE option value in the OPTIONS statement to "trick" SAS into thinking you have a smaller page size.

Variable Labels

Since SAS variable names have a maximum length of eight characters, the use of variable labels is essential for enhancing the readability of procedure output. Variable labels can be created in the DATA step or as a part of running most SAS procedures. Labels can be specified for one or more variables with a single LABEL statement. If more than one variable is used in the LABEL statement, only one semicolon (;) is used to signify the end of the statement after the final variable label description. The LABEL statement is highlighted in the following program. The program results are shown in **Output 4-1**.

```
filename svydata 'admiss.dat';

data survey;
input @1 id $3. @5 q01 1. @6 q02 1. @7 q03 1.
      @8 q04 1. @9 q05 1.;
infile svydata;

label Q01 = 'Visits by UNCA Admissions staff'
      Q02 = 'Admissions office tour of campus'
      Q03 = 'UNCA publications'
      Q04 = 'Interview with Admissions staff'
      Q05 = 'Contact with UNCA Coaches';

proc means data = survey;
title1 'Survey Item Means';
run;
```

Output 4-1: PROC MEANS with Variable Labels

```
                      Survey Item Means

Variable    Label                          N  Mean  Std Dev  Minimum  Maximum
----------------------------------------------------------------------------
Q01    Visits by UNCA Admissions staff     6   1.8    1.0      1.0      3.0
Q02    Admissions office tour of campus    6   2.0    1.3      1.0      4.0
Q03    UNCA publications                   6   2.0    1.5      1.0      5.0
Q04    Interview with Admissions staff     6   1.5    1.2      1.0      4.0
Q05    Contact with UNCA Coaches           6   1.5    0.8      1.0      3.0
----------------------------------------------------------------------------
```

Value Labels

The process of printing user-defined labels for variable values (e.g., "**Female**" for sex values of "**F**") can be confusing for beginning SAS users. The process of defining value labels and using them in procedure output requires two steps:

- First define a value label with PROC FORMAT.

- Then associate the resulting format with a variable in a FORMAT[1] statement after the PROC FORMAT statement.

---

[1] The FORMAT statement that is used to link a variable with a format is not the same as the PROC FORMAT procedure, which is used to define format labels. The FORMAT statement can be used in the DATA step, with the PUT command, or after a PROC step.

Values defined in PROC FORMAT can have up to 40 characters, but some SAS procedures (e.g., PROC FREQ) will print only the first 16 characters of a value label. PROC FORMAT can be used to create *temporary* value labels or labels that are stored *permanently*. Temporary labels are the default and can be used only during the execution of a batch program or interactive session. Permanently stored PROC FORMAT labels are stored in a SAS catalog and provide an efficient way to reuse labels in numerous SAS programs without repeating the PROC FORMAT statements in every program. The use of permanently stored formats is very helpful when working with lengthy formats such as those for country, county, state, etc.

This chapter will try to reduce the complexity of PROC FORMAT to the bare essentials needed for survey research applications. With this caveat in mind, the basic form of PROC FORMAT is as follows:

PROC FORMAT *options;*

Selected PROC FORMAT Statement Options

LIBRARY=*libref;*
    creates a permanent format catalog. The libref is used as a reference for a directory name. Working with permanently stored format catalogs is similar to creating and reading SAS permanent data sets.

Selected PROC FORMAT Statements

VALUE *name* '*range-*1' = '*label*'
               '*range-n*' = '*label*' ;

Where:

name   is a user-created format name to identify the format. Format names must be eight characters or fewer and cannot end with a number. Formats for character variables must be called *$name*. For character format names, the $ counts as one of the eight allowable characters.

*range-*1   is the first variable value (e.g., **'M'** for a variable called SEX) **'***label***'** is the formatted value label (e.g., **'Male'**)

range-n   is the last variable value for a format name.

           <u>Range Value Options:</u>
           Low
           High
           Other

Range Value Option Example

```
proc format;
   value   $sex     'M' = 'Male'
                    'F' = 'Female'
                  Other = 'Error';


   value gpagrp   low-1.99 = 'Below 2.00'
            2.00 -high = '2.00- 4.00'
```

Temporary Format Example

In the following PROC FORMAT example, the format name RATING is defined as a *numeric* format and DEALER is defined as a *characte*r format. Even though the actual values of DEALER are numbers, the $ prefix in the format $DEALER tells SAS that this is a character format. Character formats must be used with character variables and numeric formats with numeric variables. Note the use of double quotes (") in the labels for DEALER values '0003' and '0004' to handle labels that have an apostrophe in the text string. The results of this program are shown in **Output 4-2**.

```
proc format;
   value rating 1 = 'Poor''
                2 = 'Fair'
                3 = 'Good'
                4 = 'Excellent';


Value $dealer '0001' = 'Jones Chevrolet'
              '0002' = 'Smith Pontiac'
              '0003' = 'Jim''s Ford'
              '0004' = 'Harry''s Toyota';

data cars;
infile dealer;
input @1 dealer $4. @6 q01 1. @8 q02 1. @10 q03 1. ;
label Q01 = 'Price Rating'
      Q02 = 'Sales Staff'
      Q03 = 'Service';

proc freq data = cars;
   tables dealer*q03;
format dealer $dealer. q03 rating. ;
title1 'Rating of Dealership Service';
run;
```

Output 4-2: PROC FORMAT Example

```
                         Rating of Dealership Service

                          TABLE OF DEALER BY Q03

         DEALER              Q03(Service)

         Frequency        |
         Percent          |
         Row Pct          |
         Col Pct          |Poor   |Fair   |Good   |Excellent|   Total
         ----------------+-------+-------+-------+---------+
         Jones Chevrolet |    0  |    0  |    4  |    0    |      4
                         | 0.00  | 0.00  | 21.05| 0.00    |  21.05
                         | 0.00  | 0.00  |100.00| 0.00    |
                         | 0.00  | 0.00  | 57.14| 0.00    |
         ----------------+-------+-------+-------+---------+
         Smith Pontiac   |    3  |    0  |    1  |    0    |      4
                         | 15.79 | 0.00  | 5.26 | 0.00    |  21.05
                         | 75.00 | 0.00  | 25.00| 0.00    |
                         | 50.00 | 0.0   | 14.29| 0.00    |
         ----------------+-------+-------+-------+---------+
         Jim's Ford      |    3  |    1  |    1  |    1    |      6
                         | 15.79 | 5.26  | 5.26 | 5.26    |  31.58
                         | 50.00 | 16.67 | 16.67| 16.67   |
                         | 50.00 | 50.00 | 14.29| 25.00   |
         ----------------+-------+-------+-------+---------+
         Harry's Toyota  |    0  |    1  |    1  |    3    |      5
                         | 0.00  | 5.26  | 5.26 | 15.79   |  26.32
                         | 0.00  | 20.00 | 20.00| 60.00   |
                         | 0.00  | 50.00 | 14.29| 75.00   |
         ----------------+-------+-------+-------+---------+
         Total                6       2       7       4         19
                          31.58   10.53   36.84   21.05    100.00
```

Grouping Observations with PROC FORMAT

The analysis of subgroups is a key element in survey research design and analysis. Observations can be grouped using DATA step statements such as IF/THEN/ELSE to create new variables representing group membership. PROC FORMAT can also be used as a more efficient alternative to DATA step processing by grouping variables into discrete ranges or categories. This technique will be illustrated with the following survey item.

Figure 4-1: Survey Item for Creating Subgroups with PROC FORMAT

Q01. How many hours a week are you employed?

_____ Hours

The variable Q01 (hours employed) is measured as a continuous variable and the researcher wants to use PROC FORMAT to create three mutually exclusive categories of employment status: not employed, employed part-time, and employed full-time. The following SAS program will illustrate the use of PROC FORMAT to group observations. Additionally, this example uses the HIGH value option to represent the maximum value that may be found in the data set. (Additional value options are LOW and OTHER.) The results of this program are shown in **Output 4-3**.

SAS Code to Create Subgroups with FORMAT

```
options nodate nonumber ps=65 ls=70;

data work;
input q01 2. ;
cards;
10
 0
50
40
23
45
 0
 5
 7
40
;
```

```
proc format;
   value q01f    0 = 'Not Employed'
              1-39 = 'Part-time'
          40-high = 'Full-time';

proc freq data = work;
   tables q01;
title1 'Frequency Distribution of Employment';
format q01 q01f. ;
label q01='Hours Employed';
run;
```

Output 4-3: Subgroups Created with PROC FORMAT

```
              Frequency Distribution of Employment

                         Hours Employed

                                  Cumulative   Cumulative
          Q01   Frequency   Percent   Frequency    Percent
-------------------------------------------------------------
Not Employed        2       20.0          2         20.0
Part-time           4       40.0          6         60.0
Full-time           4       40.0         10        100.0
```

Permanent Formats

The use of permanently stored formats is a convenient way to save time, key-strokes, and disk space. Permanent formats can also enhance standardization when multiple users work with the same data. To store formats permanently, two additional steps are needed beyond what is required to create temporary formats:

- Use the LIBNAME statement to identify the library to hold the formats.

- Use the LIBRARY= option on the PROC FORMAT statement to direct the saved format to the directory that you identified.

Permanent Format Example

```
libname saveit 'hard drive:survey';

proc format library = saveit;
     value $sex 'M' = 'Male'
                'F' = 'Female'
              other = 'Error';

    value $race 'B' = 'Black'
                'W' = 'White'
    'A','I','S', 'O' = 'Other';
    value age  low-12 = 'Child'
               13-19 = 'Teen'
             20-high = 'Adult';
```

The preceding SAS program does not produce printed output, so it is important to check the log file to ensure that no errors were made.

To use a permanently stored format, you must identify the directory that holds the format catalog by using a LIBNAME statement.[2] When using the LIBNAME statement to create and read a SAS permanent data set (see Chapter 2), the *libref* can be any character string of up to eight characters.[3] However, when you are using LIBNAME to access permanently stored format catalogs, the *libref* must be set to LIBRARY. SAS will automatically search all directories that have LIBRARY as the *libref* value. When working with SAS permanent data sets and permanent formats, it is convenient to store both formats and data sets in the same library so that the same LIBNAME statement can access both files. Programs that use permanent formats can also create and use temporary formats in the same job. The following program shows how to use the formats created in the previous example.

Using Permanently Stored Formats

```
libname library  'hard drive:survey'

proc freq data = library.survey97;
   tables sex race age;
format sex $sex. race $race. age age. ;
```

---

[2] The LIBNAME statement is used to specify directories, while the FILENAME statement is used to reference ASCIII files.

[3] Example:
```
libname svy  ' [survey.data]';
data report;
     set svy.data97;
```

TIP: Creating and Maintaining Permanent Formats

It's helpful to put all permanent FORMAT statements into one file called FORMAT.SAS or a name that you can standardize and recognize instantly. As you add new formats or modify old ones, delete the existing format catalog and simply rerun your FORMAT.SAS file.

Chapter

5

Data Manipulation

Introduction

The SAS System provides a powerful set of tools for handling survey research data and variable manipulation tasks. The use of these tools is an important component of efficient survey practice. This chapter will illustrate the use of the DATA step to perform a variety of operations.

Creating Summated Scales

Many survey applications (especially in the social sciences) use summated scale variables that are created from individual responses to multiple survey items. These scale scores usually take the form of a respondent's mean or summated score of a set of questionnaire items designed to measure a single attitudinal dimension. These operations can be performed using SAS operators (+ = / -) as shown in the following example:

$$avg1 = (q01 + q02 + q03 + q04)/4;$$
$$scale1 = (q05 + q06 + q07 + q08);$$

In the example, if any of the Q01-Q08 variables have missing data then the result for a given observation will be set to missing as well. Incomplete responses are inevitable in the survey business and rather than lose observations, the researcher may want to create adjusted scale scores using available data. Minimal response thresholds can be established before an observation is included in an analysis or in a calculation of summated scale scores. Work-around solutions can be devised for handling missing data with the use of SAS operators, but they usually require tedious coding to account for the all the various missing-data possibilities. An easy method of creating summated or mean scales scores *within* an observation is to use the SAS SUM and MEAN functions. These functions provide two major advantages compared to the use of SAS expressions using arithmetic operators:

- SUM and MEAN results are not set to missing[1] when specified variables have missing values.

- The MEAN function automatically adjusts the denominator if a specified variable has a missing value.

The use and comparison of SUM and + operators are illustrated in the following example.

Data Set: Q1=1 Q2=2 Q3=3 Q4=.
(Note that Q4 is missing.)

SUM Examples

	Result
`scale1 = sum(q1,q2,q3);`	6
`scale2 = q1 + q2 + q3;`	6
`scale3 = sum(q1,q2,q3,q4);`	6
`scale4 = q1 + q2 + q3 + q4;`	. (missing value)

The following example illustrates the differences between the MEAN function and SAS arithmetic operators.

Data Set: Q1=1 Q2=2 Q3=3 Q4=.
(Note that Q4 is missing.)

MEAN Examples

	Result
`xbar1 = mean(q1,q2,q3);`	2
`xbar2 = (q1 + q2 + q3)/3);`	2
`xbar3 = mean(q1,q2,q3,q4);`	2
`xbar4 = (q1 + q2 + q3 + q4)/4;`	. (missing value)

---

[1] Good survey practice would suggest that the researcher establish some minimum level of response to a set of scale items before a subject is included in the analysis. For example, if a scale is based on responses to ten items, you may not want to calculate a scale score for any respondents who did not answer some minimal number of questions. In this case, it would be necessary to override the SUM and MEAN functions and set them to missing if more than a specified number of variables are missing.

Array Processing

SAS array processing is a convenient tool for performing the same operation on a number of variables by using a single variable name. Arrays can greatly reduce the amount of SAS code that is required to accomplish a task, and they can reduce the potential for coding errors and misspellings that can occur in long blocks of repetitive code. Some common survey research array applications include:

- Performing character and numeric variable conversions

- Recoding negatively worded survey items

- Redefining missing value indicators

- Creating new variables.

Array Example

In the following example (**Figure 5-1**), the survey questions have positive values associated with negative responses and the researcher wants to recode or reverse the scaling system before computing summary measures.

Figure 5-1: Survey Items for Reverse Scale Example

			How UNCA Compared to Other Colleges			
Information Sources	**Not Offered or Used**	**Best**	**Better Than Most**	**About the Same**	**Poorer Than Most**	**Worst**
1. Visits by Admissions staff	0	1	2	3	4	5
2. Admissions office tour of campus	0	1	2	3	4	5
3. UNCA publications	0	1	2	3	4	5
4. Interview with Admissions staff	0	1	2	3	4	5
5. Contact with UNCA coaches	0	1	2	3	4	5

```
                      TIP: Establishing Item Scale Values

  Use increasingly positive scale values to represent positive response cate-
  gories. In reporting item means or scale scores, it is much more intuitive for
  readers to associate higher numerical scores with positive responses than
  the reverse.
```

Using Array Processing to Reverse Survey Item Values

SAS Code	Comments
`libname db '[admiss.survey]';`	Directory containing survey data stored as permanent SAS data set

`data survey;`
`set db.svy90(keep=q01 q02 q03 q04`
`           q05);`
	Q01-Q05 variables represent survey questions on survey form shown on previous page

`array old {5} q01 q02 q03 q04 q05;`	Array "Old" represents original survey variables; {5} indicates the number of variables in the array
`array new {5} r01 r02 r03 r04 r05;`	Array "New" represents variables to be created with recoded values
`do x = 1 to 5;`	Tells SAS to perform operations on all five variables specified in ARRAY statement

`     if old{x} = 1 then new{x} = 5;`
`else if old{x} = 2 then new{x} = 4;`
`else if old{x} = 3 then new{x} = 3;`
`else if old{x} = 4 then new{x} = 2;`
`else if old{x} = 5 then new{x} = 1;`
	Creates new set of variables (R01-R05) with reversed values compared to Q01-Q05

`else if old{x} = 0 then new{x} = .;` `end;`	Sets values coded as "0" (Not Offered or Used) to missing

In this example, a new set of variables R01-R05 is created to represent the reversed scale variables of the original Q01-Q05 items. These operations could have been performed directly on the Q01-Q05 elements without creating a new set of variables, but the use of new variables allows you to cross-tabulate the new set with the old set to ensure that the recoding was done correctly.

Alternative Approach to Reversing Scale Values

An alternative to using arrays to reverse scale values is to subtract the original variable from a constant that is equal to the number of scale values plus one. To illustrate, we will use a typical Likert survey item named Q01:

1 Strongly Disagree
2 Disagree
3 Agree Somewhat
4 Strongly Agree

To reverse this scale the following code, a new variable R01 is created:

```
r01 = 5 - q01;
```

A comparison of Q01 and R01 values is shown in the following table.

Q01 Values	R01 Values
1	4
2	3
3	2
4	1

If the original scale has 5 values, then you would subtract the variable from 6. This logic continues for any number of scale values. A generalized statement of this scale-reversal technique is as follows:

recoded variable = $(n + 1)$ - original variable

where n = number of scale values

Variable Type Conversions

SAS has two separate functions for converting character variables to numeric and converting numeric variables to character. The need to perform this type of operation occurs when a variable is stored in a SAS permanent data set as one data type, and you need to convert it to perform certain operations. Perhaps the most frequent application in survey work occurs when variables have been stored as character values, and you need to perform arithmetic operations such as sums or means. Additionally, you may need to extract a subset of a numeric variable (SUBSTR) but these operations should only be performed on character variables.

Character variables are converted to numeric using the INPUT function, and numeric variables are converted to character with the PUT function. The PUT function can also be used to create a new variable that takes the value of a user-defined format as defined in a PROC FORMAT statement. Both of the functions can also be used in arrays for greater efficiency when you are performing the same operations on a number of variables. The PUT and INPUT functions are described by examples in the sections to follow.

Character Conversions - Using PUT

In this example, we have a group of survey items Q01-Q05 that have been defined in the INPUT statement as numeric, and we want to convert them to character. The following program illustrates the use of the PUT function to accomplish this task. The Q01C-Q05C variables that were created with the PUT function are the character equivalents of the original Q01- Q05 numeric variables.

Example 1: PUT Function Basics

```
data survey;
infile filename;
input @1   id   $3. @4 (n01- n05) (1.) ;
  c01 = put(n01,$1);
  c02 = put(n02,$1);
  c03 = put(n03,$1);
  c04 = put(n04,$1);
  c05 = put(n05,$1);
```

Example 2: PUT Function Combined with Array

This example is based on the same variables used in Example 1. The difference is that the PUT statements are handled with array processing. Array processing allows us to perform operations on numerous variables at the same time.

```
data survey;
infile filename;
input @1 id   $3. @4 (n01-n05) (1.) ;
  array qn{5}   n01-n05;
  array qc{5} $ c01-c05;
do i= 1 to 5;
  qc{i} = put(qn{i},$1.);
end;
```

Example 3: PUT Function - Create Variable Based on Format Value

In some situations, it is useful to sort and print observations by *formatted* values or labels rather than the *actual* variable values. In the following example, we have a variable named DEPTCODE that is represented by a two-digit numerical code. Sorting and printing this variable as currently defined will not produce an alphabetized list of DEPTCODE by formatted label. One solution to this problem is to create a new variable to represent the user-defined value labels that were created with PROC FORMAT. This conversion can be accomplished with the PUT function as shown in the following program. Results are shown in **Output 5-1**.

SAS Code to Create New Variables with Format Values

```
options nodate nonumber;

    proc format;
       value $code '01' = 'Service'
                   '02' = 'Finance'
                   '03' = 'Marketing'
                   '04' = 'Sales';
   data report;
      input @1 deptcode $2. @4 rating 1. ;
      dept = put(deptcode,$code.);

drop deptcode;
cards;
01 3
02 4
03 2
04 4
;
proc sort data = report; by dept;
proc print; id dept;
var rating;
title1 'Department Ratings';
```

Output 5-1: Value Labels Created with the PUT Function

```
        Department Ratings

        DEPT        RATING

        Finance        4
        Marketing      2
        Sales          4
        Service        3
```

INPUT - Numeric Conversions

The conversion of character to numeric variables can be accomplished with the INPUT function. The use of this function is very similar to the PUT function character conversions that were described in the previous section. In the examples to follow, the variables Q01-Q05 are initially defined with character formats, and the INPUT function is used to create new numeric variables N01-N05.

Example 1: INPUT Function Basics

```
data survey;
infile filename;
input @1  id  $3. @4 (q01- q05) ($1.) ;
  n01 = input(q01,1.);
  n02 = input(q02,1.);
  n03 = input(q03,1.);
  n04 = input(q04,1.);
  n05 = input(q05,1.);
```

Example 2: INPUT Function Combined with Array

```
data survey;
infile filename;
input @1 id  $3. @4 (q01-q05) (1.) ;
  array qc{5} $ q01-q05;
  array qn{5}   n01-n05;
do i= 1 to 5;
  qn{i} = input(qc{i},1.);
end;
```

TIP: Character-to-Numeric Conversion Alternative
Character variables can also be converted to numeric by performing arithmetic operations on the original variable. For example, if C01 is defined as character with values "1" ... '10", you can make a numeric version by multiplying C01 by 1. The following code creates a numeric representation of C01 called N01: $$N01 = C01*1;$$

Advanced Character Manipulation Techniques

This section will illustrate the use of the SAS programming language to perform a number of character manipulation tasks that are sometimes required to implement a personalized mail survey project. In this example, we have been asked to conduct a personalized mail survey, but the sample name information is stored as a one-variable, uppercase character string. To generate personalized form letters, we need to separate the combined first name, middle name, and last name field into *three* distinct variables. Additionally, we need to translate the all uppercase characters into the appropriate upper- and lowercase configuration required for personalized correspondence. The original data set is shown in **Figure 5-2**.

Figure 5-2: NAME.DAT File

```
THOMAS REAZER COCHRAN
CAROLINE B. MILLER
KERN ARTHUR PARKER
SHIRLEY S. BROWNING
JAMES R. PITTS
ELAINE A. FOX
MALCOLM E. BLOWERS
MERRITT W. MOSELEY
```

Our approach to converting the uppercase one-variable name field into three separate name variables with appropriate upper- and lowercase characters will be done using the following steps.

1. Convert uppercase text to lowercase text.

2. Identify the character position number of the blank spaces that separate first name, middle name, and last name in the original name field.

3. Use the position numbers of these blanks or separators as a guide or pointer to extract the three distinct name elements.

4. Convert the first character of each newly created name field to uppercase.

The following program makes these data conversions. The results are shown in **Output 5-2**.

Converting Name Example

SAS Code	Comments

```data test;```
```   infile 'name.dat';```
``` input name $35. ;```	

```spacel = 0;```
```space2 = 0;```
```space3 = 0;```
	Create variables with an initial value of 0 to identify location of spaces between first name, middle name, and last name

```name = lowcase(name);```	Convert original uppercase name values to lowercase
```do x = 1 to 35;```	The DO statement repeats commands based on the value of the index variable (X, which represents each character position of NAME) until SAS encounters the END command
```if substr(name,x,1) = ' ' then do;```	Checks each character position of NAME for a blank When ' ' or a blank character is found, the following statements are executed
``` if spacel = 0 then spacel = x;```	SPACE1 is assigned the value of character position (1-35) in which the first blank is found.
``` else if space2 = 0 then space2 = x;```	SPACE2 is assigned the character position number of the second blank
``` else if space3 = 0 then space3 = x;```	SPACE3 is assigned the character position number of the third blank
```end;``` ```end;```	

Name Converting Example (*continued*)

SAS Code	Comments
`fname = substr(name,1,space1-1);`	Defines FNAME as an extract of NAME from position 1 to the position before the first blank
`mname = substr(name,space1+1,((space2-1)-space1));` `lname = substr(name,space2+1,((space3-1)-space2));`	Defines MNAME as an extract of NAME from the first character position after the first blank to the position before the third blank

`if lname = ' ' then do;`
`   lname=mname;`
`   mname = ' ';`
`end;`
	The code up to this point assumes that all records have a first, middle, and last name. This IF statement adjusts the data for records that do not have a middle name

`substr(fname,1,1) =`
`upcase(substr(fname,1,1));`
`substr(mname,1,1) =`
`upcase(substr(mname,1,1));`
`substr(lname,1,1) =`
`upcase(substr(lname,1,1));`
`proc print; var fname mname lname;`
`title1 'Creation of New Name Variables';`
`run;`
	Converts first character of FNAME, MNAME, and LNAME to uppercase while leaving the remaining characters as lowercase

Output 5-2: Name Conversion

```
        Creation of New Name Variables

    OBS     FNAME        MNAME        LNAME

     1      Thomas       Reazer       Cochran
     2      Caroline     B.           Miller
     3      Kern         Arthur       Parker
     4      Shirley      S.           Browning
     5      James        R.           Pitts
     6      Elaine       A.           Fox
     7      Malcolm      E.           Blowers
     8      Merritt      W.           Moseley
```

It should be noted that name conversions of this type usually do not work perfectly for several reasons. One, you will sometimes encounter records with four names when your code assumes three names; and two, you may find inconsistent spacing between names in the original data file. The previous example can be augmented with additional SAS code to handle names with mixed upper- and lowercase (e.g., McDowell). When you are using conversions of this type, it is important to *proof-read* the name and address information (see "Name and Address Files" in Chapter 3) before printing individualized letters and envelopes. Personalization features that are poorly handled may have a more deleterious effect on response rates than a mistake-free, but crude "DEAR ALUMNI" or "DEAR CUSTOMER" letter.

Reshaping Data - Converting Variables to Observations

In the analysis and reporting of survey results, it is often necessary to reshape your data to create multiple observations from existing observations based on responses to one or more variables. There are two general applications for this type of data manipulation in survey work.

* A common survey technique is to have multiple-response type questions in which respondents are instructed to *check all that apply*. While this type of question may appear on the survey form as a single question with *n* response categories, it is usually coded as *n* variables with dichotomous response coding (Y/N, 1/0 , etc.).

* In the analysis of a series of questions related to a single dimension, an effective presentation of the results may be made by reporting the data in a single table or graph rather than in multiple tables or graphs.[2] With the SAS System, this type of presentation is facilitated by reshaping multiple variables into a single variable whose values are represented by the creation of new observations.

The process for reshaping data under either of these two scenarios is based on using the OUTPUT statement. The SAS System executes an implicit OUTPUT statement by default at the end of every DATA step to write observations to one or more SAS data sets. When specified by a user, the OUTPUT statement directs SAS to write the current observation to the SAS data set immediately rather than at the end of the DATA step. A good practice is to use DROP or KEEP statements to eliminate unnecessary variables as part of the data-reshaping process. The example to follow is based on the multiple-response type question shown in **Figure 5-3**.

---

2 See the concept of the *supertable* in E. R. Tufte, *The Visual Display of Quantitative Information,* (Cheshire, Conn: Graphics Press, 1983), 179.

Figure 5-3: Multiple Response Example Survey Items

1. The following statements reflect the goals of many college students. Which of these goals is important to you? (*Circle all that apply*)

   01 To prepare for a career or good job
   02 To take part in college social life
   03 To develop an appreciation and enjoyment of art, music, and literature
   04 To develop an understanding and appreciation of science and technology

In the original data set, each ID or case has one observation with four goal variables coded as 1 or 0. The following program reshapes the multiple-response survey items (GOAL01-GOAL04) into a pair of new variables named GOAL and FREQ. GOAL captures the original GOAL01-GOAL04 label information and FREQ represents the response (1/0) for each goal. In the transformed data set, the observation count for each ID is expanded to four so that we have a separate value of GOAL for each record. The information previously contained in four variables per record now resides on two variables stored on four records. The new data set is not efficient for storage purposes, but it has advantages for generating custom tables and graphs where we need to treat multiple variables as a single dimension to facilitate the reader's ability to make quick comparisons. For this example, PROC TABULATE is used to report a frequency count of the new variable GOAL in a single table as shown in **Output 5-3**.

SAS Code to Reshape Data

```
libname library 'pb hd:new student svy';


options nonumber nodate ps=65 ls=80;

data survey(keep=goal freq);
length goal $40;
  set library.db966(keep=goal01-goal04);

goal = 'Prepare For Career or Good Job';
if goal01 = '1' then freq = 1;
else freq = 0;
output;

goal = 'Take Part in College Social Life';
if goal02 = '1' then freq = 1;
else freq = 0;
output;

goal = 'Dev Apprec, Enjoy of Art, Music, & Lit';
if goal03 = '1' then freq = 1;
else freq = 0;
output;

goal = 'Dev Understand of Science and Tech';
If goal04 = '1' then freq = 1;
else freq = 0;
output;

proc tabulate data = survey;
class goal;
var freq;
table goal= ' ', freq = 'Frequency'*sum=' '*f=11.0/
      box = 'Goals for Attending College' RTS=42;
title1 'Reshaping Data Example Output';
run;
```

Output 5-3: Variables Reshaped into Observations

```
                    Reshaping Data Example Output


--------------------------------------------------------------
|Goals for Attending College               | Frequency |
|------------------------------------------+-----------|
|Dev Apprec, Enjoy of Art, Music, & Lit    |       280|
|------------------------------------------+-----------|
|Dev Understand of Science and Tech        |       242|
|------------------------------------------+-----------|
|Prepare For Career or Good Job            |       580|
|------------------------------------------+-----------|
|Take Part in College Social Life          |       380|
--------------------------------------------------------------
```

Chapter

6

Analyzing Survey Data

"If the statistics are boring, then you've got the wrong numbers."
Edward R. Tufte
The Visual Display of Quantitative Information

Introduction

This chapter will illustrate, by example, the use of the SAS System to perform basic analyses of survey research data. Topics include frequency distributions, descriptive statistics, *t*-tests, correlation, scale reliability, analysis of variance, multiple regression, scatter plots, and histograms. The SAS System provides a relatively easy-to-use set of procedures (procs) for "getting answers" to basic questions. The following SAS procs will be covered in this chapter:

- FREQ
- TTEST
- MEANS
- GLM
- UNIVARIATE
- REG
- SUMMARY
- PLOT
- CORR
- CHART

These analytical procedures have many options, and this chapter will describe those that are most commonly used in the analysis of survey data. For a full discussion of the options for these procs, see the *SAS Procedures Guide* (FREQ, MEANS, UNIVARIATE, CORR, SUMMARY, CHART, and PLOT procedures) and the *SAS/STAT User's Guide, Volume 1* and *Volume 2* (TTEST, GLM, and REG procedures). The final section of this chapter will illustrate the use of SAS data manipulation techniques for processing qualitative responses to survey open-ended items.

Frequency Distributions and Chi Square Analysis

PROC FREQ is one of the most often-used procedures in the SAS System. This procedure is used to generate one-way frequency distributions and cross-tabulations of two or more variables. For two-way tables, PROC FREQ can compute measures of association (e.g., Chi Square and other statistical tests). In the following example, a Chi Square analysis is used to determine if male college students seek employment more often than females. Anticipated employment is estimated with the survey question shown in **Figure 6-1** and response values are stored as the variable EMPLOYED in a SAS data set (DB96). The variable SEX is also stored in the same data set. This example also illustrates the use of PROC FORMAT to generate value labels for SEX and EMPLOYED. The results of the PROC FREQ analysis are shown in **Output 6-1**.

Figure 6-1: Chi Square Analysis Survey Item

Q10. Do your plans include employment during your first semester?

  1 No

  2 Yes

PROC FREQ SAS Code

```
libname library 'pb hd:new student svy';
options nonumber nodate ps=65 ls=80;
proc format;
   value $yesno '1' = 'No'
                '2' = 'Yes';
   value $sex
                'F' = 'Female'
                'M' = 'Male';
proc freq data = library.db96;
tables employed*sex/chisq;
format employed $yesno. sex $sex. ;
title1 'Anticipated Employment by Sex - Chi Square Analysis';
run;
```

Output 6-1: PROC FREQ - Chi Square Output

```
           Anticipated Employment by Sex - Chi Square Analysis
                      TABLE OF EMPLOYED BY SEX

              EMPLOYED    SEX
              Frequency|
              Percent  |
              Row Pct  |
              Col Pct  | Female | Male    | Total
              ---------+--------+--------+
              No       |    184 |    113 |    297
                       |  31.35 |  19.25 |  50.60
                       |  61.95 |  38.05 |
                       |  52.27 |  48.09 |
              ---------+--------+--------+
              Yes      |    168 |    122 |    290
                       |  28.62 |  20.78 |  49.40
                       |  57.93 |  42.07 |
                       |  47.73 |  51.91 |
              ---------+--------+--------+
              Total        352      235      587
                         59.97    40.03   100.00
              Frequency Missing = 15

               STATISTICS FOR TABLE OF EMPLOYED BY SEX
   Statistic                    DF       Value        Prob
   ------------------------------------------------------------
   Chi-Square                    1        0.989       0.320
   Likelihood Ratio Chi-Square   1        0.989       0.320
   Continuity Adj. Chi-Square    1        0.828       0.363
   Mantel-Haenszel Chi-Square    1        0.987       0.320
   Fisher's Exact Test (Left)                         0.860
                      (Right)                         0.181
                      (2-Tail)                        0.354
   Phi Coefficient                        0.041
   Contingency Coefficient                0.041
   Cramer's V                             0.041

   Effective Sample Size = 587
   Frequency Missing = 15
```

Interpretation

As shown in **Output 6-1**, 47.73% of females and 51.91% of males anticipate being employed during their first semester of college. The Chi Square analysis provides a test statistic of 0.989 with a probability value of 0.320. Thus, using the standard .05 or .01 level of statistical significance, we have insufficient evidence to reject the null hypothesis that men and women have equivalent first-semester employment plans.

Measures of Central Tendency

PROC MEANS and PROC UNIVARIATE are easy-to-use SAS procedures for generating measures of central tendency and other descriptive statistics. PROC SUMMARY can also produce means, standard deviations, and summated totals. A major difference between PROC SUMMARY and the MEANS and UNIVARIATE procedures is that the former produces a SAS data set and no printed output by default. While this feature of PROC SUMMARY may be initially confusing to beginners, PROC SUMMARY is an extremely useful procedure for collapsing data in summarized data sets. This type of data manipulation and analysis is often a first step for

- Reporting survey results with multiple breakdown or class variables in a condensed form
- Creating files with aggregated results for use in tables and graphs.

The survey items shown in **Figure 6-2** will be used to illustrate PROC MEANS, PROC UNIVARIATE, and PROC SUMMARY.

Figure 6-2: Survey Items for PROC MEANS, UNIVARIATE, and SUMMARY

Q1. How well do you feel that UNCA met your needs in the following areas?				
	Poorly	Somewhat Adequately	Adequately	Very Well
a. Intellectual growth	1	2	3	4
b. Career training	1	2	3	4
c. Personal growth	1	2	3	4

PROC MEANS

In this section, PROC MEANS is used to compute item means for survey items
Q1A (intellectual growth), Q1B (career training), and Q1C (personal growth). These
variables are defined on the survey form shown in **Figure 6-2**. The example to follow illustrates the use of PROC MEANS with the optional CLASS statement. The
CLASS statement is used to identify subgroups for reporting the results of the
MEANS procedure. In this example, DISCIP (academic discipline) is used as a
class variable. A nice feature of PROC MEANS is that you can specify the
number of decimal positions for display by using the MAXDEC option on the
PROC statement. The results of the following program are shown in **Output 6-2**.

PROC MEANS SAS Code

```
libname svy 'pb hd:gss';

data report;
  set svy.data96(keep=discip qla qlb qlc);
  label qla = 'Intellectual Growth'
        qlb = 'Career Training'
        qlc = 'Personal Growth';

proc format;
  value $discip 'NS' = 'Natural Sciences'
                'SS' = 'Social Sciences'
                'HM' = 'Humanities'
                'PR' = 'Professional';

proc means data = report maxdec=1;
  class discip;
  var qla qlb qlc ;
format discip $discip. ;
title1 'Mean Satisfaction Scores by Academic Discipline';
run;
```

Output 6-2: PROC MEANS - Output with Class Variable

```
              Mean Satisfaction Scores by Academic Discipline

DISCIP              N Obs   Variable    Label              N    Mean Std Dev
-----------------------------------------------------------------------------
Humanities           56     Q1A      Intellectual Growth   56   3.6    0.6
                            Q1B      Career Training       53   2.4    1.0
                            Q1C      Personal Growth       53   3.5    0.7

Natural Sciences     83     Q1A      Intellectual Growth   83   3.5    0.7
                            Q1B      Career Training       82   2.7    0.9
                            Q1C      Personal Growth       83   3.3    0.8

Professional        143     Q1A      Intellectual Growth  141   3.5    0.6
                            Q1B      Career Training      141   2.9    0.8
                            Q1C      Personal Growth      141   3.2    0.8

Social Sciences     146     Q1A      Intellectual Growth  146   3.5    0.7
                            Q1B      Career Training      143   2.5    0.8
                            Q1C      Personal Growth      145   3.3    0.8
-----------------------------------------------------------------------------
```

PROC UNIVARIATE

PROC UNIVARIATE and PROC MEANS are similar procedures, but PROC UNIVARIATE provides a more complete set of descriptive statistics. The primary advantages of PROC UNIVARIATE include

- Percentile distributions including the median statistic (default)

- Test of normality (NORMAL option)

- Plots - both stem and leaf and normal probability (PLOT option)

- Measures of kurtosis, skewness (default).

UNIVARIATE is one of three SAS procedures[1] that will produce the median statistic. When the NORMAL option is specified on the PROC UNIVARIATE statement, the procedure will test the null hypothesis that the observed data for a specified vari-

---

[1] The median statistic can be determined from PROC FREQ (base SAS software) and PROC CAPABILITY (SAS/QC software). In Version 7 of the SAS System, PROC TABULATE will compute the median statistic.

able are taken from a normal distribution. If the probability associated with the test statistic[2] is less than the level chosen (e.g., p=.05), then the null hypothesis can be rejected, and you would conclude that the observed data are *not* normally distributed. Many commonly used statistical procedures (e.g., ANOVA, regression) assume that the data are normally distributed.

The PROC UNIVARIATE example to follow is based on the same survey items used in the PROC MEANS example (**Figure 6-2**). In this example, the three survey items (Q1A, Q1B, Q1C) are combined in a single summated scale measure of "overall satisfaction." The NORMAL option is used to test the hypothesis that the summated scale values are taken from a normal distribution. The results of the following program are shown in **Output 6-3**.

PROC UNIVARIATE SAS Code

```
libname svy 'pb hd:gss';

data report;
  set svy.data96(keep=q1a q1b q1c);

if (q1a = . or q1b = . or q1c = . ) then delete;
overall = sum(q1a,q1b,q1c);
label overall = 'Overall Satisfaction';

proc univariate data = report normal;
  var overall;
title1 'Overall Satisfaction Scale: Descriptive Statistics';
run;
```

---

2 For sample sizes of 2,000 or less, the normality test is the Shapiro-Wilk statistic. For sample sizes greater than 2,000, the Kolmogorov-Smirnoff statistic is used to test the null hypothesis that the data are taken from a normal distribution.

Output 6-3: PROC UNIVARIATE - Output with NORMAL Option

```
                Overall Satisfaction Scale: Descriptive Statistics

                            Univariate Procedure

    Variable=OVERALL        Overall Satisfaction

                 Moments                           Quantiles(Def=5)

    N                 428  Sum Wgts       428   100%  Max  12      99%    12
    Mean         9.422897  Sum           4033    75%  Q3   11      95%    12
    Std Dev      1.746496  Variance  3.050247    50%  Med  10      90%    11
    Skewness     -0.57408  Kurtosis  -0.02368    25%  Q1    8      10%     7
    USS             39305  CSS       1302.456     0%  Min   3       5%     6
    CV           18.53459  Std Mean   0.08442                      1%     5
    T:Mean=0     111.6192  Pr>|T|      0.0001        Range    9
    Num ^= 0          428  Num > 0        428        Q3-Q1    3
    M(Sign)           214  Pr>=|M|     0.0001        Mode    11
    Sgn Rank        45903  Pr>=|S|     0.0001
    W:Normal     0.923764  Pr<W        0.0001


                Overall Satisfaction Scale: Descriptive Statistics

                            Univariate Procedure

    Variable=OVERALL     Overall Satisfaction

                                   Extremes

                     Lowest   Obs    Highest   Obs
                        3(    14)      12(    391)
                        4(    41)      12(    401)
                        4     23)      12(    410)
                        5    380)      12(    417)
                        5    374)      12(    420)
```

Interpretation

From **Output 6-3**, we note the following key statistics on the summated overall satisfaction scale:

```
        N = 428
     Mean = 9.4
   Median = 10.0
      Min = 3
      Max = 12
  Std Dev = 1.7
 W:Normal = 0.9
     Pr<W = 0.0001
```

The probability associated with the Wilkes-Shapiro normality statistic (Pr <W) is highly significant ($p <= .0001$), which provides sufficient evidence to reject the null hypothesis that the satisfaction scores are normally distributed.

PROC SUMMARY

Like the MEANS and UNIVARIATE procedures, PROC SUMMARY can compute descriptive statistics (mean and standard deviation) and sum amounts. The major difference between PROC SUMMARY and the MEANS and UNIVARIATE procedures is that PROC SUMMARY does not generate printed output by default, but instead outputs a new SAS data set that contains the results of the analysis. PROC SUMMARY and PROC MEANS allow the use of CLASS statement to facilitate the analysis of numeric variables by one or more subgroups. The UNIVARIATE procedure does not have a CLASS statement, but groups could be analyzed with BY-group processing. The basic form of the SUMMARY procedure is

PROC SUMMARY DATA = *name*;

Selected PROC SUMMARY Statements

VAR *variable-list*;
CLASS *variable-list*;
OUTPUT OUT = *name*
        statistic-list;
Where:
        statistic-list is one or more of the following:
        mean
        std
        sum

> min
> max
>   *name-list;*

Where:

name-list are user-defined variable names to represent statistical measures.

The output files that are created by PROC SUMMARY always contain two automatic variables called _FREQ_ and _TYPE_. The _FREQ_ variable contains the number of observations included for a given line of output or combination of class variables. The _TYPE_ variable is used to represent the combination of class variables or the level of analysis. A _TYPE_ value of 0 is always used to represent the grand total for all class variables combined. As each class variable is included in the analysis, the _TYPE_ variable is incremented by one. The _TYPE_ variable is very useful for manipulating the output data set created by the SUMMARY procedure. For example, the user may want to print or graph only a set of summary observations for a particular combination of class variables. This type of operation is performed with a subsetting IF statement in a DATA step (e.g., `if _type_ = 2;`). It is important to note that PROC SUMMARY will exclude observations that have missing data for one or more class variables unless the MISSING option is specified on the PROC SUMMARY statement.

TIP: PROC SUMMARY Statistic Short-cut

If only one statistic (e.g., mean) is requested, *name-list* can be eliminated with a shortcut default *statistic* = option. The result of using this option is to use the original names of the variables specified in the VAR statement as the names used to represent the summary statistic. This shortcut cannot be used if more than one statistic is requested, as at least two or more names will be needed to represent the statistics requested for each variable.

```
proc summary data = survey;
    var income
    educ score1;
    class race sex;
    output out = stats
    mean = ;
```

PROC SUMMARY Example

The example to follow is based on the same survey items used in the PROC MEANS example. The only difference is that the present example is expanded to include two years of data stored in separate permanent SAS data sets (DATA95 and DATA96). Mean scores for Q1A, Q1B, and Q1C are reported by academic discipline and year. Note that PROC PRINT is used to display the file (named STATS in this example) that was created by PROC SUMMARY. The results of the analysis are shown in **Output 6-4**.

PROC SUMMARY SAS Code

```
libname svy 'pb hd:gss';

data report;
 set svy.data96(keep=discip qla qlb qlc year)
     svy.data95(keep=discip qla qlb qlc year);

        label qla = 'Intellectual Growth'
              qlb = 'Career Training'
              qlc = 'Personal Growth';

proc format;
   value $discip 'NS' = 'Natural Sciences'
                 'SS' = 'Social Sciences'
                 'HM' = 'Humanities'
                 'PR' = 'Professional';

proc summary data = report;
   class discip year;
   var qla qlb qlc ;
   output out = stats
   mean = ;

proc print data = stats label;
format discip $discip. ;
title1
'Mean Satisfaction Scores by Academic Discipline & Year';
run;
```

Output 6-4: PROC SUMMARY - Output to Display STATS File

```
            Mean Satisfaction Scores by Academic Discipline & Year

                                            Intellectual   Career     Personal
    OBS DISCIP            YEAR   _TYPE_  _FREQ_   Growth    Training     Growth

     1                              0     646    3.47196    2.71203    3.30551
     2                      95      1     368    3.47397    2.76816    3.33889
     3                      96      1     278    3.46931    2.63869    3.26182
     4  Humanities                  2      93    3.54348    2.55056    3.38202
     5  Natural Sciences            2     134    3.45113    2.74809    3.31818
     6  Professional                2     211    3.45455    2.91866    3.24519
     7  Social Sciences             2     208    3.47115    2.54680    3.32524
     8  Humanities          95      3      55    3.46296    2.62745    3.38462
     9  Humanities          96      3      38    3.65789    2.44737    3.37838
    10  Natural Sciences    95      3      75    3.51351    2.80822    3.35616
    11  Natural Sciences    96      3      59    3.37288    2.67241    3.27119
    12  Professional        95      3     122    3.42975    2.90083    3.25833
    13  Professional        96      3      89    3.48864    2.94318    3.22727
    14  Social Sciences     95      3     116    3.50000    2.66372    3.39130
    15  Social Sciences     96      3      92    3.43478    2.40000    3.24176
```

TIP: PROC SUMMARY NWAY Option

Use the PROC SUMMARY NWAY option to reduce unnecessary output detail. The NWAY option instructs SAS to output only the highest level of interaction among class variables as represented by the _TYPE_ value. In many cases this is the only _TYPE_ value needed. For example, if the NWAY option were used in the preceding example, **Output 6-5** would contain only the records with a _TYPE_ value of 3. The use of the NWAY option is illustrated as follows:

```
proc summary data = survey nway;
```

Mathematical Trick for Calculating Percentages

In many survey research projects, percentages are the statistic of choice for summarizing and reporting the results. For most social science survey projects that are based on Likert type scales (1 = Strongly Disagree; 2 = Disagree; 3 = Agree; 4 = Strongly Agree) the use of percentages has two major advantages over reporting mean scores.

- For interval level measurements the use of means, while frequently reported, may not be statistically appropriate.

- A good practice is to report Likert-type survey items as the percentage of respondents that "agree" or are "satisfied" with some dimension. This percentage statistic has much more intuitive meaning to users of the survey data than mean scores.

PROC FREQ provides an easy-to-use procedure for generating percentages in one-way and *n*-way tables, but the output can be lengthy and awkward to work with. PROC TABULATE provides an enhanced capability to report percentages in custom tables, but this procedure can involve considerable complexity (see Chapter 7). A quick and easy way to compute percentages is based on the mathematical "trick" of creating a new variable with two possible values: 100 to represent the presence of some characteristic and 0 to indicate the absence of the characteristic. The mean of this new variable is the percentage of observations with the characteristic represented by the value of 100. If a proportion, rather than a percentage, is desired the new variable can be represented by 1 or 0.

This process of creating dummy variables to report percentages is illustrated in the program to follow. This example is based on the survey items (Q1A, Q1B, Q1C) shown in **Figure 6-2**. The analysis to follow creates new variables (PCT1-PCT3) to represent the percentage of those who responded either "adequately" or "very well" to the three items (intellectual growth, career training, personal growth) that are represented by Q1A-Q1C. The new PCT1-PCT3 variables are assigned a value of either 100 or 0 based on the values of the Q1A-Q1C variables. PROC SUMMARY is used to compute means for PCT1-PCT3 by YEAR and DISCIP (academic discipline). The "mean" scores that are computed by the SUMMARY procedure are actually the *percentage* of subjects who reported "adequately" or "very well." This process of creating dummy variables to calculate percentages will work with any SAS procedure that computes means (the MEANS, UNIVARIATE, and TABULATE procedures). The results of the program are shown in **Output 6-5**.

SAS Code for Calculating Percentages with Mean of 100 or 0

```
libname svy 'pb hd:gss';

data report;
 set svy.data96(keep=discip q1a q1b q1c year)
     svy.data95(keep=discip q1a q1b q1c year);

     if q1a = 4          then pct1 = 100;
else if (1 <= q1a <= 3) then pct1 =   0;

     if q1b = 4          then pct2 = 100;
else if (1 <= q1b <= 3) then pct2 =   0;

     if q1c = 4          then pct3 = 100;
else if (1 <= q1c <= 3) then pct3 =   0;

label pct1 = 'Intellectual Growth'
      pct2 = 'Career Training'
      pct3 = 'Personal Growth';

proc format;
   value $discip 'NS' = 'Natural Sciences'
                 'SS' = 'Social Sciences'
                 'HM' = 'Humanities'
                 'PR' = 'Professional';

proc summary data = report;
   class discip year;
   var pct1 pct2 pct3 ;
   output out = stats
   mean = ;

proc print data = stats label;
format discip $discip. ;
title1 'Satisfaction Scores by Academic Discipline & Year';
title3 'Percent Reporting "Adequately" or "Very Well"';
run;
```

Output 6-5: PROC SUMMARY - Calculating Percentages

```
              Satisfaction Scores by Academic Discipline & Year
                 Percent Reporting "Adequately" or "Very Well"

                                         Intellectual   Career    Personal
 OBS DISCIP            YEAR    _TYPE_   _FREQ_   Growth    Training    Growth
                                  0      646     94.3925   62.3418    86.1417
  2                     95        1      368     94.7945   66.4804    87.2222
  3                     96        1      278     93.8628   56.9343    84.7273
  4   Humanities                  2       93     93.4783   53.9326    87.6404
  5   Natural Sciences            2      134     94.7368   64.8855    84.0909
  6   Professional                2      211     97.1292   73.6842    85.5769
  7   Social Sciences             2      208     91.8269   52.7094    87.3786
  8   Humanities        95        3       55     92.5926   58.8235    86.5385
  9   Humanities        96        3       38     94.7368   47.3684    89.1892
 10   Natural Sciences  95        3       75     97.2973   68.4932    87.6712
 11   Natural Sciences  96        3       59     91.5254   60.3448    79.6610
 12   Professional      95        3      122     97.5207   73.5537    87.5000
 13   Professional      96        3       89     96.5909   73.8636    82.9545
 14   Social Sciences   95        3      116     91.3793   61.0619    86.9565
 15   Social Sciences   96        3       92     92.3913   42.2222    87.9121
```

Correlation and Scale Reliability

Correlation matrices are generated with the CORR procedure. By default, PROC CORR computes both descriptive statistics and Pearson product-moment correlations for all numeric variables that are included on the VAR statement. The CORR procedure has a number of options that are useful in survey research projects. An estimate of *internal consistency* or scale reliability can be estimated with Cronbach's coefficient alpha. This statistic is computed when the ALPHA option is specified on the PROC CORR statement. For example:

```
proc corr alpha data = test;
var q1 q2 q3;
```

When you specify the ALPHA option, specify only the variables that define a single scale on the VAR statement. If it is desired to generate Cronbach's coefficient alpha for multiple scales, then a separate procedure will need to be run for each scale. You may also use PROC CORR to compute the following non-parametric correlations: (1) Spearman's rank-order; (2) Kendall's tau-b; and (3) Hoeffding's measure of dependence. Lastly, PROC CORR can be used to compute a number of partial correlations. The use of PROC CORR with Cronbach's coefficient Alpha is illustrated using the survey items shown in **Figure 6-3**.

Figure 6-3: PROC CORR Survey Example

How do you rate your instructor on the following dimensions?	Instructor Rating *Circle Response*			
1. Fairness in assigning grades	Poor	Fair	Good	Excellent
2. Variety of teaching methods	Poor	Fair	Good	Excellent
3. Useful feedback in reviewing your work	Poor	Fair	Good	Excellent
4. Willingness to meet with you outside class	Poor	Fair	Good	Excellent

In the program to follow, the **Figure 6-3** survey items (Q01-Q04) are stored in a SAS data set (FAC_EVAL). The CORR procedure is performed on the SAS data set without using a DATA step. The results are shown in **Output 6-6**.

PROC CORR SAS Code

```
libname library 'pb hd:prog assess svy';
options nonumber nodate ps=65 ls=80;

proc corr data = library.fac_eval alpha;
var q01 q02 q03 q04;
title1 'Perceived Quality of Teaching Scale';
title2 'Correlation Matrix and Reliability';
run;
```

Output 6-6: PROC CORR - Output without a DATA Step

```
                    Perceived Quality of Teaching Scale
                    Correlation Matrix and Reliability


                          Correlation Analysis


              4 'VAR' Variables: Q01    Q02    Q03    Q04


                            Simple Statistics
    Variable      N        Mean      Std Dev      Sum     Minimum    Maximum

    Q01         1156     2.95069     0.72086     3411    1.00000    4.00000
    Q02         1154     3.02253     0.71011     3488    1.00000    4.00000
    Q03         1154     2.97920     0.71382     3438    1.00000    4.00000
    Q04         1140     3.17018     0.75600     3614    1.00000    4.00000
```

Output 6-6: PROC CORR (continued)

```
                Perceived Quality of Teaching Scale
                Correlation Matrix and Reliability

                       Correlation Analysis

                    Cronbach Coefficient Alpha

             for RAW variables      : 0.777455
             for STANDARDIZED variables: 0.779217


                  Raw Variables              Std. Variables

       Deleted    Correlation              Correlation
       Variable   with Total    Alpha      with Total      Alpha
       ----------------------------------------------------------

       Q01        0.606166    0.710630    0.610048       0.711848
       Q02        0.626980    0.700159    0.628216       0.702249
       Q03        0.594678    0.716760    0.595698       0.719357
       Q04        0.502335    0.765844    0.502637       0.766502

     Pearson Correlation Coefficients / Prob > |R| under Ho: Rho=0
     / Number of Observations

               Q01            Q02            Q03            Q04

  Q01        1.00000        0.59309        0.49942        0.36518
             0.0            0.0001         0.0001         0.0001
             1156           1154           1146           1132

  Q02        0.59309        1.00000        0.47498        0.42397
             0.0001         0.0            0.0001         0.0001
             1154           1154           1144           1132

  Q03        0.49942        0.47498        1.00000        0.45583
             0.0001         0.0001         0.0            0.0001
             1146           1144           1154           1135

  Q04        0.36518        0.42397        0.45583        1.00000
             0.0001         0.0001         0.0001         0.0
             1132           1132           1135           1140
```

Interpretation

The first table shown in **Output 6-6** provides descriptive statistics for all variables that are listed on the VAR statement. The second table in the CORR output provides both raw and standardized item-total scale correlations for each variable that is included on the VAR statement. The table also includes the Cronbach's coefficient alpha[3] correlations that would be obtained if each item were dropped from the scale. We note that the lowest item-total correlation was found for Q04 (r = .50). This would suggest that the Q04 variable should be considered for deletion or rewording. In the correlation matrix that follows the second table, there are three numbers in each cell. The top or first number is the Pearson product-moment correlation coefficient for the pair of variables represented in the matrix. The second or middle number is the probability value for testing the null hypothesis that the observed r value is equal to zero. The bottom number is the sample size for that cell.

Analysis of Group Means

SAS/STAT software provides an excellent set of statistical tools for data analysis. This section will describe the SAS procedures for conducting independent *t*-tests (PROC TTEST), paired comparisons *t*-tests (PROC MEANS), and analysis of variance (PROC GLM). PROC GLM is a widely used procedure for the analysis of general linear models.

Paired Comparisons T-Test

SAS has separate procedures for conducting *t*-tests for paired comparisons and *t*-test for independent samples. The TTEST procedure is designed for *independent* samples. PROC MEANS is used for the analysis of *dependent* or paired samples (e.g., the comparison of individual pre- and post-measures). The first step in the analysis of paired comparisons is to create a variable to represent the difference between two variables. A paired comparison *t*-test can be computed with PROC MEANS by using the T and PRT options to test the null hypothesis that the difference score is equal to zero. To illustrate this process, we present the example data set in **Figure 6-4**, which contains two SAT scores for each of ten individuals. The null hypothesis is that SAT2 - SAT1 = 0; alternatively, we would expect SAT2 - SAT1 > 0. The data for this example are stored in a comma-delimited ASCII file (SAT.DAT) shown in **Figure 6-4**. Note the use of the DSD option on the INFILE statement to read this comma-delimited file. The results of this program are shown in **Output 6-7**.

---

3 Cronbach's coefficient alpha provides a measure of instrument reliability that is based on internal consistency or the degree to which scale items are homogenous. Measures of internal consistency can be visualized in the following way. Randomly split an instrument or scale into two sets of items, then correlate the two subscales for each subject. The average of these correlations provides a measure of internal consistency or scale reliability.

Figure 6-4: SAT.DAT File

ID	SAT1	SAT2
001,	0900,	0950
002,	0750,	0850
003,	1200,	1240
004,	1000,	1050
005,	0820,	0950
006,	1400,	1350
007,	1150,	1200
008,	1050,	1110
009,	1350,	1300
010,	1175,	1375

PROC MEANS - SAS Code for Paired Comparisons

```
filename sat 'pb hd:sat.dat';

data compare;
infile sat dsd;
input id $ sat1 sat2 ;
diff = sat2-sat1;

proc means data = compare mean t prt stderr;
var diff;
title1
'T-Test of difference between 1st SAT Test and 2nd SAT Test';
run;
```

Output 6-7: PROC MEANS - Paired Comparisons T-Test

```
T-Test of difference between 1st SAT Test and 2nd SAT Test
  Analysis Variable : DIFF

      Mean              T  Prob>|T|     Std Error
------------------------------------------------------
  58.0000000     2.4374434    0.0375    23.7954244
------------------------------------------------------
```

Interpretation

From **Output 6-7**, we note that the mean SAT gain score (SAT2-SAT1) is 58 points. The T statistic is 2.44 with $p <= .0375$. It is important to note that SAS computes the *two-tailed* probability level and since we specified a directional null hypothesis a priori, the correct p value is (.0375/2) or .01875. Thus, we reject the null hypothesis that the difference score is equal to 0, and we conclude that the observed increase in SAT scores for the second administration of the test is statistically significant.

Independent T-Test

The TTEST procedure can be used to compare means of two *independent* samples or groups. The form for PROC TTEST is nearly identical to PROC MEANS:

> PROC TTEST DATA = *name*;

Selected PROC TTEST Statements

> CLASS *variable*;
> VAR *variables*;

The CLASS statement in PROC TTEST is used to specify the variable that represents the comparison group. The VAR statement is used to identify the analysis variable(s) for the TTEST procedure. PROC TTEST tests the assumption of equal variances and computes appropriate test statistics for both equal and unequal variance conditions. Consistent with the preceding PROC MEANS example, the TTEST procedure computes a two-tailed probability value. If you have a directional alternative hypothesis, the p value that SAS computes should be divided by two to adjust for a one-tailed test.

In the following example, we wish to test the null hypothesis that male and female college graduates have equal self-reported gains in the development of computer skills. The analysis variable (self-reported gain) is defined by the survey question shown in **Figure 6-5**. The class variable (SEX) and the survey variable (Q3) are stored in a permanent SAS data set (DATA96). The results of the TTEST procedure are shown in **Output 6-8**.

Figure 6-5: PROC TTEST Survey Item

> 3. To what extent do you think your college education contributed to your development of computer skills?
>
>   1 Not at all
>   2 Very Little
>   3 Somewhat
>   4 Very Much

PROC TTEST SAS Code

```
libname svy 'pb hd:gss';

data report;
set svy.data96(keep=sex q3);

label q3 = 'Developing Computer Skills';

proc format;
   value $sex 'F' = 'Female'
              'M' = 'Male';

proc ttest data = report;
class sex;
var q3;
format sex $sex. ;
title1
'T-Test Analysis of Self-Reported Gain in Computer
Skills by Sex';
run;
```

Output 6-8: PROC TTEST Results

```
            T-Test Analysis of Self-Reported Gain in Computer Skills by Sex

                              TTEST PROCEDURE

   Variable: Q3          Developing Computer Skills

   SEX        N   Mean       Std Dev     Std Error    Minimum     Maximum
   ------------------------------------------------------------------------
   Female    360  3.05277778  0.90494959  0.04769503  1.00000000  4.00000000
   Male      260  3.19615385  0.82666972  0.05126788  1.00000000  4.00000000


   Variances       T    DF   Prob>|T|
   -----------------------------------------
   Unequal  -2.0476  585.1   0.0410
   Equal    -2.0179  618.0   0.0440

   For H0: Variances are equal, F' = 1.20   DF = (359,259)   Prob>F' = 0.1204
```

Interpretation

From **Output 6-8**, we note that male college graduates have a slightly higher mean Q3 score (3.19) than female graduates (3.05). Assuming equal Q3 variance among males and females, we have a T value of -2.05, and we can reject the null hypothesis that men and women do not differ on self-reported gain in computer skills ($p <= .04$). Our understanding of this relationship will be increased when we use analysis of variance procedures described in the next section to expand this one-variable model to include the effects of academic discipline.

Analysis of Variance - PROC GLM

In addition to the TTEST procedure, the SAS System has six additional procedures for performing analysis of variance (the GLM, ANOVA[4], NESTED, VARCOMP, NPAR1WAY, and PLAN procedures). In the analysis of survey data, PROC GLM (General Linear Models) is widely used for conducting one-way to *n*-way analysis of variance procedures. PROC GLM can also be used to conduct regression analyses.[5]

---

4 ANOVA is designed for the analysis of balanced designs where there are an equal number of subjects in each cell, a condition that almost never exists in survey research projects.

5 For regression analyses using PROC GLM, the CLASS statement is not used.

The basic form of the PROC GLM for conducting analysis of variance is as follows:

PROC GLM DATA = *name*;
CLASS *variables*;
MODEL *dependents* = *independents*;
LSMEANS *effects/options*;
MEANS *effects/options*;

The CLASS statement is used to specify the classification or group variables that are used in the analysis. For a one-way analysis of variance problem, only one group or classification variable is listed on the CLASS statement. For a two-way analysis of variance, two variables are listed on the CLASS statement and so on. The MODEL statement is used to identify both dependent and independent variables. The independent variables are the same classification variables that are listed on the CLASS statement. Interaction effects are specified with an asterisk(*), e.g., VAR1*VAR2. The LSMEANS statement is optional and is used to request least square or group means for all effects listed. For nonorthogonal or unbalanced designs, GLM will compute least square means as if a balanced design were used. The MEANS statement requests GLM to compute means for any effect listed. A useful option for the MEANS statement is to specify a multiple-range test (e.g., Duncan, Scheffe, Tukey) and the alpha level. Multiple-range tests have a default alpha level of .05. This default *p* value can be overridden with the ALPHA = .*xx* option, where *xx* is the desired probability level. Consult the *SAS/STAT User's Guide* for a full discussion of PROC GLM and available options.

Two-Way ANOVA Example

In the previous PROC TTEST example, our SAS researcher found that male college graduates had a statistically significant higher level of self-reported gains in computer skills than female graduates. In an effort to explain this observed difference based on sex, our researcher decided to include academic discipline in the model. This type of analysis can be conducted by using a two-way analysis of variance procedure. The dependent variable is Q3 (computer skills) and the group variables are SEX and DISCIP. To assess the impact of SEX on Q3 (computer skills), SEX is included in the model as both a main effect and an interaction[6] term DISCIP*SEX. The program to conduct a two-way analysis of variance procedure by using PROC GLM is shown in the following example. The GLM results are shown in **Output 6-9**.

---

6 The inclusion of the interaction term in the model SEX*DISCIP will test the null hypothesis that men and women within a particular academic discipline do not differ in self-reported computer skills.

PROC GLM SAS Code

```
libname srsvy 'pb hd:gss';

data report;
 set srsvy.data96(keep=sex q3);

label q3 = 'Developing Computer Skills';

proc format;
    value $discip 'NS' = 'Natural Sciences'
                  'SS' = 'Social Sciences'
                  'HM' = 'Humanities'
                  'PR' = 'Professional';

        value $sex    'F' = 'Female'
                      'M' = 'Male';

proc glm data = report;
class sex discip;
model q3 = discip sex sex*discip;
means sex discip/duncan alpha=.01;
format sex $sex. discip $discip. ;
title1 'Two-Way ANOVA of Gain in Computer Skills by Discipline & Sex';
run;
```

Output 6-9 : PROC GLM Results

```
Two-Way ANOVA of Self-Reported Computer Skills by Discipline & Sex    1

                    General Linear Models Procedure
                        Class Level Information


Class   Levels  Values

SEX        2    Female Male

DISCIP     4    Humanities Natural Sciences Professional Social Sciences

            Number of observations in data set = 624

NOTE: Due to missing values, only 622 observations can be used in this
      analysis.
```

Output 6-9: PROC GLM (*continued*)

```
     Two-Way ANOVA of Self-Reported Computer Skills by Discipline & Sex    2

                        General Linear Models Procedure

Dependent Variable: Q3G    Developing computer skills

Source              DF       Sum of Squares     F Value     Pr > F

Model                7          21.13142077       4.08       0.0002

Error              614         453.76407762

Corrected Total    621         474.89549839

                 R-Square              C.V.            Q3G Mean

                 0.044497           27.60525         3.11414791

Source              DF          Type I SS      F Value     Pr > F

DISCIP               3         18.87854608       8.52       0.0001
SEX                  1          1.68414489       2.28       0.1317
SEX*DISCIP           3          0.56872980       0.26       0.8567

Source              DF         Type III SS     F Value     Pr > F

DISCIP               3         17.74685191       8.00       0.0001
SEX                  1          1.39047829       1.88       0.1707
SEX*DISCIP           3          0.56872980       0.26       0.8567
```

Output 6-9: PROC GLM (*continued*)

```
      Two-Way ANOVA of Self-Reported Computer Skills by Discipline & Sex    3

                         General Linear Models Procedure

                   Duncan's Multiple Range Test for variable: Q3G

    NOTE: This test controls the type I comparisonwise error rate, not the
          experimentwise error rate

                       Alpha= 0.01 df= 614 MSE= 0.739029
                       WARNING: Cell sizes are not equal.
                       Harmonic Mean of cell sizes= 302.9614

                             Number of Means    2
                             Critical Range .1805

          Means with the same letter are not significantly different.

                  Duncan Grouping        Mean    N   SEX

                              A       3.19923   261   Male
                              A
                              A       3.05263   361   Female
```

Output 6-9: PROC GLM (*continued*)

```
    Two-Way ANOVA of Self-Reported Computer Skills by Discipline & Sex    4

                         General Linear Models Procedure

                 Duncan's Multiple Range Test for variable: Q3G

  NOTE: This test controls the type I comparisonwise error rate, not the
        experimentwise error rate

                    Alpha= 0.01 df= 614 MSE= 0.739029
                    WARNING: Cell sizes are not equal.
                  Harmonic Mean of cell sizes= 137.4239

                     Number of Means   2     3     4
                     Critical Range .2680 .2793 .2870

      Means with the same letter are not significantly different.

          Duncan Grouping       Mean    N   DISCIP

                          A     3.3301  209  Professional
                          A
                      B   A     3.1318  129  Natural Sciences
                      B
                      B   C     2.9898  197  Social Sciences
                          C
                          C     2.8506   87  Humanities
```

Interpretation

As shown in **Output 6-9**, the GLM results are printed on four pages. The first page provides users with log-type information on classification variables to include number of levels, values, and observations that are included in the analysis. It is important to review the first page as a check for possible errors in defining groups, handling missing values, etc.

On the first half of the second page of output, SAS prints a summary ANOVA table to show sums of squares information, degrees of freedom, the R^2 statistic, the F value and associated probability level for the overall model. In this example, we have obtained an overall F value of 4.08 with $p \leq .0002$; thus we can reject the null hypothesis that the means of all groups (men, women, and four academic disciplines) are equal. At this point, we do not know the source of the statistically significant differences. On the bottom half of the second page of output, SAS provides the degrees of freedom, sum of squares, F values, and probability values for each source of variation. By default, SAS provides you with two types of sums of squares, TYPE I SS and TYPE III SS. In orthogonal or balanced designs with equal numbers of observations in each classification group, these two sums of squares are equal. With unbalanced designs or unequal group sizes, the TYPE III sum of squares and associated F statistic or probability values should be used. The TYPE I SS, also known as *sequential sums of squares*, are computed based on the order of class variables entered into the model. In the computation of TYPE III SS, every class variable is treated as if it were entered last; thus, the order of specification on the MODEL statement does not affect the SS calculations. Upon inspection of the TYPE III SS table, we note that the main effect DISCIP has an F value of 8.00 with $p <= .0001$. Thus, we can reject the null hypothesis that all discipline group means are equal. We also note that the main effect SEX and the interaction term SEX*DISCIP are not statistically significant. The question now remains as to how the four academic disciplines differ on self-reported gains in computer skills.

The results of the Duncan multiple range test are reported on the fourth page of the GLM output. As expected, based on the TYPE III SS analysis, the DUNCAN option indicates that males and females are not significantly different in self-reported computer skills. The results of the DUNCAN multiple-range option for analysis of discipline means are more difficult to interpret. In this example, the discipline means have been grouped by letters A, B, C, into three partially overlapping groups. The most significant difference in group means was found between graduates of professional and natural science programs (group A) and the social sciences and humanities (group C).

Multiple Regression

SAS/STAT software includes five different procedures (GLM, REG, STEPWISE, RSQUARE, and NLIN) for performing regression analyses; SAS/ETS and SAS/QC software include additional time-series regression procedures. This chapter will describe the use of PROC REG as a general-purpose regression tool. The general form of the REG procedure is as follows:

    PROC REG *options*;
    MODEL *dependents = predictors/options*;

SAS provides for a number of options on both the PROC REG and MODEL statements. The most commonly used options are described in the section to follow. Consult the *SAS/STAT User's Guide* for a full description of PROC REG.

PROC REG statement options

DATA = *name*
specifies the SAS data set to be used by PROC REG. If DATA = *name* is omitted, the most recently created SAS data set will be used.

SIMPLE
prints descriptive statistics for each variable used in PROC REG.

MODEL statement options

STB   prints standardized regression coefficients.

P   calculates predicted values from data analyzed and model specified.

R   provides an analysis of the actual-predicted or residuals.

PROC REG Example

The use of PROC REG will be illustrated in a example in which a researcher wants to develop a regression model for understanding the academic achievement of first-year college students. To assist the early identification of at-risk students, the regression analysis will include student socioeconomic factors and measures of academic preparation. The variables for the analysis are as follows.

Dependent Variable		Independent/Regressor Variables	
Name	**Data Source**	**Name**	**Data Source**
CUMGPA	Student Records	Mother's Education	Survey
		Father's Education	Survey
		Family Income	Survey
		Hours Employed	Survey
		High School GPA	Student Records
		SAT Score	Student Records
		Sex	Student Records

The data used in the analysis are stored in two files. Student socioeconomic information (parent education, income, work hours) have been obtained from a survey and are stored as a permanent SAS data set. The dependent variable (CUMGPA) and the admissions score information (HSGPA, SATTOTAL) and student gender are stored in an extract of the institutional student records system as a SAS data set. The first task of the analysis is to combine these two files with a merge operation using a common ID (SSN). Based on previous research, we have noted that female students earn higher GPAs than male students. The character variable SEX is treated as a predictor by dummy-coding a new variable called FEMALE in which males are assigned a value of 0 and females a value of 1. Parental education level (PARENTED) is defined as the mean of Mother's Education (MAEDUC) and Father's Education (PAEDUC). The results of the REG procedure are shown in **Output 6-10**.

PROC REG SAS Code

```
libname svy 'pb hd:new student svy';
libname db 'pb hd:student';

options ls=75 nodate;

data survey;
  set svy.fresh96(keep=ssn maeduc paeduc income hours);
 by ssn;
 if sex = 'F' then female = 1;
  else female = 0;
parented = mean(maeduc,paeduc);
drop maeduc paeduc;

data scores;
  set db.studnt96(keep=ssn sex cumgpa hsgpa sattotal);
 by ssn;

data combo;
  merge survey(in=a) scores; by ssn;
if a;
drop ssn;

proc reg data = combo;
  model   cumgpa=sattotal hsgpa parented hours female
          income/stb;
run;
title1  'Prediction of 1st Year GPA: 1996 Freshmen';
```

Output 6-10: PROC REG Results

```
              Prediction of 1st Year GPA: 1996 Freshmen        1


Model: MODEL1
Dependent Variable: CUMGPA

                        Analysis of Variance

                    Sum of          Mean
Source         DF    Squares        Square      F Value     Prob>F

Model           6   101.78555      16.96426     35.818      0.0001
Error         531   251.49531       0.47363
C Total       537   353.28087


     Root MSE      0.68820    R-square     0.2881
     Dep Mean      2.68095    Adj R-sq     0.2801
     C.V.         25.67022


              Prediction of 1st Year GPA: 1996 Freshmen        2

                        Parameter Estimates

                    Parameter      Standard     T for H0:
Variable      DF    Estimate         Error     Parameter=0    Prob > |T|

INTERCEP       1    -2.119271      0.36607028     -5.789        0.0001
SATTOTAL       1     0.001375      0.00026078      5.272        0.0001
HSGPA          1     0.799004      0.08429431      9.479        0.0001
PARENTED       1     0.067933      0.01893140      3.588        0.0004
HOURS          1    -0.008419      0.00358748     -2.347        0.0193
FEMALE         1     0.158715      0.06408622      2.477        0.0136
INCOME         1     0.000581      0.00883481      0.066        0.9476

                    Standardized
Variable      DF      Estimate

INTERCEP       1     0.00000000
SATTOTAL       1     0.20331776
HSGPA          1     0.37728342
PARENTED       1     0.14183945
HOURS          1    -0.08918838
FEMALE         1     0.09493736
INCOME         1     0.00264131
```

Interpretation

The REG procedure output is printed on two pages, both of which are shown in **Output 6-10**. The first page of output provides an analysis of variance table and an F statistic to test the null hypothesis that all predictor coefficients are equal to 0. In our example, we have a highly significant F statistic (35.818) with $p<= 0.0001$; thus, we can conclude that at least some of the regression coefficients are significantly different from 0. The most important information on the first page are the MSE (0.68820) and the R-square (0.2881). The MSE, or mean square error, represents the standard deviation of the residuals (actual-predicted). The R-square statistic is the ratio of variance in CUMGPA that is explained by the linear combination of the predictor variables. The adjusted R-square takes into consideration the number of predictor variables and provides a slightly lower estimate of R^2. The MSE and R-square statistics together tell us how well our model explains or predicts the independent variable. In this example, we are able to explain 28 percent of the variance in college academic performance by using only precollege information.

The second page of the PROC REG output provides a detailed analysis of each parameter estimate. In addition to the intercept term, SAS provides a *t*-test to test the null hypothesis that the observed regression weights are equal to 0. In this example, we note that all predictors except INCOME are statistically significant ($p <= .05$). The linear relationship between the independent variable (CUMGPA) and the predictors can be expressed as an equation using the parameter estimates.[7]

CUMGPA = (-2.12) + SATTOTAL(.0014) + HSGPA(.7990) + PARENTED(.0679) + HOURS(-.0084) + FEMALE(.1587)

It is important to note that the parameter estimates that are used in this regression equation are *raw* and not *standardized*. As raw estimates, the metric of the scale used to measure the predictor variable will influence the coefficient weight. It is often of interest to determine the relative ability of each predictor variable to explain or predict the dependent variable. The examination of standardized regression coefficients does provide meaningful comparisons for this purpose. SAS does not compute standardized beta weights by default. This analysis can be obtained by specifying the STB option on the MODEL statement. In this example, we note that the most important precollege characteristic in predicting first-year college GPA is high school GPA (.38), which is nearly twice as important as the SAT score (.20). Following these factors in importance, we find that parental education (.14) is more important than work hours (-.09) or being female (.09).

---

[7] In actual practice, we would rerun PROC REG with statistically insignificant variables removed from the model before generating the final equation.

Graphical Display of Data

The SAS System provides two levels of graphics tools. PROC PLOT and PROC CHART are part of base SAS software and are easy-to-use procedures for generating basic scatter plots and histograms. These procedures have minimal user customization features and provide low- to medium-resolution graphics output. PROC GPLOT and PROC GCHART provide high-resolution graphical output with full user control over colors, fonts, and the ability to label and annotate the graphical display. The GPLOT and GCHART procedures are part of SAS/GRAPH software and will be covered in Chapter 8). This section describes the use of PROC PLOT and PROC CHART as tools for the analysis of survey data. While the base SAS graphics procedures may not provide users with presentation-quality output, they do provide the survey research analyst with quick and easy-to-use graphical *analytical* tools. PROC GCHART and PROC GPLOT are better suited for communicating the results of a research project while PROC CHART and PROC PLOT are designed to assist in the analysis of data. Advantages of PROC CHART and PROC PLOT compared to PROC GCHART and PROC GPLOT include cost savings in

- Programming time

- Equipment needed to print and view graphics output

- Disk space for storing output files.

PROC CHART and PROC PLOT can also be used to pilot graphical applications that are later finalized with PROC GCHART or PROC GPLOT.

Plotting Data

PROC PLOT is used to create scatter plots in which the values for two variables for each observation are plotted on a vertical and a horizontal axis. The form for this easy-to-use procedure is as follows:

PROC PLOT DATA = *name*;
PLOT *vertical* *horizontal*/*options*;

where:

vertical is the name of the variable to use on the vertical axis.
horizontal is the name of the variable to use on the horizontal axis.

The default symbol for each data point in the plot is the letter A. If two data points have the same values, the letter B will be used as the plot symbol; for three data points with the same value, C will be used, etc. This default plot symbol system can be modified by the following statement:

```
plot x1*x2='character';
```

where *character* is a user-supplied text string with a length of one symbol.

Two variables can be plotted by a third variable by using the following statements:

```
proc plot data = name;
plot vertical*horizontal=variable;
```

A separate series of data points will be plotted for each value of the variable that is listed to the right of the equal sign (=). For this type of plot, the plot symbol will be the first nonblank character of the variable value. For example:

```
proc plot data = survey;
plot q01*income=region;
```

These statements will produce a separate data series of q01 by income for each *value* of region on one plot.

Some of the more commonly used options[8] for the PLOT statement are

VAXIS=/HAXIS=	Specifies values for tic marks on vertical or horizontal axis.
VZERO/HZERO	Begins the vertical or horizontal axis at 0.
VREF=/HREF=	Draws a vertical or horizontal reference line for a specified value.
OVERLAY	Prints two or more plots on the same pair of vertical or horizontal axes.

---

[8] Consult the *SAS Procedure Guide* for a complete list of the available options.

Example 1 - Basic Plot

This first example will illustrate the use of PROC PLOT with no options. This example is based on the same data that were used in the previous section on PROC REG and multiple regression. For this application, we want to evaluate how well the model is working by comparing students' actual GPAs with their predicted GPAs. The REG procedure used in the previous section is repeated with two additional features. Since we have already examined the PROC REG output, the NOPRINT option is specified on the PROC statement to suppress the printing of the standard REG output. The P option is specified on the REG MODEL statement to request that SAS compute predicted values for each observation. Lastly, we have used the OUTPUT statement with PROC REG to create a SAS data set with both actual and predicted GPAs (named PRED_GPA in this example) that can be passed to PROC PLOT. The program to compute and plot predicted versus actual GPA follows with the results shown in **Output 6-11**.

PROC PLOT Example 1 SAS Code

```
proc reg data = combo noprint;
  model cumgpa=sattotal hsgpa parented hours female/p;
  output out = stats p=pred_gpa;
proc plot data = stats;
plot cumgpa*pred_gpa;
title1 'Actual vs Predicted GPA';
run;
```

Output 6-11: PROC PLOT Example 1

```
                           Actual vs Predicted GPA

Plot of CUMGPA*PRED_GPA.  Legend: A = 1 obs, B = 2 obs, etc.

CUMGPA |
       |
     4 +                     B      ACADD  AB  AA
       |                   A AA  BBCA  B  BEABABA    A
       |                       A     A A    AAAAABBDEAC  A
       |      A              A A A C  BCCADBBACACA  A
       |                  A      A A AA CB  ACABA
       |              A     BAB AAAAB  AABB  A  AE  B
       |                  B  BBBCCABBEBCCD    CB
     3 +              A AA A   ACBACADCEDFFBEDBBAA
       |              A   A  AAAAABBAAEB  AABC BACABB
       |                 B  BB A  ABDABBAC  A  A A
       |              B AA B  CA  AAEAB  CDCCCCABCAA
       |              A AABABECABBD  CD  ADC   B  A  A
       |              A AAAAD AA  CCACAEB   D  AA
       |              A  AC BF  AB  B AAAAA  AAAA
     2 +                B  BDAB  C  CA  AAACAA  AA   A
       |          A     AABBBBBB  ABA
       |              A  ABA  BAA  AAA  AA AA  A
       |          B        AA BBA BA A A A
       |          A    AAACA   B  B  BB  AA
       |           A AA A B A   B      AA
       |          AA  A B A A    A
     1 +           A    A AA A A A   A
       |           B  AA A    A        A
       |                              A
       |
       |
       |     A              A
       |          A   AA
       |              A
     0 +                      A
       |
       --+--------+--------+--------+--------+--------+--------+--------+-
         1.0      1.5      2.0      2.5      3.0      3.5      4.0

                        Predicted Value of CUMGPA
```

Example 2: Customizing Axis Scaling and Adding Reference Lines

The default axis scaling used in the first PROC PLOT example (**Output 6-11**) can be improved with the use of the VAXIS= and HAXIS= options to control the scaling of the axes. Although both the vertical (actual GPA) and the horizontal variable (predicted GPA) have the same numerical range (0.0- 4.0), SAS used inconsistent tick-mark scale values to represent the two axes. Additionally, to facilitate discussions about admission policies, it would be very useful to divide the plot into four quadrants, above and below 2.0 for both predicted and actual GPA using reference lines drawn on the graph. The second PROC PLOT example illustrates the use of the HAXIS= and VAXIS= options to specify exact scale values and the VREF= and HREF= options to draw vertical and horizontal reference lines. An enhanced version of the program used to generate **Output 6-11** follows. The resulting graph is shown in **Output 6-12**.

PROC PLOT - Example 2 SAS Code

```
proc reg data = combo noprint;
   model cumgpa=sattotal hsgpa parented hours female/p;
   output out = stats p=pred_gpa;

proc plot data = stats;
plot cumgpa*pred_gpa/href=2.0 vref=2.0 haxis=0 to 4.0 by .5
                                        vaxis=0 to 4.0 by .5;
title1 'Actual vs Predicted GPA';
run;
```

Output 6-12: PROC PLOT Example 2

```
                         Actual vs Predicted GPA

Plot of CUMGPA*PRED_GPA.    Legend: A = 1 obs, B = 2 obs, etc.

CUMGPA |                         |
       |                         |
  4.0 +                          |   AA      AADEA AAAA
       |                         | A      AABA ADABCA A
       |                         |A    A AAAAAB CCDDBBB
       |               A         |  AA      AACCCBBADAB
  3.5 +                          | A       AAA BADDBECB A
       |                         | A AA A BAD     BAA
       |                  A  |    ADB BACABABC    ACA
       |                 AA|   B BBDBBCFFCC     ACB
  3.0 +                  A |  A    BCBACCEDEBEBAAA
       |               A A| AA    BA   CCAABC BDBAB
       |                A AACABAEACADD   ABAA
       |               AA B B BEA CCBACBCCA
  2.5 +               AA A A H BC BBADEBAA
       |              AACADCAABBBEACA CA A
       |               AB DEAABBABGC D CA
       |              AAAB AB AC B B A A A
  2.0 +---------------------------+EBBAB-AA-BB-AAA-------------
       |              A  A AABBCC ABB A
       |                 |ABAA AAAAAA B A
       |              A  A |ABACAAAA A
  1.5 +               B  | A BAAABA AA
       |              ABAD   AA AA A
       |               B  AA C A AA    AA
       |             A AA |A B  A A A
  1.0 +                   |       A
       |               B AA A AA A
       |                 A| A        A
       |                  |
  0.5 +            A     |      A
       |                  |
       |                A  AA
       |                  | A
  0.0 +                  |      A
       |                  |
       -+------+------+------+------+------+------+------+------+
       0.0    0.5    1.0    1.5    2.0    2.5    3.0    3.5    4.0

                      Predicted Value of CUMGPA
```

Multiple Data Series

Our understanding of relationships among variables is often enhanced by viewing plots with multiple data series where two variables are plotted as a function of a third variable. For example, you may want to plot income by year for each value of sex. SAS can handle this type of plot in three different ways:

- BY-group processing using PROC SORT

- OVERLAY option on the PLOT statement

- PROC PLOT subgroup request.

Each of these techniques for plotting multiple data series will be discussed in the sections to follow.

BY-Group Processing Using PROC SORT

```
proc sort; by sex;
proc plot; by sex;
plot income*year;
```

The SAS data set must first be sorted before BY-group processing can take place. These PLOT statements will create a separate plot of income by year for each value of SEX. BY-group processing with PROC PLOT is most useful when you need to produce numerous plots with identical horizontal and vertical axes, and the comparison of plots for the different values of the BY variable is of minimal interest.

OVERLAY Option on the PLOT Statement

```
proc plot;
plot m_inc*year='m' f_inc*year='f' /overlay;
```

This option will plot two or more variables with a common variable on the same output page. Using this example, the data would have to be reshaped to create separate income variables for each sex (M_INC and F_INC) for each year. On the PLOT statement, two or more separate plots can be requested, and the OVERLAY option will tell SAS to print them on the same page.

PROC PLOT Subgroup Request

```
proc plot;
plot income*year=sex;
```

This method will produce similar results to that obtained with the OVERLAY option. The structure of the data will determine which method requires fewer SAS statements to implement. For example, if the data set has the variable YEAR as the unit of analysis, one income variable, and a sex variable to capture gender, then the subgroup method will be easiest to accomplish. On the other hand, if there is no sex variable, but you have two income variables to represent each sex, then the OVERLAY method would require less data manipulation. In using SAS/GRAPH software, you have some built-in features for printing legends to describe the data series for each subgroup. These features make the PLOT A*B=C statement more attractive than the use of the OVERLAY option.

Example 3: Plotting Subgroups

In this example, we wish to plot mean HOURS of employment by YEAR and TSTUDENT (F=Freshman/T=Transfer). A separate survey has been conducted for each year 1990-1996 and the data are stored in seven SAS permanent data sets - one for each year. Before plotting these data, we must first compute the mean hours of employment by student type for each year. This is accomplished with PROC SUMMARY using the NWAY option. The NWAY option requests that only the highest _TYPE_ value representing the most detailed level of analysis be output. The aggregated data set created by PROC SUMMARY is shown in **Output 6-13** and the results of the PROC PLOT procedure are shown in **Output 6-14**.

PROC PLOT Example 3 SAS Code

```
libname db 'PB HD:new student svy';

options ls=65 nodate nonumber ps=50;

data hist;
  set db.db90(keep=tstudent hours year)
      db.db91(keep=tstudent hours year)
      db.db92(keep=tstudent hours year)
      db.db93(keep=tstudent hours year)
      db.db94(keep=tstudent hours year)
      db.db95(keep=tstudent hours year)
      db.db96(keep=tstudent hours year);
  yr='19'||year;

proc summary nway data = hist;
  class tstudent yr;
    var hours;
    output out = stats
    mean = ;
```

```
proc print data = stats;
title1 'PROC SUMMARY Output File';

proc plot data = stats;
plot hours*yr=tstudent/vzero;
label yr='Fall Semester';
title1 'Mean Hours of Employment by Student Type: 1990-1996';
run
```

Output 6-13 - PROC SUMMARY Results

```
                        PROC SUMMARY Output File
   OBS      TSTUDENT        YR       _TYPE_       _FREQ_       HOURS
    1          F          1990          3          360        8.8474
    2          F          1991          3          328        8.6559
    3          F          1992          3          358        8.2696
    4          F          1993          3          338        6.5258
    5          F          1994          3          388        7.7791
    6          F          1995          3          387        7.0029
    7          F          1996          3          411        5.9129
    8          T          1990          3          219       18.2163
    9          T          1991          3          248       18.5268
   10          T          1992          3          294       16.9926
   11          T          1993          3          237       15.2321
   12          T          1994          3          295       15.3534
   13          T          1995          3          305       18.7570
   14          T          1996          3          191       16.6484
```

Output 6-14: Plotting Subgroups

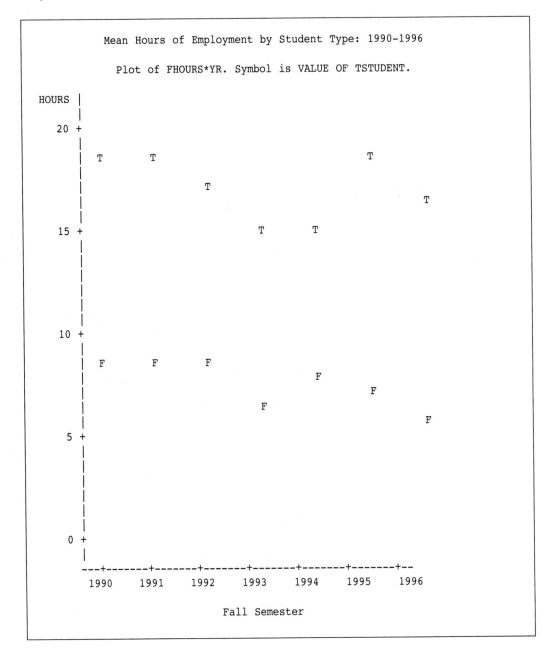

Example 4: Overlay

The OVERLAY option is used to print two or more variables with a comon variable on the same plot page. To illustrate the use of the OVERLAY option, the same graph plotted in **Output 6-14** with the statement PLOT HOURS*YEAR = TSTU-DENT will be plotted as two plots on the same page with OVERLAY. The first step is to modify the data structure so that we have two HOUR variables to represent this dimension for each of the two possible TSTUDENT values (freshman or transfer). PROC SUMMARY is then used to calculate means for each year. This summary data set (see **Output 6-15**) is then passed to the PLOT procedure. Other than some minor differences in labeling, the resulting plot produced with the OVERLAY option shown in **Output 6-16** is identical the plot shown in **Output 6-14**.

PROC PLOT- Overlay SAS Code

```
libname db 'PB HD:new student svy';

options ls=65 nodate nonumber ps=50;

data hist;
   set db.db90(keep=tstudent hours employed year)
       db.db91(keep=tstudent hours employed year)
       db.db92(keep=tstudent hours employed year)
       db.db93(keep=tstudent hours employed year)
       db.db94(keep=tstudent hours employed year)
       db.db95(keep=tstudent hours employed year)
       db.db96(keep=tstudent hours employed year);
 if employed = '1' then hours = 0;
  yr='19'||year;
  if tstudent = 'F' then fhours = hours;
  else if tstudent = 'T' then thours = hours;

proc summary nway data = hist;
 class yr;
  var fhours thours;
  output out = stats
  mean = ;

proc print data = stats;

proc plot data = stats;
plot fhours*yr='F' thours*yr='T'/overlay vzero;
label yr='Fall Semester'
      fhours='Hours';
title1 'Mean Hours of Employment by Student Type: 1990-1996';
run;
```

Output 6-15: PROC SUMMARY - Overlay Example

OBS	YR	_TYPE_	_FREQ_	FHOURS	THOURS
1	1990	1	579	8.84735	18.2163
2	1991	1	576	8.65591	18.5268
3	1992	1	652	8.26959	16.9926
4	1993	1	575	6.52577	15.2321
5	1994	1	683	7.77907	15.3534
6	1995	1	692	7.00293	18.7570
7	1996	1	602	5.91293	16.6484

Output 6-16: PROC PLOT - Overlay Example

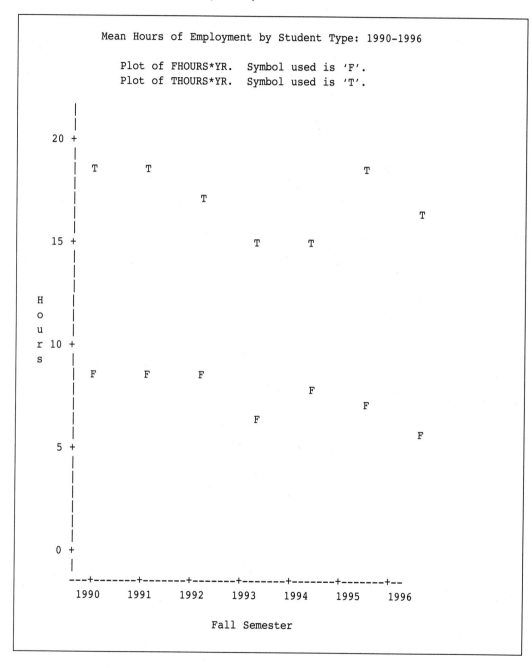

```
            Mean Hours of Employment by Student Type: 1990-1996

               Plot of FHOURS*YR.   Symbol used is 'F'.
               Plot of THOURS*YR.   Symbol used is 'T'.

       |
       |
    20 +
       |
       |    T         T                                   T
       |
       |                   T
       |                                                      T
    15 +
       |                        T         T
       |
   H   |
   o   |
   u   |
   r 10 +
   s   |
       |    F         F         F
       |                                  F
       |                                        F
       |                   F
     5 +                                              F
       |
       |
       |
       |
       |
     0 +
       |
        ---+-------+-------+-------+-------+-------+-------+--
          1990    1991    1992    1993    1994    1995    1996

                            Fall Semester
```

Histograms

PROC CHART will produce vertical and horizontal histograms (or bar charts), pie charts, block charts, and star charts. This section will focus on the use of histograms for reporting survey data. Based on the principles of graphical excellence articulated by Edward Tufte (1983), histograms are far superior to pie charts, block charts, and star charts for communicating quantitative information. (See Chapter 7 for further discussion of graphical design.) The basic form for PROC CHART is as follows:

PROC CHART DATA = *name*;
   VBAR *variable/options*;
   HBAR *variable/options*;

Vertical histograms are created with the VBAR statement and horizontal bar charts are generated with the HBAR statement. There is evidence to suggest that horizontal bar charts are more effective presentation devices than the more common vertical bar charts. Readers are perceptually able to read *down* with less effort than it takes to scan *across*. Another advantage of horizontal bar charts is that SAS will print a table of descriptive statistics by default to the right of the bars. Some of the most commonly used options with HBAR and VBAR are shown in the following section. Consult the *SAS Procedures Guide* for a full discussion of PROC CHART options.

GROUP =	Specifies class variable for generating a set of bars for each value of the GROUP variable.
G100	Requests that SAS compute percent statistics separately for each group, i.e., the cumulative percent will be 100% for each group specified. This option must be used in conjunction with the GROUP option.
ASCENDING	Prints bars in ascending order.
DESCENDING	Prints bars in descending order.
MIDPOINTS =	Specifies order of bars. If this option is not used, SAS will print the bars in sort order.
SUMVAR =	Specifies an analysis variable for computing means, sums, percents, or frequencies.

TYPE =   Specifies the type of statistic (sum, mean, frequency, percent)
                that is represented by the bar. The default TYPE value is FREQ.
                The statistics (keywords) that can be requested using TYPE = are

>   CFREQ   Cumulative frequency
>
>   CPCT   Cumulative percent
>
>   MEAN   Each bar represents the mean of the variable
>   specified by SUMVAR=
>
>   PCT   Percent
>
>   SUM   Each bar represents the sum of the variable
>   specified by SUMVAR=.

Example 1: Vertical Histogram

This example will illustrate the basic vertical bar chart where each bar represents a
frequency count for the HBAR variable. The TYPE= option is not specified since
TYPE = FREQ is the default. The survey question shown in **Figure 6-6** will be
graphed in a vertical histogram using the SAS code that follows. Note the use
of the MIDPOINTS option to control the order of the bars. In this example,
MIDPOINTS is used to override the default order. When using formatted values, the
values specified on the MIDPOINTS statement are the format labels and *not* the
original values. The PROC CHART output is shown in **Output 6-17**.

Figure 6-6: PROC CHART Survey Item

> 6. With how many students have you developed a close personal relationship?
>
>   0 None
>   1 One
>   2 Two
>   3 Three or more

PROC CHART Example 1 SAS Code

```
libname db 'PB HD:stud exp svy';

options ls=67 nodate nonumber ps=50;

proc format;
  value $q06f '0' = 'None'
              '1' = 'One'
              '2' = 'Two'
              '3' = 'Three +';

proc chart data =db.survey96;
vbar q06/midpoints= 'None' 'One' 'Two' 'Three +' ;
label q06 = 'Number';
format q06 $q06f. ;
title1
'With How Many Students Have You Developed a Personal Relationship?';
run;
```

Output 6-17: Vertical Histogram

```
   With How Many Students Have You Developed a Personal Relationship?
   Frequency
        |                                            * * * * *
   200 +                                             * * * * *
        |                                            * * * * *
        |                                            * * * * *
        |                                            * * * * *
   180 +                                             * * * * *
        |                                            * * * * *
        |                                            * * * * *
        |                                            * * * * *
   160 +                                             * * * * *
        |                                            * * * * *
        |                                            * * * * *
        |                                            * * * * *
   140 +                                             * * * * *
        |                                            * * * * *
        |                                            * * * * *
        |                                            * * * * *
   120 +                                             * * * * *
        |                                            * * * * *
        |                                            * * * * *
        |                                            * * * * *
   100 +                                             * * * * *
        |                                            * * * * *
        |                                            * * * * *
        |                                            * * * * *
    80 +                                             * * * * *
        |                                            * * * * *
        |                                            * * * * *
        |                                            * * * * *
    60 +                                             * * * * *
        |                                            * * * * *
        |                                            * * * * *
        |                                            * * * * *
    40 +                                             * * * * *
        |                                  * * * * *  * * * * *
        |                                  * * * * *  * * * * *
        |          * * * * *               * * * * *  * * * * *
    20 +          * * * * *               * * * * *  * * * * *
        |          * * * * *   * * * * *   * * * * *  * * * * *
        |          * * * * *   * * * * *   * * * * *  * * * * *
        |          * * * * *   * * * * *   * * * * *  * * * * *
        ----------------------------------------------------------
                   None         One         Two       Three +
                               Number
```

Example 2: Horizontal Bar Chart

The second PROC CHART example is based on the same survey question and data used in the first example, but it uses the HBAR statement to produce a horizontal bar chart instead of the vertical chart shown in **Output 6-17**. As shown in **Output 6-18**, a table of descriptive statistics is generated by default with the HBAR statement.

PROC CHART - Example 2 SAS Code

(SAS DATA step - same as Example 1)

```
proc chart data = db.survey96;
hbar q06/midpoints= 'None' 'One' 'Two' 'Three +' ;
label q06 = 'Number';
format q06 $q06f. ;
title1
'With How Many Students Have You Developed a Personal Relationship?';
run;
```

Output 6-18: Horizontal Histogram

```
With How Many Students Have You Developed a Personal Relationship?

   Number                                   Cum.              Cum.
                                     Freq   Freq   Percent   Percent

                |
   None         |***                   25    25     8.99      8.99
                |
   One          |**                    16    41     5.76     14.75
                |
   Two          |***                   34    75    12.23     26.98
                |
   Three +      |******************   203   278    73.02    100.00
                |
                -----+----+----+----+
                    50   100 150   200

                     Frequency
```

Example 3: Bar Chart of Analysis Variables

PROC CHART generates a separate bar for each value of the variable specified on the VBAR or HBAR statement. In the absence of the SUMVAR and TYPE options, each bar will represent a frequency count of the variable listed on the HBAR or VBAR statement. The SUMVAR option is used to identify an analysis variable that is represented by the length of the bar. A separate bar will still be generated for each value of the HBAR or VBAR variable. The TYPE option is used to request the statistic (SUM, MEAN, FREQ, PCT, CPCT) used to describe the SUMVAR variable. We will generate a horizontal bar chart of the two survey items shown in **Figure 6-7** to illustrate the use of the SUMVAR and TYPE options. The first question (Q07), the number of student organizations, is the analysis variable, and it will be specified by SUMVAR. The second item, (Q08), will be used on the HBAR statement, and a bar will be generated for each value. The PROC CHART results are shown in **Output 6-19**.

Figure 6-7: Bar Chart of Analysis Variable Survey Items

7. To how many student organizations do you belong?

_____ Number

8. Are you a full-time or part-time student?

1 Full-Time
2 Part-Time

PROC CHART Example 3 SAS Code

```
libname db 'PB HD:stud exp svy';

options ls=67 nodate nonumber ps=50;

proc format;
  value $q08f '1' = 'Full-time'
              '2' = 'Part-time';

proc chart data =db.survey96;
hbar q08/sumvar=q07 type=mean;
label q07 = 'Student Organiz.';
format q08 $q08f. ;
title1 'To How Many Student Organizations Do You Belong?';
run;
```

Output 6-19: Use of SUMVAR and TYPE Options

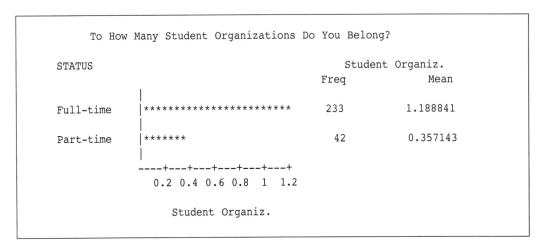

Example 4: Analysis of Subgroups

It is often instructive to use histograms to show group comparisons with a separate set of bars for each group. This type of analysis is requested with the GROUP= option. It is important to note that most analysts will *always* want to use the G100 option when using the GROUP= option. By default, SAS calculates percentages and cumulative totals by using the total for all groups as the base for computing simple percents, cumulative percents, and cumulative frequencies. For most applications, users will want to use the G100 option to request SAS to use the individual group total rather than the grand total as the base for computing frequency and percentage totals.

The example to follow is based on the two survey items shown in **Figure 6-8**. The HBAR variable is the frequency of attending athletic events (Q12), and a separate bar will be printed for each value. The GROUP= variable is residence hall or commuter status (Q13), and SAS will create a separate set of bars for each of the two Q13 values. In the interest of eliminating unnecessary detail and conserving space, the FREQ and PCT options have been specified so that only these statistics will be printed in the table to the right of the bars. If no statistics are requested, SAS will print the FREQ, PCT, CFREQ, and CPCT statistics by default when TYPE=FREQ or no TYPE request is made since TYPE=FREQ is the default. The results of the following program are shown in **Output 6-20**.

Figure 6-8: PROC CHART Subgroup Survey Items

> 12. How often have you attended a University athletic event?
>
>   0 Never
>   1 Occasionally
>   2 Often
>   3 Very Often
>
> 13. Do you live in a residence hall or commute to campus?
>
>   1 Residence Hall
>   2 Commuter

PROC CHART Example 4 SAS Code

```
libname db 'PB HD:stud exp svy';

options ls=67 nodate nonumber ps=50;

proc format;
   value $freq '0' = 'Never'
               '1' = 'Occasionally'
               '2' = 'Often'
               '3' = 'Very Often';

   value $live '1' = 'Residence Hall'
               '2' = 'Commmuter';

proc chart data = db.survey96;
   hbar q12/group = q13 g100 freq percent;
   label   q13 = 'Living Status'
           q12 = 'Frequency';
format q12 $freq. q13 $live. ;
title1 'How Often Have You Attended a Univ Athletic Event?';
run;
```

Output 6-20: Histogram with Grouped Bars

```
            How Often Have You Attended a Univ Athletic Event?

     Living Status       Frequency
                                                            Freq   Percent
                                     |
        Commmuter        Never       |**************         104    72.73
                         Occasionally|****                    29    20.28
                         Often       |                         3     2.10
                         Very Often  |*                        7     4.90
                                     |
     Residence Hall      Never       |****                    29    21.17
                         Occasionally|*****                   36    26.28
                         Often       |***                     26    18.98
                         Very Often  |******                  46    33.58
                                     |
                                     ----+---+---+--
                                       30  60  90

                                     Frequency
```

Open-Ended Comments

The analysis and reporting of open-ended responses can provide an important qualitative dimension to the survey research product. We have found it very useful to take the time to type qualitative responses and report them as appendices. In evaluative type research, open-ended responses can help readers understand the reasons underlying the numerical results reported in tables and graphs. In some cases, the power of the narrative will overshadow the numbers.

Data-processing techniques can assist in the reporting of comments in a targeted fashion to facilitate the integration of the information by the reader. For example, readers of a survey report on college graduates are more likely to gain a better understanding of qualitative issues by reading comments that are sorted by academic major or some other key classification variable. To enable this type of presentation, you can type comments as character strings in a text file and tag them with an ID variable. SAS can then read the comments as *data* and merge them with other files to add information for sorting and printing in a way to most effectively focus the reader's attention. The resulting output can be loaded into any word-processing or spreadsheet program. Depending upon the need for presentation quality, survey comments can also be printed as SAS output.

Example

To illustrate the use of SAS to process open-ended comments, we have provided a typical evaluative type survey item in **Figure 6-9**. Respondents assigning "Poor" or "Fair" responses for any of the three departments are asked to write reasons for their dissatisfaction in survey item B.

Figure 6-9: Open-Ended Survey Items

A. Based on your experience at the ABC Car Dealership, how do you rate the:

1 Sales Staff	Poor	Fair	Good	Excellent
2 Service Dept	Poor	Fair	Good	Excellent
3 Front Office	Poor	Fair	Good	Excellent

B. Please describe reasons for any ratings of "Poor" or "Fair" below:

Using a text editor, the comments to survey item B in **Figure 6-9** have been typed as a comma-delimited ASCII data file (COMMENT.DAT). This file contains three variables: ID, DEPT, and COMMENT. In reporting these responses, the analyst wants to print all comments for a given department in one list and indicate to the reader whether the respondent purchased a truck or car. The vehicle purchase information is stored in a separate file called SAMPLE.DAT. The two files are merged using a common ID variable that is present in both files. The two data sets are shown in **Figure 6-10** and **Figure 6-11**.

Figure 6-10: COMMENT.DAT File

ID	DEPT	COMMENT
001,	1,	I couldn't get anyone to wait on me
001,	2,	Vehicle was not ready when promised
001,	3,	I didn't get the interest rate I was promised
002,	1,	Salesman was not knowledgeable
002,	3,	I resent the extended warranty rip-off
003,	1,	My salesman was less than honest
003,	2,	I am tired of having to bring the car back for repair
004,	1,	Couldn't get waited on - seem short handed
004,	2,	Price of service is too high!
005,	1,	Salesman promises were not kept
005,	2,	Why is shop not open on weekends?
005,	3,	The paperwork was not handled well

Figure 6-11: SAMPLE.DAT File

```
ID      TYPE

001,    T
002,    C
003,    C
004,    T
005,    C
```

The SAS program that combines these two files and prints a report showing the comments for each department is shown on the following page. The comment list generated by PROC PRINT is shown in **Output 6-21**. This example illustrates the use of SAS to

* Read a comma-delimited data set with the DSD INFILE option

* Merge files

* Concatenate and trim variables

* Use the PUT statement to assign a formatted value label to a variable value.

SAS Code to Analyze Open-Ended Comments

```
options ls=65 ps=65 nodate;

filename cdata 'pb hd:survey:comments.dat';
filename iddata 'pb hd:survey:sample.dat';

data comments;
length id $3 dept $2 comment $60 ;
infile cdata dsd;
input id $ dept $ comment $ ;

data sample;
length id $3 ;
infile iddata dsd;
input id $ type $;
```

```
proc sort data = comments; by id;
proc sort data = sample;  by id;

proc format;
  value $type 'T' = 'Truck'
              'C' = 'Car';

  value $dept '1' = 'Sales'
              '2' = 'Service'
              '3' = 'Front Office';

data report;
 merge sample comments(in=a); by id;
if a;
comment=trim(comment)||' '||'('||trim(put(type,$type.))||')'
;

proc sort data = report; by dept type;

proc print data = report n uniform noobs; by dept;
 var comment;
format dept $dept. ;
Title1 'Open-Ended Responses to New Car Owner Survey';
run;
```

Output 6-21: Reporting of Open-Ended Survey Comments

```
                    Open-Ended Responses to New Car Owner Survey

        ------------------------- DEPT=Sales -----------------------------
        COMMENT


        Salesman was not knowledgeable (Car)
        My salesman was less than honest (Car)
        Salesman promises were not kept (Car)
        I couldn't get anyone to wait on me (Truck)
        Couldn't get waited on - seem short handed (Truck)


                              N = 5


        ------------------------- DEPT=Service ---------------------------
        COMMENT


        I am tired of having to bring the car back for repair (Car)
        Why is shop not open on weekends? (Car)
        Vehicle was not ready when promised (Truck)
        Price of service is too high! (Truck)


                              N = 4


        ----------------------- DEPT=Front Office -----------------------
        COMMENT


        I resent the extended warranty rip-off (Car)
        The paperwork was not handled well (Car)
        I didn't get the interest rate I was promised (Truck)


                              N = 3
```

7

Creating Custom Tables with PROC TABULATE

"Words are for those who cannot understand tables; graphs are for those who cannot read."

Unattributed quote, *Journal of the Royal Statistical Society*

Introduction

The first six chapters of this book have concentrated on the use of SAS to accomplish the mechanics of the survey research process: reading and creating files, taking random samples, generating personalized form letters, tracking respondents, and analyzing data. We now turn to the communication of survey results in tabular form. Chapter 8 will discuss the use of SAS as a medium for cognitive art, the presentation of survey data in graphical form.

This chapter will begin with a review of basic design principles for reporting data in tabular form. We begin with how to use PROC TABULATE to generate custom tables for reporting survey research results. Survey examples will be used to demonstrate the specification of row and column variables, the reporting of descriptive statistics to include percentages, and the control of a table's appearance. This chapter will also illustrate the use of the SAS macro language to automate the specification of files and title information to report longitudinal survey data.

The importance of *communicating* survey research findings to decision-makers is often overlooked, and it cannot be overstated. The quality of presentation can determine whether a research report is used to make informed decisions, or misinterpreted, or ignored. Tufte (1997) presents two fascinating case studies to illustrate how the quality of data presentation has contributed to life and death decisions.

- Poor-quality data presentation obscured the relationship between cold temperatures and the failure of rubber O-rings. The failure of the rings to seal properly caused the 1986 Challenger space shuttle disaster.

- Excellence in data presentation enabled Dr. John Snow to discover the cause of the 1854 London cholera epidemic. The causes of the spread of cholera had been a mystery for centuries.

The researcher has three main tools to convey the message of his or her work: graphs, words, and tables. Like a woodworker's chisels, saws, and planes, these tools are best used to perform distinct functions, but all are usually required in combination to produce a quality piece of work. Mahon (1977) points out a corollary principle that graphs, words, and tables should be used in mutually supporting ways. Some general guidelines for their effective use include the following:

- Tables are the medium of choice for conveying numerical values.

- Graphs are best suited for depicting relationships among variables.

- Sentences are used to summarize information.

- When small numerical differences have important implications, graphs tend to do a poor job of communicating the findings.

- Tables do a much better job than words in comparing more than two numbers.

- For reporting small data sets, tables are more effective than graphs.

Elements of Effective Table Design

The hallmark of a well-designed table is the degree to which readers are able to detect data trends and anomalies with *minimal* effort. The researcher should never overestimate the reader's attention span or interest in the data. Moreover, in some cases, readers will passively, or even actively, resist legitimate survey findings because of preconceived bias, politics, or an unwillingness to accept the message conveyed by the findings. Given these inherent communication difficulties, it is imperative for the analyst to avoid unwittingly contributing to the problem by presenting tabular results in a way that diminishes the reader's ability to understand the study's key findings. Based on a synthesis of Ehrenberg's (1977) and Tufte's (1983) ideas, we suggest six basic rules for designing statistical tables.

- Eliminate unnecessary digits.

- Use row and column means and totals.

- Use columns for data comparisons.

- Order rows and columns by size.

- Use space and layout to maximize readability.

- Use *supertables* for many localized comparisons.

Rule 1: Eliminate Unnecessary Digits

SAS default procedure output typically provides you with four or five decimal places. In most survey applications, this level of detail is problematic for two reasons: it grossly exaggerates the precision of the data, and it reduces the readability of tables. In reporting large whole numbers with values in the tens of thousands or millions, it is good practice to reduce the scale by reporting the data in units of 1,000 or some other appropriate figure. The elimination of unnecessary detail removes artificial precision, enhances the ability of the reader to compare and contrast tabular figures, and provides the analyst with more flexibility in table layout and design. The rounding principle also assists the reader in performing mental arithmetic and retaining information in short-term memory. With the SAS System, you can control the number of decimal places in both the DATA step (with the ROUND function) and in the procedures (with options or formatting features). For example, some procedures such as PROC MEANS and PROC TABULATE have ROUND options.

Rule 2: Use Row and Column Means and Totals

The use of row and column summary measures provides the reader with benchmarks for detecting trends and outliers. When you are reporting percentages, row and column totals provide the reader with a visual aid to immediately understand the base or denominator definition that was used in the calculations. With PROC TABULATE, row and column total measures are easily obtained using the internal ALL classification variable. The row and column total principle is illustrated in **Figure 7-1** and **Figure 7-2**.

Figure 7-1: Basic Table without Row and Column Totals

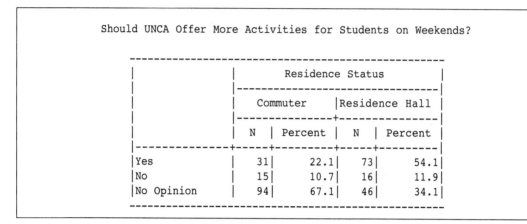

```
          Should UNCA Offer More Activities for Students on Weekends?

               ---------------------------------------------------
               |                   |          Residence Status         |
               |                   |-----------------------------------|
               |                   |   Commuter    |Residence Hall |
               |                   |---------------+---------------|
               |                   | N  | Percent  | N  | Percent |
               |-------------+-----+---------+-----+---------|
               |Yes          |   31|     22.1|   73|     54.1|
               |No           |   15|     10.7|   16|     11.9|
               |No Opinion   |   94|     67.1|   46|     34.1|
               ---------------------------------------------------
```

Figure 7-2: Improved Table with Row and Column Totals

```
        Should UNCA Offer More Activities for Students on Weekends?

   ----------------------------------------------------------------------
   |               |          Residence Status         |           |
   |               |-----------------------------------|           |
   |               |   Commuter    |Residence Hall |      Total      |
   |               |---------------+---------------+---------------|
   |               | N  | Percent  | N  | Percent  | N  | Percent |
   |---------------+-----+---------+-----+---------+-----+---------|
   |Yes            |   31|     22.1|   73|     54.1| 104|     37.8|
   |No             |   15|     10.7|   16|     11.9|  31|     11.3|
   |No Opinion     |   94|     67.1|   46|     34.1| 140|     50.9|
   |Total          |  140|    100.0| 135|    100.0| 275|    100.0|
   ----------------------------------------------------------------------
```

Rule 3: Use Columns for Data Comparisons

There are perceptual advantages to displaying key table values in columns rather than in rows, as the eye can read *down* a column with less effort than it takes to scan *across* a row. In reading down a column there is less distance for the eye to travel and it is much easier to focus on the first two digits in a string of numbers. Compare the ease of detecting the downward trend in the two tables shown in **Figure 7-3** and **Figure 7-4**.

Figure 7-3: Comparisons Shown in Rows

	1990	1991	1992	1993	1994	1995
Mean Age	28.0	27.6	27.5	26.4	26.0	25.3

Figure 7-4: Comparisons Shown in Columns

Year	Mean Age
1990	28.0
1991	27.6
1992	27.5
1993	26.4
1994	26.0
1995	25.3

Space limitations often make the column rule hard to implement, as it is usually easier to fit more text on the row dimensions. This problem can be partially alleviated by printing column text on multiple lines and by printing reports in landscape mode.

Rule 4: Order Rows and Columns by Size[1]

The ordering of table row and column dimensions in *ascending* or *descending* order of variable values helps the reader quickly grasp the structure of the data. The commonly used technique of ordering rows and columns by heading alphabetical order often diminishes the reader's ability to see trends and detect outliers. In reporting time-series data, a common practice is to show the time variable increasing from left to right or from top to bottom. This is almost always done in graphical displays and consistency in the accompanying communication has a considerable amount of virtue. In ordering values, there are advantages to using descending (or high-to-low order) rather than ascending order. The ordering of numbers that are not in time-series order from top (high) to bottom (low) or from left (high) to right (low) seems to have a greater intuitive appeal than the reverse order. Ehrenberg (1977) notes that descending order facilitates mental arithmetic. This principle is illustrated in the following two tables.

Try to calculate the difference between Group A and Group B by using ascending order as shown in **Figure 7-5a** and **Figure 7-5b**.

[1] This rule does not apply to tables that have a time-series or natural order embedded in the row/column dimension. For example, natural CLASS values like Jan, Feb, Mar, or Freshman, Sophomore, Junior, Senior should be used to order the table rather than the actual values of a response variable.

Figure 7-5a: Comparisons Shown in Ascending Order

Group	Percent
Group A	58
Group B	85

In the following table, it is easier to mentally calculate the 27-point difference between the two groups listed in *descending* order:

Figure 7-5b: Comparisons Shown in Descending Order

Group	Percent
Group B	85
Group A	58

PROC TABULATE, by default, will order row and column headings by the same order as would be obtained by PROC SORT. To override this default, use the ORDER = *value* option on the PROC TABULATE statement to specify the order in which headings for class variables are printed. Some possible values for order are

- DATA

- FORMATTED

- FREQ

Techniques for ordering row and column dimensions with the TABULATE procedure will be covered in detail later in this chapter.

Rule 5: Use Spacing and Layout to Maximize Readability

A key aspect of enhancing the readability of tables is to minimize the distance the eye has to travel to make comparisons among table cells. As a general rule, white space makes the best separator, but lines can be useful in separating distinctive components of a table. A sample of PROC TABULATE default output is provided in **Figure 7-6**. Notice the negative effects of all upper case labels, unnecessary row/column headings, table cells with too much white space, unnecessary decimals, and horizontal separator lines on the readability of the table. An improved version of this table is provided in **Figure 7-7**.

Figure 7-6: PROC TABULATE Default Table

```
  Should UNCA Offer More Activities for Students on Weekends?

  -----------------------------------------------------------------
  |               |               STATUS             |           |
  |               |----------------------------------|           |
  |               |              | RESIDENCE |        |           |
  |               |  COMMUTER    |   HALL    |     TOTAL          |
  |               |--------------+-----------+-------------|       |
  |               |    PCTN      |   PCTN    |    PCTN     |       |
  |---------------+--------------+-----------+-------------|       
  |Q17            |              |           |            |       |
  |---------------|              |           |            |       |
  |YES            |       22.14|      54.07|      37.82|          |
  |---------------+--------------+-----------+-------------|       
  |NO             |       10.71|      11.85|      11.27|          |
  |---------------+--------------+-----------+-------------|       
  |NO OPINION     |       67.14|      34.07|      50.91|          |
  |---------------+--------------+-----------+-------------|       
  |TOTAL          |      100.00|     100.00|     100.00|          |
  -----------------------------------------------------------------
```

Figure 7-7: Enhanced PROC TABULATE Table

```
  Should UNCA Offer More Activities for Students on Weekends?

  ------------------------------------------------------
  |             |          |Residence|           |
  |             |Commuter  |  Hall   |  Total    |
  |             |----------+---------+---------|       
  |             | Percent  | Percent | Percent |       
  |-------------+----------+---------+---------|       
  |Yes          |     22.1|     54.1|     37.8|        
  |No           |     10.7|     11.9|     11.3|        
  |No Opinion   |     67.1|     34.1|     50.9|        
  |Total        |    100.0|    100.0|    100.0|        
  ------------------------------------------------------
```

Rule 6: Use *Supertables* for Many Localized Comparisons

According to Tufte (1983), the supertable is an ideal format when "the data presentation requires many localized comparisons." See **Figure 7-8**, which shows the rate of returning college freshmen over a five-year period according to 25 dimensions. According to Tufte (1983, p. 179), a supertable will "... attract and intrigue readers through its organized, sequential detail and reference-like quality. One supertable is far better than a hundred little bar charts."

Figure 7-8: Supertable Example

```
                  Percentage of New Freshmen Returning for 2nd Year

     ----------------------------------------------------------------------
     Demographic Factor   |   P E R C E N T     R E T U R N I N G   |
                          ------------------------------------------- All
                          | 1991  | 1992  | 1993  | 1994  | 1995  | Years
     ---------------------+-------+-------+-------+-------+-------+-------
     Commuter             | 67.5  | 74.8  | 72.0  | 71.4  | 70.3  | 71.2
     Res Hall             | 83.2  | 79.1  | 82.2  | 80.5  | 78.4  | 80.6
     ---------------------+-------+-------+-------+-------+-------+-------
     Black                | 69.2  | 85.7  | 83.3  | 83.3  | 64.5  | 75.5
     Other                | 100.0 | 85.7  | 40.0  | 81.8  | 72.7  | 77.5
     Hispanic             | 100.0 | 66.7  | 83.3  | 100.0 | 100.0 | 90.0
     White                | 77.5  | 77.4  | 79.9  | 77.4  | 77.5  | 78.0
     ---------------------+-------+-------+-------+-------+-------+-------
     Female               | 76.0  | 77.0  | 78.9  | 77.4  | 81.1  | 78.2
     Male                 | 80.3  | 78.7  | 80.5  | 79.1  | 69.8  | 77.7
     ---------------------+-------+-------+-------+-------+-------+-------
     Other NC             | 77.0  | 80.4  | 83.8  | 83.2  | 78.7  | 80.9
     Western              | 78.1  | 78.4  | 75.4  | 75.0  | 77.0  | 76.8
     Out-of-State         | 77.3  | 70.0  | 82.5  | 76.3  | 71.2  | 75.8
     ---------------------+-------+-------+-------+-------+-------+-------
     Cum GPA Range:       |       |       |       |       |       |
     0.00 - 0.99          | 18.2  | 22.2  | 15.0  | 21.1  | 12.5  | 17.4
     1.00 - 1.99          | 63.0  | 65.1  | 74.0  | 63.5  | 62.3  | 65.4
     2.00 - 2.99          | 80.7  | 82.3  | 86.8  | 86.8  | 83.9  | 84.1
     3.00 - 4.00          | 90.0  | 84.8  | 82.9  | 85.4  | 85.9  | 85.6
     ---------------------+-------+-------+-------+-------+-------+-------
     SAT Range:           |       |       |       |       |       |
     400 - 890            | 66.7  | 100.0 | 75.0  | 33.3  | 54.5  | 57.7
     900 - 990            | 63.9  | 76.9  | 68.8  | 87.1  | 78.4  | 75.3
     1,000 - 1,090        | 74.5  | 79.6  | 76.4  | 77.5  | 75.6  | 76.7
     1,100 - 1,600        | 81.8  | 78.0  | 82.8  | 79.9  | 78.3  | 80.1
     ---------------------+-------+-------+-------+-------+-------+-------
     HS Rank Percentile   |       |       |       |       |       |
     1  - 49              | 80.0  | 33.3  | 60.0  | 83.3  | 50.0  | 63.6
     50 - 69              | 69.8  | 70.5  | 78.8  | 71.1  | 63.4  | 70.3
     70 - 79              | 72.7  | 76.2  | 75.3  | 86.8  | 72.9  | 77.1
     80 - 89              | 72.0  | 78.1  | 81.4  | 72.5  | 78.5  | 76.8
     90 - 99              | 86.9  | 83.3  | 83.3  | 79.8  | 85.6  | 83.8
     ---------------------+-------+-------+-------+-------+-------+-------
     Cohort Total         | 77.7  | 77.8  | 79.6  | 78.1  | 76.6  | 78.0
     ----------------------------------------------------------------------
```

Introduction to PROC TABULATE

The utility of PROC TABULATE as a tool for reporting survey data cannot be overstated. This procedure enables intermediate-level SAS users to generate custom tables without rekeying survey results into a word-processing and spreadsheet program or without using advanced SAS DATA step programming to generate reports with exact specifications. Compared to the use of advanced report-writing techniques (e.g., RETAIN and PUT statements), PROC TABULATE requires less programming time, and the code can easily be modified.

Experienced SAS users, comfortable with advanced report-writing techniques, should resist the temptation to avoid learning PROC TABULATE. In our extensive survey research experience, we have only rarely found table-reporting needs that could not be handled well with the TABULATE procedure. The major limitation of PROC TABULATE is that it will not produce output that looks as good as tables printed with a word-processing or spreadsheet program. PROC TABULATE does not give you control over font, shading, color, etc. However, in most cases, the presentation quality of TABULATE output is more than adequate for reporting survey research findings, given the relatively short life span of these data, and the labor costs associated with reworking the results in a spreadsheet or word-processing program. In those cases where the highest print quality is needed, TABULATE output can be imported into a spreadsheet or word-processing program. With Version 6, this is done with cut and paste techniques. Version 7 of the SAS System will enable users to create a true output file directly with the TABULATE procedure.

The price of powerful computing procedures is invariably paid for in complexity. We recommend that you learn

1. Basic PROC TABULATE syntax for creating row and column table dimensions

2. How to control table appearance

3. How to report descriptive statistics (n, means, standard deviations, sums)

4. How to calculate percentages.

Of these, only reporting percentages offers much of a challenge to advanced beginner- or intermediate-level SAS users. The first three can be mastered with little difficulty. Our approach will be to help you understand the basics of the TABULATE procedure and then to move on to a more complete discussion of its full features.

PROC TABULATE Basics

As a way of introducing PROC TABULATE, we will first describe and then illustrate by example the procedure's structural elements. PROC TABULATE is identical to the MEANS and SUMMARY procedures in the use of class variables to specify groups and VAR statements to identify analysis variables. These three procedures also share many of the same statistical keywords, (e.g., N, MEAN, SUM, STD), but PROC TABULATE has unique statistical keywords (PCTN, PCTSUM) for generating percentages. The major difference between the SUMMARY and MEANS procedures and PROC TABULATE is the ability of PROC TABULATE to *combine* class dimensions, VAR analysis variables, and statistical measures into user-specified page, row, and column dimensions. Additionally, PROC TABULATE provides users with the ability to control cell widths and formats.

Here is the basic form of PROC TABULATE:

PROC TABULATE *options*;
CLASS *variables*;
VAR *variables*;
TABLE *page_expression, row_expression, col_expression / table-option list*;
KEYLABEL keyword = *'label text'*;

Selected PROC TABULATE Statement Options

DATA = *SAS-data-set*
specifies the data set to be analyzed by PROC TABULATE. If you omit the DATA= option, PROC TABULATE will use the most recently created SAS data set.

MISSING
instructs SAS to include observations with missing class variables and show missing values in a row or column header. By default, SAS will *eliminate* observations with missing class variables. Note that SAS does not eliminate observations with missing analysis variables from the output table.

NOSEPS
removes horizontal separator lines from row titles and the table body. Note that horizontal separator lines do remain in the column heading section of the table. Given that white space is generally the best separator, this is a very useful option.

ORDER = *order*

specifies the order of printing row and column headings. The default order is the same as would be produced by PROC SORT. The possible values for *order* are

- DATA (the order of class values is kept in the order that is found in the data set).

- FORMATTED (class headings are ordered by formatted values as defined by a PROC FORMAT step and referenced with a FORMAT statement).

- FREQ (headings for class variables are in descending order by frequency count so that class values that occur in the greatest number of observations come first).

Selected PROC TABULATE Statements

CLASS Statement

specifies grouping variables that can be character or numeric. Usually these classification variables have a small number of values. It is important to note that observations with missing class variables are not included in the analysis unless the MISSING option is specified on the PROC statement.

VAR Statement

specifies analysis variables that must be numeric. The VAR statement is not required to report frequency counts or percentages of class variables.

TABLE Statement

specifies the page, row, and column dimension of the table. The TABLE statement must have at least one dimension expression specified. In our experience, page dimensions are rarely used in reporting survey results. The form of the TABLE statement is

TABLE *page_expression, row_expression, column_expression / table-options*;

This TABLE statement will produce a three-dimensional table. For two-dimensional tables (rows and columns), *page_expression* is not included on the TABLE statement:

TABLE *row_expression, column_expression / table-options*;

The following elements can be used in TABLE statements:

- class variables as defined in the CLASS statement.

- the universal SAS class variable ALL, used to represent a row or column. (Note: ALL is not defined in the CLASS statement.)

- analysis variables that are defined in the VAR statement. (Note: all analysis variables must be on either the row or column dimension.)

- format modifiers.

- labels.

- statistics referenced by keywords.

Row and column dimensions are specified by connecting TABLE elements with operators. The following are four of the operators that can be used in the TABLE statement.

Operator	Symbol	Action
Comma	,	Separates row, column, and page dimensions
Asterisk	*	Crosses elements within a row or column
Blank space		Concatenates elements within a row or column
Parentheses	( )	Group elements within a crossing statement

Selected TABLE Statement Options[2]

BOX = *value*

enables you to write text in the empty box above the row titles. The possible values are

PAGE (*page-dimension-text*)
variable-name
'*character-string*'

---

2 These options are the most commonly used in survey reporting applications. See the *SAS Procedures Guide* or the *SAS Guide to TABULATE Processing* for a complete description of all TABLE statement options.

INDENT = *n*

allows you to specify the number of spaces to indent each level of row nesting. Class variable names and labels are not used as row titles with the INDENT= option.[3] This option is very useful for reducing the amount of space needed to print the table without detracting from readability.

MISSTEXT = *'text'*

allows you to specify a character string of up to 20 characters in table cells with missing data.

RTSPACE = *n*
RTS = n

The *n* value represents the number of print positions used in the row title space. The default setting is one-fourth of the LINESIZE value minus two (spaces for table outline characters). The default RTS value will often produce a row heading space that is too small which causes the heading label to wrap or print on multiple lines or, conversely, to allocate row heading space that is longer than necessary for the row title.

KEYLABEL Statement

The KEYLABEL statement is a special feature of PROC TABULATE for creating variable labels for statistics or for the universal class variable ALL. The form of the KEYLABEL is

KEYLABEL *keyword* = *'text'*;

The text label can be up to 40 characters long. The KEYLABEL statement can save you work in that you can label a statistic keyword once rather than each time it appears in the TABLE statement. Example 1 and Example 2 illustrate. They will have the identical label results.

Example 1

```
table dept all,
      n*year*mean all*sum;
keylabel all = 'Total'
           n = 'Number Employees'
         mean = 'Avg Sales'
          sum = 'Total Sales';
```

Example 2

```
table dept all='Total',
      n='Number Employees' year*mean='Avg Sales'
      all='Total'*sum='Total Sales';
```

---

[3] The INDENT= option was made available starting with Release 6.10.

Selected Statistics Available with PROC TABULATE[4]

The most commonly used statistics are

N	Number of observations with nonmissing values
MEAN	Arithmetic mean
MIN	Minimum value
MAX	Maximum value
PCTN	Percentage based on frequency count
PCTSUM	Percentage based on sum amounts
RANGE	Maximum value - minimum value
STD	Standard deviation
SUM	Sum total
VAR	Variance.

Constructing Table Expressions

The TABLE statement is used to define the page, row, and column dimensions of TABULATE output. The use of TABLE statement operators will be illustrated in the examples to follow.

Comma - Identify Table Dimensions

The comma is used to identify page, column, and row dimensions. The following example TABLE statement produces the three-dimensional table layout shown in **Output 7-1**.

```
TABLE YEAR,
      RACE ,
      SEX ;
```

---

4 See the *SAS Procedures Guide* or the *SAS Guide to TABULATE Processing* for a complete description of statistics available and their definitions.

Output 7-1: Use of Commas to Create Page, Row, and Column Dimensions

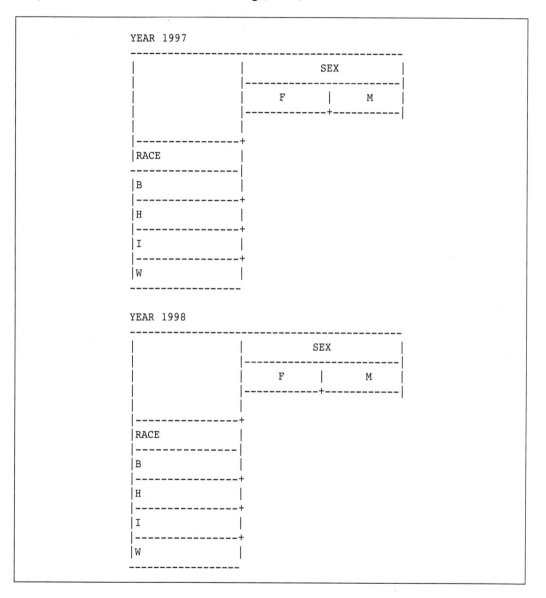

A two-dimensional TABLE statement would have two variables separated by a comma:

```
TABLE RACE,
      SEX;
```

The result of this table definition would be the same as that shown in **Output 7-1**, but only one table would be generated for all years combined.

Asterisk - Crossing Elements

The asterisk is used to cross elements *within* a row or column dimension. (The comma crosses row and column dimensions.) Variables can be crossed with variables and variables can be crossed with one or more statistics. Here are some crossing examples:

```
TABLE RACE*SEX,
      YEAR;
```

Output 7-2: Crossing Two Class Variables

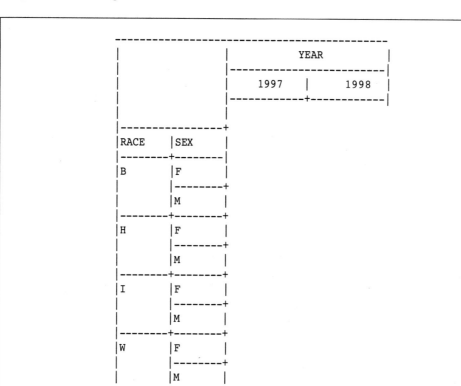

```
TABLE RACE*SEX,
        YEAR*INCOME*MEAN;
```

Output 7-3: Crossing Class Variables, Analysis Variables, and Statistics

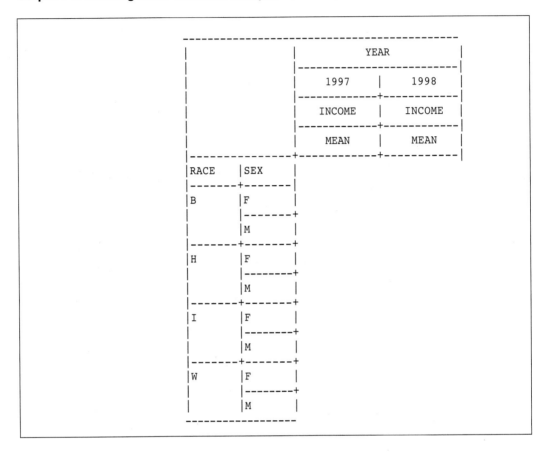

Blank Spaces - Concatenation of Elements

Blanks are used to concatenate or stack elements *within* a dimension. This is often a useful technique for making many data comparisons on one table. The following TABLE statement will produce a layout with two row variables (RACE, SEX) and the column dimension will be the crossing of YEAR with MEAN and INCOME. Variables can be concatenated on either row or column dimensions.

```
TABLE RACE SEX,
      YEAR*INCOME*MEAN;
```

Output 7-4: Concatenated Table

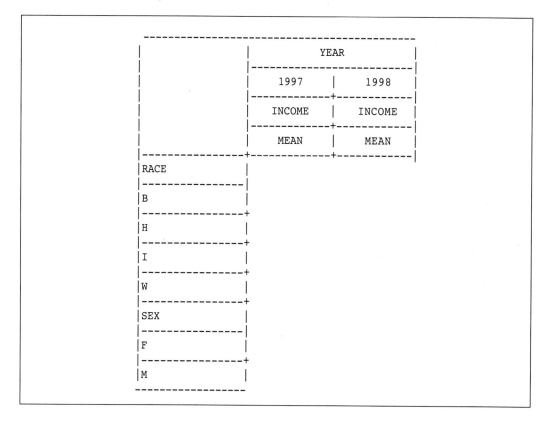

Parentheses - Nesting Elements within a Dimension

Parentheses are used on the TABLE statement to group or nest multiple elements with the same operator. In the following example, we wish to report mean income and standard deviations separately for each year for each race and sex category. The results of the following TABLE statement are shown in **Output 7-5**.

```
TABLE RACE*SEX,
      YEAR*(INCOME*(MEAN STD));
```

Output 7-5: Grouping TABLE Elements with Parentheses

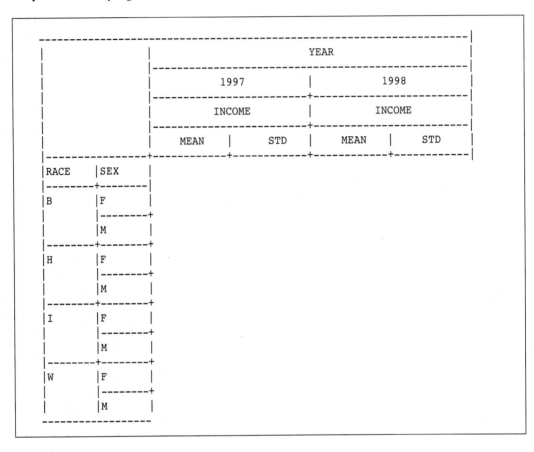

ALL-Creating Row/Column Totals

SAS provides a built-in class variable called ALL than can be used to represent row or column totals. The ALL class variable can also be used capture subtotals for nested[5] groups. The first ALL example is an extension of the program used to generate **Output 7-3** and demonstrates the use of ALL to create a row total field to capture the two-year total.

```
TABLE RACE*SEX,
        YEAR*INCOME*MEAN ALL*INCOME*MEAN;
```

---

[5] An example of class variable "nesting" is illustrated by the RACE*SEX row dimension shown in Output 7-5.

Output 7-6: Row Totals with ALL

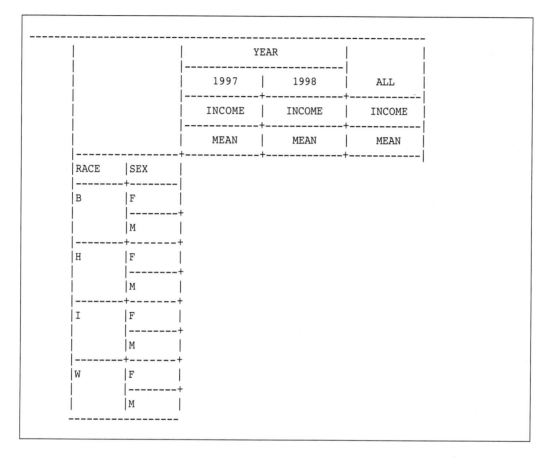

The first ALL example will be extended by adding both column totals and column subgroup totals. The following TABLE statement produces the results shown in **Output 7-7**.

```
TABLE RACE*(SEX ALL) ALL,
       YEAR*INCOME*MEAN ALL*INCOME*MEAN;
```

Output 7-7: Row, Column, and Subgroup Totals with ALL

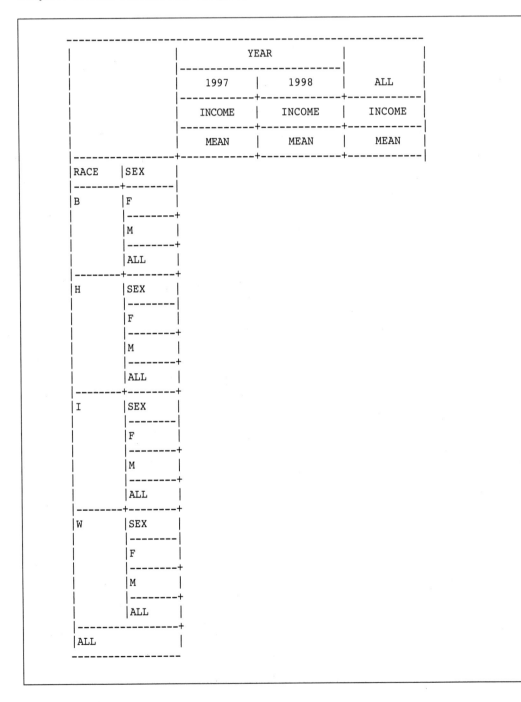

Basic PROC TABULATE Examples

This section will provide three examples to illustrate the fundamental elements of PROC TABULATE. All three examples are based on the two survey questions shown in **Figure 7-9** plus two demographic variables, SEX and TSTUDENT (freshmen and transfer) that are stored in a permanent SAS data set.

Figure 7-9: One-dimensional Table Survey Example

1. How many colleges did you apply to this year, including UNCA?

   _____ Number

2. Is UNCA your: (*Circle One*)

   1 First Choice
   2 Second Choice
   3 Less Than Second Choice

Example 1: One-dimensional Table

In this example, note the use of the CLASS and VAR statements to specify grouping and analysis variables. On the TABLE statement, the comma (,) is used to distinguish between the row and column variables. The universal ALL class variable is used to request a total for the row dimension. The asterisk crossing symbol (*) is used to request statistical measures (MEAN MAX STD) be computed for N_COLL. The results of this program are shown in **Output 7-8**.

SAS Code for a One-dimensional Table

```
libname svy 'pb hd:new student svy';

options ls=65 ps=60 nonumber;

proc format;
   value $choice '1' = 'First Choice'
                 '2' = 'Second Choice'
                 '3' = 'Third Choice';
```

```
proc tabulate data = svy.db96;
 class choice;
 var n_coll;
 table choice all,
       n_coll*(mean max std);
 format choice $choice.;
titlel 'Mean College Applications by Selection Choice of UNCA';
run;
```

Output 7-8: One-dimensional Table Example

```
    Mean College Applications by Selection Choice of UNCA

          ---------------------------------------------------------
          |              |              N_COLL                    |
          |              |-----------------------------------------|
          |              |    MEAN    |    MAX     |    STD       |
          |--------------+------------+------------+------------|
          |CHOICE        |            |            |              |
          |--------------|            |            |              |
          |First Choice  |      2.09|      10.00|        1.51|
          |--------------+------------+------------+------------|
          |Second Choice |      3.56|      16.00|        2.01|
          |--------------+------------+------------+------------|
          |Third Choice  |      4.00|       8.00|        1.64|
          |--------------+------------+------------+------------|
          |ALL           |      2.39|      16.00|        1.71|
          ---------------------------------------------------------
```

Example 2: Two-dimensional Table

This example is based on the same two survey items used in Example 1. A new variable SEX is added to the analysis to create a second dimension or column variable. Note the crossing (*) of SEX (column dimension) with mean values of N_COLL. ALL is used to report both row and column totals. The results of this program are shown in **Output 7.9**.

SAS Code for a Two-dimensional Table

```
libname svy 'pb hd:new student svy';

options ls=65 ps=60 nonumber;

proc format;
  value $choice '1' = 'First Choice'
                '2' = 'Second Choice'
                '3' = 'Third Choice';

  value $sex  'M' = 'Male'
              'F' = 'Female';

proc tabulate data = svy.db96;
 class choice sex;
 var n_coll;
 table choice all,
       sex*n_coll*mean all*N_coll*mean;
 format choice $choice. sex $sex.;
title1
'College Applications by Sex & Selection Choice of UNCA';
run;
```

Output 7-9: Two-dimensional Table Example

```
College Applications by Sex & Selection Choice of UNCA

   --------------------------------------------------------
   |              |              SEX           |          |
   |              |----------------------------|          |
   |              |   Female    |    Male      |   ALL    |
   |              |-------------+--------------+----------|
   |              |   N_COLL    |   N_COLL     |  N_COLL  |
   |              |-------------+--------------+----------|
   |              |    MEAN     |    MEAN      |   MEAN    |
   |--------------+-------------+--------------+----------|
   |CHOICE        |             |              |          |
   |--------------|             |              |          |
   |First Choice  |        2.11 |         2.05 |     2.09 |
   |--------------+-------------+--------------+----------|
   |Second Choice |        3.39 |         3.77 |     3.56 |
   |--------------+-------------+--------------+----------|
   |Third Choice  |        4.30 |         3.63 |     4.00 |
   |--------------+-------------+--------------+----------|
   |ALL           |        2.36 |         2.42 |     2.39 |
   --------------------------------------------------------
```

Example 3: Three-dimensional Table

PROC TABULATE creates three-dimensional tables as a series of two-dimensional tables for each value of a third dimension variable. The use of PROC TABULATE to generate three-dimensional tables will be illustrated by using the same variables in the preceding two-dimensional example plus a third variable (TSTUDENT).

Similar results could be obtained by sorting the data set and using BY-group processing on the PROC TABULATE statement. The comma (,) is used as a separator for page, row, and column dimensions. The third dimension variable is shown at the top left of the table. The results of the following program are shown in **Output 7-10**.

SAS Code for a Three-dimensional Table

```
libname svy 'pb hd:new student svy';

options ls=65 ps=60 nonumber;

proc format;
  value $choice '1' = 'First Choice'
                '2' = 'Second Choice'
                '3' = 'Third Choice';

  value $sex   'M' = 'Male'
               'F' = 'Female';

  value $tstudent 'F' = 'Freshmen'
                  'T' = 'Transfer';

proc tabulate data = svy.db96;
  class choice sex tstudent;
  var n_coll;
  table tstudent all,
      choice,
      sex*n_coll*mean all*n_coll*mean;
  format choice $choice. sex $sex. tstudent $tstudent. ;
title1
'College Applications by Type, Sex, & Selection Choice of UNCA';
run;
```

Output 7-10: Three-dimensional Table Example

```
     College Applications by Sex & Selection Choice of UNCA

TSTUDENT Freshmen
   --------------------------------------------------------------
   |               |               SEX               |          |
   |               |---------------------------------|          |
   |               |   Female   |    Male    |   ALL             |
   |               |------------+------------+------------|      |
   |               |   N_COLL   |   N_COLL   |   N_COLL   |      |
   |               |------------+------------+------------|      |
   |               |    MEAN    |    MEAN    |    MEAN    |      |
   |---------------+------------+------------+------------|
   |CHOICE         |            |            |            |
   |---------------|            |            |            |
   |First Choice   |       2.52 |       2.58 |       2.54 |
   |---------------+------------+------------+------------|
   |Second Choice  |       3.59 |       3.84 |       3.70 |
   |---------------+------------+------------+------------|
   |Third Choice   |       4.30 |       3.63 |       4.00 |
   |---------------+------------+------------+------------|
   |ALL            |       2.80 |       2.95 |       2.85 |
   --------------------------------------------------------------
```

```
     College Applications by Sex & Selection Choice of UNCA

TSTUDENT Transfer
   --------------------------------------------------------------
   |               |               SEX               |          |
   |               |---------------------------------|          |
   |               |   Female   |    Male    |   ALL             |
   |               |------------+------------+------------|      |
   |               |   N_COLL   |   N_COLL   |   N_COLL   |      |
   |               |------------+------------+------------|      |
   |               |    MEAN    |    MEAN    |    MEAN    |      |
   |---------------+------------+------------+------------|
   |CHOICE         |            |            |            |
   |---------------|            |            |            |
   |First Choice   |       1.30 |       1.34 |       1.32 |
   |---------------+------------+------------+------------|
   |Second Choice  |       1.40 |       3.33 |       2.45 |
   |---------------+------------+------------+------------|
   |ALL            |       1.30 |       1.48 |       1.38 |
   --------------------------------------------------------------
```

Controlling the Appearance of PROC TABULATE Output

Up to this point, we have concentrated on learning the basic mechanics of defining PROC TABULATE row and column dimensions. Now that we have an understanding of PROC TABULATE fundamentals, we will describe the process of creating custom tables. The previous examples are based on the PROC TABULATE default settings for column and row headings and for cell width. You will probably want to alter the default heading labels and format the table cells to create an attractive, well-designed table that is easy to read. The formatting of table cells enables you to eliminate unnecessary detail by rounding decimals, to add special formatting features such as dollar signs and commas, and to enhance readability by controlling cell widths. Controlling the width of table cells is especially important as the default width is often longer than necessary and will cause PROC TABULATE output to wrap so that it does not fit the page correctly. This section will explain how to control the appearance of output by manipulating row and column headings and by formatting cells.

Defining PROC TABULATE Headings

The designation of row and column headings with exact specifications is an important first step in creating a well-designed table. SAS will automatically create row and column headings for

- class variable names

- class variable values

- analysis variable names that are specified on the VAR statement

- statistical keywords.

By default, the TABULATE procedure will represent row and column dimensions with variable names printed in all uppercase letters and class variable unformatted values. You will almost always want to override these default headings to enhance the appearance and readability of the table. There are six different ways to override the default heading for row and column variables.

1. Use LABEL statements in the DATA step or immediately after the PROC TABULATE statements (see Chapter 4).

2. Use PROC FORMAT to create value labels that are referenced with a FORMAT statement after the PROC TABULATE step (see Chapter 4).

3. Assign variable labels to variables and statistics as part of the PROC TABULATE TABLE statement.

4. Assign variable labels with the PROC TABULATE KEYLABEL statement.

5. Use the BOX = *value* option on the TABLE statement to specify a label or variable name to appear in the empty box above the row headings.

6. Use the INDENT = *n* option on the TABLE statement to suppress the printing of class variable names and labels and to indent each level of row nesting.

LABEL Statement

The use of the LABEL statement to label variable names and of PROC FORMAT to create temporary or permanent value labels is discussed in detail in Chapter 4, "Labeling SAS Output."

KEYLABEL Statement

The KEYLABEL statement works much like the LABEL statement, but the KEYLABEL is restricted for use with TABULATE statistical keywords and with the universal class variable ALL. Here is an example KEYLABEL statement:

```
keylabel mean = 'Mean'
         all = 'Total'
         sum = 'Sum Amt';
```

TABLE Statement Labels

Statement can be defined as part of the TABLE statement for class variables, analysis variables, and PROC TABULATE statistics as follows:

```
table Q01 = 'Occupation' all='Total',
      Q02 = 'Annual Salary'*(mean='Mean' min='Min'
            max='Max');
```

It is often desirable to suppress the printing of column or row headings to eliminate superfluous detail. For example, it is usually not necessary to have a column heading "Sex" to describe subordinate columns labeled "Male" and "Female". Column or row labels can be suppressed in the TABLE statement by setting the label value to blank as follows:

```
table race=' ',
      sex=' '*N;
```

Note that there must be at least one blank space between the single quotes (' '). Note that blank or null LABEL statements outside the TABLE statement cannot be used to eliminate a table heading.

Example: Define Row and Column Headings

The example to follow will illustrate the specification of row and column labels using the following:

* PROC FORMAT and the FORMAT statement

* KEYLABEL statement

* Assignment of labels to elements in the TABLE statement

* BOX = *value.*

Note the use of NOSEPS option on the PROC TABULATE statement to eliminate horizontal row separators in the body of the table. The result of the following program are shown in **Output 7-11**.

SAS Code for Specifying Row and Column Headings

```
libname svy 'pb hd:new student svy';

options ls=65 ps=60 nonumber nodate;

proc format;
  value $choice '1' = 'First Choice'
                '2' = 'Second Choice'
                '3' = 'Third Choice';

  value $sex    'M' = 'Male'
                'F' = 'Female';

proc tabulate data = svy.db96 noseps;
 class choice sex;
 var n_coll;

table choice=' ' all,
      sex=' '*n_coll = 'Number Colleges'*mean
      all*N_coll = 'Number Colleges'*MEAN/Box = 'Choice';

keylabel MEAN = 'Mean'
         ALL = 'Total';
  format choice $choice. sex $sex. ;
title1
'College Applications by Sex & Selection Choice of UNCA';
run;
```

Output 7-11: Labeling Row and Column Headings

```
    College Applications by Sex & Selection Choice of UNCA


    ----------------------------------------------------------
    |Choice         |    Female   |     Male    |    Total    |
    |               |-------------+-------------+-------------|
    |               |   Number    |   Number    |   Number    |
    |               |  Colleges   |  Colleges   |  Colleges   |
    |               |-------------+-------------+-------------|
    |               |    Mean     |    Mean     |    Mean     |
    |---------------+-------------+-------------+-------------|
    |First Choice   |        2.11|        2.05|        2.09|
    |Second Choice  |        3.39|        3.77|        3.56|
    |Third Choice   |        4.30|        3.63|        4.00|
    |Total          |        2.36|        2.42|        2.39|
    ----------------------------------------------------------
```

Formatting PROC TABULATE Cells and Values

Now that we have learned how to specify row and column headings, the next step in creating custom tables with PROC TABULATE is to format table cells and values. The formatting of table cells enables you to specify the number of character positions to define the *width* of table cells, which in turn determine how the table fits the page. Each PROC TABULATE table cell has a default format width of 12.2. In most cases, this default value is either too big or too small for the optimal table presentation. A frequent consequence of not overriding the default cell width is that the cells are too wide to fit on the page, forcing PROC TABULATE to print a continuation table to show all cells. With a little planning, you can reduce the cell widths to provide sufficient white space and to allow the table to be printed as one table without wrapping.

The example to follow is based on the SAS code used to generate **Output 7-11**. We will add a new variable to this table by reporting the N statistic for each value of the variable SEX and of the ALL class variable. The problems that can occur with using the default cell width are shown in **Output 7-12**.

```
proc tabulate data = svy.db96 noseps;
   class choice sex;
   var n_coll;
   table choice=' ' all,
         sex=' '*(n n_coll='Number Colleges'*mean)
         all*(n N_coll='Number Colleges'*MEAN)/Box='Choice';
keylabel MEAN = 'Mean'
         ALL = 'Total';
   format choice $choice. sex $sex. ;
title1 'College Applications by Sex & Selection Choice of UNCA';
run;
```

Output 7-12: Default Cell Width with Resulting Table Wrapping

```
          College Applications by Sex & Selection Choice of UNCA

     --------------------------------------------------------------
     |Choice        |            Female            |              |
     |              |-----------------------------|              |
     |              |              | Number       |              |
     |              |              | Colleges     |  Male        |
     |              |              |--------------+--------------|
     |              |     N        |    Mean      |     N        |
     |--------------+--------------+--------------+--------------|
     |First Choice  |       298.00|          2.11|       186.00|
     |Second Choice |        54.00|          3.39|        44.00|
     |Third Choice  |        10.00|          4.30|         8.00|
     |Total         |       362.00|          2.36|       238.00|
     --------------------------------------------------------------


     (CONTINUED)

          College Applications by Sex & Selection Choice of UNCA

     --------------------------------------------------------------
     |Choice        |     Male     |            Total            |
     |              |--------------+-----------------------------|
     |              | Number       |              | Number       |
     |              | Colleges     |              | Colleges     |
     |              |--------------|              |--------------|
     |              |    Mean      |     N        |    Mean      |
     |--------------+--------------+--------------+--------------|
     |First Choice  |         2.05|        484.00|         2.09|
     |Second Choice |         3.77|         98.00|         3.56|
     |Third Choice  |         3.63|         18.00|         4.00|
     |Total         |         2.42|        600.00|         2.39|
     --------------------------------------------------------------
```

The PROC TABULATE results shown in **Output 7-13** are far from ideal. The use of the default cell width format (12.2) creates columns wider than necessary and causes the output to wrap or print as two tables. We also note that the default cell width has created some unnecessary detail in reporting N with two decimals even though N is always a whole number in the data set. The mean statistics reported for **Number Colleges** also has two decimals which is one more than needed for this type of data.

There are two approaches you can take to controlling the width of PROC TABU-LATE table cells.

* Use the FORMAT= option on the PROC TABULATE statement.

* Use format modifiers in the TABLE statement dimension expression.

PROC TABULATE FORMAT= Option

This method is easy to use, but it has the major limitation of applying the same format definition to *all* cells. Some examples include

```
proc tabulate data = survey format = 9.1;
proc tabulate data = survey format = comma7.;
proc tabulate data = survey format = dollar10.2;
```

The new default format values that are defined in these statements can be selectively overridden with the *F= format modifier on the TABLE statement dimension expression. In our experience, the use of a single format modifer as defined in the FORMAT = option will not usually produce the desired table appearance, and rather than selectively override this format, it easier to just assign all formats in the TABLE statement dimension expression as described in the next section.

Format Modifiers in TABLE Statement Dimension Expression

The heart of the TABULATE procedure is the TABLE statement dimension expression. We have illustrated the crossing and concatenation of CLASS variables, analysis variables, statistics, and labels to form expressions that define row and column dimensions. We will now add format modifiers (F=) as a new element to the TABLE dimension expression. The F= format modifier can be crossed with analysis variables or with PROC TABULATE statistical keywords (N, MEAN, MIN, MAX, etc.) to specify both cell widths and formats. Here are some examples of TABLE statement format modifiers:

```
table team,
      batting*mean='Average'*f=9.2  errors*sum=' '*f=8.0
      attend='Attendance'*mean='Average'*f=comma12.0
      salary=' '*mean='Average'*f=dollar12.0;
```

The following SAS code will illustrate the use of the F= format modifiers with the same basic program that was used to generate **Output 7-12**. In this example, format modifiers are used to selectively reduce the width and number of decimals places so that the resulting table can be printed without wrapping. The improved table is shown in **Output 7-13**.

SAS Code for Formatting Table Cell Width and Decimals

```
proc tabulate data = svy.db96 noseps;
  class choice sex;
  var n_coll;
table choice=' ' all,
      sex=' '*(n*f=5. n_coll='Number Colleges'*mean*f=9.1)
      all*(n*f=5. N_coll='Number Colleges'*mean*f=9.1)/Box='Choice';

keylabel MEAN = 'Mean'
         ALL = 'Total';
  format choice $choice. sex $sex. ;
title1 'College Applications by Sex & Selection Choice of UNCA';
run;
```

Output 7-13: Controlling Table Cell Width and Decimals

College Applications by Sex & Selection Choice of UNCA

Choice	Female		Male		Total	
		Number Colleges		Number Colleges		Number Colleges
	N	Mean	N	Mean	N	Mean
First Choice	298	2.1	186	2.1	484	2.1
Second Choice	54	3.4	44	3.8	98	3.6
Third Choice	10	4.3	8	3.6	18	4.0
Total	362	2.4	238	2.4	600	2.4

Controlling Row Heading Space

As discussed in the previous section, the PROC TABULATE FORMAT option and the TABLE statement format modifier (F=) commands are used to control the width and appearance of column cells. Neither of these formatting commands have any effect on the *width* of row title space. By default, SAS uses the following formula to determine how much space, as measured by character positions, is assigned for row column headings:

(LINESIZE/4) -2

The purposeful assignment of space to row headings is as important to the well-designed table as the appearance of column cells. The PROC TABULATE default as determined in this formula usually provides either too much or not enough white space. There are two PROC TABULATE TABLE statement options that can be used to customize the appearance of the row dimension. The RTSPACE = *n* (RTS=) option can be used to override the default row title space width. The INDENT = *n* option specifies the number of character spaces to indent each level of row nesting and suppresses the printing of row variable names and labels. For tables with nested (e.g., RACE*SEX) row dimensions, both of these options are often used together to provide the optimal table appearance.

RTS = Option Example

The following program will illustrate the default RTS value for a line size of 80 as shown in **Figure 7-10**.

```
options ls=80 nonumber nodate;
proc tabulate data = library.carsvy noseps;
   class make;
   var rating;
   table make=' ',
     n*f=5 rating='Customer Rating'*mean='Mean'*f=9.1;
run;
```

Figure 7-10: Default Row Title Space

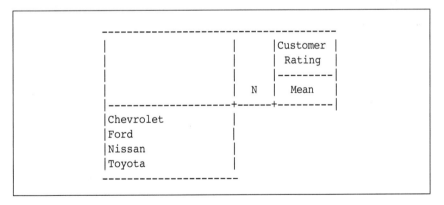

As shown in **Figure 7-10**, the default RTS value, (80/4) -2 = 18 characters, provides more white space than needed for the row headings. Since the longest heading label **Chevrolet** is 9 characters long, an RTS value of 13 would provide a more attractive row width value. Note that two row character positions are always used by the column vertical dividers (|). Two blank spaces beyond the maximum header value width seems to provide the ideal minimum amount of white space for maximizing readability. The following program illustrates the use of the RTS= option with the preceding example to customize the number of character positions that are allocated to row headings.

```
options ls=80 nonumber nodate;

proc tabulate noseps data=library.carsvy;
   class make;
   var rating;
   table make=' ',
   n*f=5. rating='Customer Rating'*mean='Mean'*f=9.1/
      rts=13;
run;
```

Figure 7-11: Customized Row Title Space

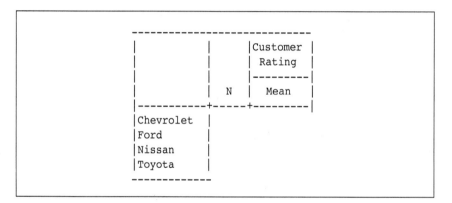

The RTS = option works very well for controlling the amount of space allocated to one-dimensional row headings. One of the few limitations of PROC TABULATE is that you cannot directly control the amount of space allocated to multiple dimensional row headings. SAS will divide *equally* among all row headings the amount of space allocated by the default RTS= option or the default value based on the linesize value if RTS= is not specified. To illustrate the dynamics of this process, we will expand the example shown in **Output 7-11** to include a second row variable TYPE (car or truck). It is necessary to increase the RTS value of 13 that was used to generate **Output 7-11** to 25 character positions to handle a second row dimension as shown in **Output 7-12**. RTS values of less than 25 will generally force the relatively short values of the variable MAKE to print on more than one line. With more than two row dimensions, you usually have to experiment with different RTS values to reach a compromise between overall table readability, use of

multiple lines to print row headings, and the overall space requirements of the
table to fit the page correctly.

```
options ls=80 ps=65 nonumber nodate;

proc tabulate data = library.carsvy;
  class make type;
  var rating;
  table make=' '*(type=' ' all='Make Total'),
        n*f=5. rating='Customer Rating'*mean='Mean'/
  rts=25;
run;
```

Figure 7-12: Use of RTS Option with Multidimensional Row Headings

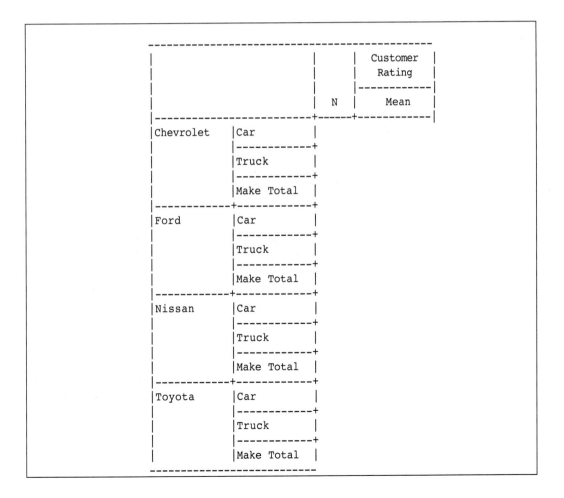

INDENT= Option Example

The INDENT= option enables you to generate easy-to-read multidimensional (nested) row tables that require far fewer *horizontal* and *vertical* character positions than is possible without this TABLE statement option. The default multidimensional row table creates a separate column for each row variable. The INDENT= option allows you to indent nested row variables by a specified number of column positions within the same column, thereby reducing the amount of horizontal space needed to display the table. Without the INDENT= option, it usually necessary to use the default horizontal separator lines to delineate between row class variables. The problem with horizontal separator lines is that they increase the vertical space requirements of the table. For long tables, these lines may determine if the table fits on one page or not. These horizontal and vertical space-saving features of the INDENT= option are very useful given the twin challenges of maximizing readability and making the table fit the page properly. The following program offers an improved version of the preceding example, and the results are shown in **Figure 7-13**.

```
proc tabulate noseps library.carsvy;
   class make type;
   var rating;
   table make*(type all='Make Total'),
   n*f=5. rating='Customer Rating'*mean='Mean'/
   rts=16 indent=3;
```

Figure 7-13: Use of INDENT= and RTS Options with Multidimensional Row Headings

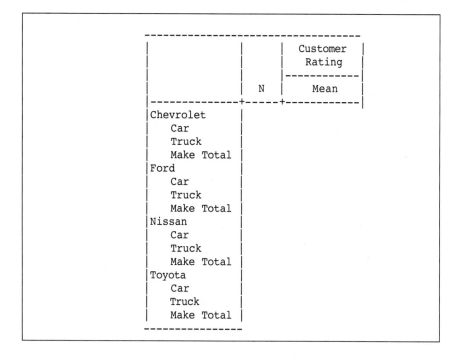

Computing Percentages with PROC TABULATE

Percentages are the most commonly used statistic for reporting survey research results. PROC TABULATE provides two types of percentage statistics. The PCTN keyword is used to calculate percentages based on frequency counts. When you are using PCTN to calculate percentages based on the frequency of class values, analysis variables (specified on the VAR statement) are not required. The PCTSUM keyword calculates percentages based on sums and requires the specification of an analysis variable. The challenge of computing percentages with PROC TABULATE is in the specification of the denominator definition. This definition determines the table cells that are used to calculate the percentage. If no denominator definition is specified, the default denominator is the sum of all cells for PCTSUM or the frequency count for all cells for PCTN. The survey item shown in **Figure 7-14** will be used to illustrate the default PCTN denominator.

Figure 7-14: PCTN Default Denominator Survey Item

How well do you like living in Asheville?

1   I am enthusiastic about it
2   I like it
3   I am more or less neutral about it
4   I don't like it

SAS Code for PROC TABULATE Default Denominator: One-dimensional Table

```
libname db 'PB HD:stud exp svy';

options ls=70 nodate nonumber;

proc format;
  value $q01f '1' = 'I am enthusiastic'
              '2' = 'I like it'
              '3' = 'More or less neutral'
              '4' = 'I don''t like it';

  value $region 'W' = 'Western NC'
                'P' = 'Other NC'
                'X' = 'Out-of-State' ;
```

```
proc tabulate data = db.survey96 noseps;
  class q01 region;
  table q01=' ' all,
        n*f=7.0 pctn*f=9.1 /rts=25;
  keylabel pctn = 'Percent'
           all = 'Total';
format q01 $q01f.;
title1 'How Well Do You Like Living in Asheville?';
run;
```

Output 7-14: One-dimensional Table Using PCTN Default Denominator Definition

```
How Well Do You Like Living in Asheville?


------------------------------------------------
|                       |   N   | Percent |
|-----------------------+-------+---------|
|I am enthusiastic      |    80|    30.4|
|I like it              |   114|    43.3|
|More or less neutral   |    52|    19.8|
|I don't like it        |    17|     6.5|
|Total                  |   263|   100.0|
------------------------------------------------
```

As shown in **Output 7-14**, the default PCTN denominator definition provides the desired result when reporting percentages for a single class dimension or column. With more complex tables, the default denominator will usually *not* calculate percentages for all cells in the most useful way. To illustrate the use of the default denominator definition on two-dimensional tables, we will add a second class variable (REGION) to the preceding example as shown in the following program.

SAS Code for PROC TABULATE Default Denominator: Two-dimensional Table

```
proc tabulate data = survey noseps;
  class q01 region;
  table q01=' ' all,
        region='Geographical Region'*
        (n*f=5.0 pctn*f=5.1) all*(n*f=5.0 pctn*f=5.1) /rts=22;
  keylabel pctn = 'Pct'
           all = 'Total';
format q01 $q01f. Region $region. ;
title1 'How Well Do You Like Living in Asheville?';
title3 'By Student''s Home Geographical Region';
```

Output 7-15: Two-dimensional Table with Default PCTN Denominator

```
                    How Well Do You Like Living in Asheville?

                    By Student's Home Geographical Region
```

		Geographical Region						
		Other NC		Western NC		Out-of-State		Total
	N	Pct	N	Pct	N	Pct	N	Pct
I am enthusiastic	29	11.0	45	17.1	6	2.3	80	30.4
I like it	32	12.2	71	27.0	11	4.2	114	43.3
More or less neutral	22	8.4	20	7.6	10	3.8	52	19.8
I don't like it	3	1.1	8	3.0	6	2.3	17	6.5
Total	86	32.7	144	54.8	33	12.5	263	100.0

The percentages shown in **Output 7-15** are based on the default denominator or total frequency count for *all* CLASS variables. The column percentages for each geographical region do not sum to 100%, which would be a more useful data presentation. Since the default denominator was used, each column percentage is based on the *total* N (263) rather than the N for each geographical region. It is instructive to note that, unlike the individual region columns, the percentages in the far right **TOTAL** column do sum to 100% when the default denominator definition is used.

Specifying Denominator Definitions

As illustrated in the preceding example, the default denominator definition may not calculate percentages in the desired manner. Continuing with this example, the solution to making the region column percentages sum to 100% is to specify a denominator based on the *column total*. Denominator definitions are specified in *angle brackets* (< >) not parentheses, which are concatenated with the PCTN or PCTSUM keywords. There are two steps (Keene, 1991) to follow in determining PROC TABULATE denominator definitions:

1. Visualize the structure of the table and determine which total or subtotals represent the denominator for calculating the desired percentage statistic.

2. Determine which class variables must be summed to create the total or subtotal denominator definition.

   a) Column totals are based on the sum of all *row* values for a given column. The universal class variable ALL is included in the definition to represent the sum of all rows.

   b) Row totals are based on the sum of all *column* values for a given row. The universal class variable ALL is included in the definition to represent the sum of all columns.

The logic involved in defining denominators begins with understanding the cell you want to represent the denominator. Then work backwards to understand the class variables that are summed by SAS to create the specified total or subtotal. We will now provide some examples for reporting percentages based on column and row totals. These programs will provide models that will cover most of your PROC TABULATE percentage reporting needs.

Percentages Based on Column Totals

In general, the denominator definition for a column total is

PCTN<*Row_variable* ALL>
PCTSUM<*Row_variable* ALL>

Note that this denominator definition includes both the *row variable* and the class variable ALL to represent the total of all rows, which is the column total. The SAS code used to generate **Output 7-15** is modified in the program to follow by specifying a denominator to compute percentages based on column totals. Note that different denominator definitions are used for the region percentage statistics and for the ALL or total region percentages. For the ALL column, the default denominator will compute percentage figures that sum to 100% since the default is equal to the grand total frequency count. The results are shown in **Output 7-16**.

```
proc tabulate data = db.survey96 noseps;
  class q01 region;
  table q01=' ' all,
        region='Geographical Region'*(n*f=5.0 pctn<q01 all>*f=5.1)
        all*(n*f=5.0 pctn*f=5.1)/rts=22;
  keylabel pctn = 'Pct'
           all = 'Total';
format q01 $q01f. Region $region. ;
title1 'How Well Do You Like Living in Asheville?';
title3 'By Geographical Region';
run;
```

Output 7-16: Percentages Based on Column Totals

```
                    How Well Do You Like Living in Asheville?

                         By Geographical Region

    ------------------------------------------------------------------------
    |                       |         Geographical Region         |        |
    |                       |-------------------------------------|        |
    |                       |          |            | Out-of-     |        |
    |                       | Other NC |Western NC  |  State      | Total  |
    |                       |----------+------------+-------------+--------|
    |                       |  N | Pct |  N | Pct | N  | Pct |  N | Pct |
    |-----------------------+----+-----+----+-----+----+-----+----+-----|
    |I am enthusiastic      | 29| 33.7| 45| 31.3|  6| 18.2| 80| 30.4|
    |I like it              | 32| 37.2| 71| 49.3| 11| 33.3|114| 43.3|
    |More or less neutral   | 22| 25.6| 20| 13.9| 10| 30.3| 52| 19.8|
    |I don't like it        |  3|  3.5|  8|  5.6|  6| 18.2| 17|  6.5|
    |Total                  | 86|100.0|144|100.0| 33|100.0|263|100.0|
    ------------------------------------------------------------------------
```

Percentages of Column Totals with Subtotals

We will extend the use of PROC TABULATE to compute column percentages by
adding a subtotal dimension. Our example will be based on the survey item
(**Figure 7-15**) used in a survey of college drop-outs.

Figure 7-15: Column Total and Subtotal Percentages Survey Item

1. Was your faculty advisor helpful?

    1 Yes, very helpful
    2 Yes, somewhat helpful
    3 No, not particularly helpful
    4 No, not at all helpful
    5 I did not consult with my advisor

The survey is repeated each year and it is of interest to track response patterns over time as a reflection of changes in institutional advising effectiveness. PROC TABULATE will be used to report the **Figure 7-15** survey item responses as percentages for two dimensions YEAR and STUDTYPE (freshmen or transfer). Note these elements in the program to follow:

- The denominator definition for the column totals and subtotals is similar to that used in the preceding two-dimensional table, but includes the subtotal class variable.

- The default denominator definition used for the ALL column in the preceding two-dimensional example will not work with subtotals.

- PROC FORMAT has been used to collapse the original survey response categories from five to three.

- The INDENT and RTS TABLE statement options have been used to control the appearance of row variables.

- The BOX= option was used to create a column heading.

- Format modifiers (F=) in the TABLE statement were used to precisely control the width of the output to fit the page without wrapping. The results are shown in **Output 7-17**.

SAS Code for Column Percentages with Subtotals

```
libname db 'pb hd:non ret svy';
options ps=65 nodate nonumber ls=70 missing=' ';

data report;
 set db.cohort91
     db.cohort93
     db.cohort95;

proc format;
   value $type 'F' = 'Freshmen'
               'T' = 'Transfer';

   value $q01f  '1','2' = 'Yes, Helpful'
                '3','4' = 'Not Helpful'
                    '5' = 'Did Not Consult';

proc tabulate data = report noseps;
class q01 cohort studtype;
table q01 * (studtype all='Subtotal') all='Total',
cohort='Fall Semester'*(n*f=5.0 pctn<q01 studtype all>='Pct'*f=5.1)
all = '3-Yr Total'*(n*f=5.0 pctn<q01 studtype all>='Pct'*f=5.1)/
Box='Student Rating' rts=17 indent=3;
format q01 $q01f. studtype $type. ;
title1 'Non-Returning Student Perception of Faculty Advising';
run;
```

Output 7-17: Column Percentages with Subtotals

```
        Non-Returning Student Perception of Faculty Advising

------------------------------------------------------------------
|Student Rating |        Entering Fall Semester         |        |
|               |---------------------------------------|        |
|               |    91    |    93    |    95    |3-Yr Total |
|               |----------+----------+----------+-----------|
|               | N  | Pct | N  | Pct | N  | Pct | N  | Pct |
|---------------+-----+-----+-----+-----+-----+-----+-----+-----|
|Yes, Helpful   |     |     |     |     |     |     |     |     |
|   Freshmen    | 21| 67.7| 25| 69.4| 27| 64.3| 73| 67.0|
|   Transfer    | 27| 61.4| 22| 68.8| 35| 71.4| 84| 67.2|
|   Subtotal    | 48| 64.0| 47| 69.1| 62| 68.1|157| 67.1|
|Not Helpful    |     |     |     |     |     |     |     |     |
|   Freshmen    | 10| 32.3| 11| 30.6| 13| 31.0| 34| 31.2|
|   Transfer    | 12| 27.3|  6| 18.8| 12| 24.5| 30| 24.0|
|   Subtotal    | 22| 29.3| 17| 25.0| 25| 27.5| 64| 27.4|
|Did Not Consult|     |     |     |     |     |     |     |     |
|   Freshmen    |     |     |     |     |  2|  4.8|  2|  1.8|
|   Transfer    |  5| 11.4|  4| 12.5|  2|  4.1| 11|  8.8|
|   Subtotal    |  5|  6.7|  4|  5.9|  4|  4.4| 13|  5.6|
|Total          | 75|100.0| 68|100.0| 91|100.0|234|100.0|
------------------------------------------------------------------
```

Column Percentages for Concatenated Tables

Concatenated tables have multiple class variables appearing as row dimensions. This type of table can be a very useful device for reporting survey data on a group of related variables. A well-organized supertable with many localized comparisons is a much better presentation than a host of small tables or bar charts. To illustrate the reporting of percentages for concatenated supertables, we will use the survey items shown in **Figure 7-16**.

Figure 7-16: Survey Items for Column Percentages

16. How would you rate each of the following at UNCA?				
		Quality Rating		
	Poor	Fair	Good	Excellent
a. Your academic experience?	1	2	3	4
b. Your social experience?	1	2	3	4
c. Your overall experience?	1	2	3	4

The survey items shown in **Figure 7-16** are defined as three variables Q16A, Q16B, and Q16C. The data are stored in a permanent SAS data set for each of three years (91,93,95). The program to follow will combine all three evaluative dimensions into a single concatenated table. The row variables will be Q16A - Q16C and a column will be generated to show percentages for each year. Note these elements in the following program:

- Listing of the Q16A - Q16C as class variables separated by a blank prior to the comma (,) to indicate the end of the row dimension and the beginning of the column dimension.

- The denominator definitions are a simple restatement of the row dimension.

- A single PROC FORMAT value ($RATING) has been used to represent the values of three different CLASS variables (Q16A - Q16C).

The results are shown in **Output 7-18.**

SAS Code for Column Percentages with Concatenated Variables

```
libname db 'pb hd:non ret svy';

options ps=65 nodate nonumber ls=70;

data report;
 set db.cohort91
     db.cohort93
     db.cohort95;

proc format;
 value $rating  '1' = 'Poor'
                '2' = 'Fair'
                '3' = 'Good'
                '4' = 'Excellent';

proc tabulate data = report;
class q16a q16b q16c cohort;
table q16a = 'Academic Exper: '
      q16b = 'Social Exper: '
      q16c = 'Overall Exper: ',
cohort = 'Fall Semester'*(n*f=5.0 pctn<q16a q16b q16c>='Pct'*f=5.1)
   all = '3-Yr Total'*(n*f=5.0 pctn<q16a q16b q16c>='Pct'*f=5.1)/
   Box = 'Student Rating' rts=18;
format q16a $rating. q16b $rating. q16c $rating. ;
title1 'Non-Returning Student Rating of UNCA Experience';
run;
```

Output 7-18: Column Percentages for a Concatenated Table

```
             Non-Returning Student Rating of UNCA Experience

--------------------------------------------------------------------
|Student Rating  |                Fall Semester         |          |
|                |--------------------------------------|          |
|                |    91     |    93     |    95     |3-Yr Total |
|                |-----------+-----------+-----------+-----------|
|                |  N  | Pct |  N  | Pct |  N  | Pct |  N  | Pct |
|----------------+-----+-----+-----+-----+-----+-----+-----+-----|
|Academic Exper: |     |     |     |     |     |     |     |     |
|----------------|     |     |     |     |     |     |     |     |
|Poor            |   5 | 6.7 |   3 | 4.5 |  10 |11.1 |  18 | 7.8 |
|----------------+-----+-----+-----+-----+-----+-----+-----+-----|
|Fair            |  13 |17.3 |  12 |17.9 |  17 |18.9 |  42 |18.1 |
|----------------+-----+-----+-----+-----+-----+-----+-----+-----|
|Good            |  40 |53.3 |  35 |52.2 |  35 |38.9 | 110 |47.4 |
|----------------+-----+-----+-----+-----+-----+-----+-----+-----|
|Excellent       |  17 |22.7 |  17 |25.4 |  28 |31.1 |  62 |26.7 |
|----------------+-----+-----+-----+-----+-----+-----+-----+-----|
|Social Exper:   |     |     |     |     |     |     |     |     |
|----------------|     |     |     |     |     |     |     |     |
|Poor            |  20 |26.7 |  11 |16.4 |  28 |31.1 |  59 |25.4 |
|----------------+-----+-----+-----+-----+-----+-----+-----+-----|
|Fair            |  25 |33.3 |  22 |32.8 |  19 |21.1 |  66 |28.4 |
|----------------+-----+-----+-----+-----+-----+-----+-----+-----|
|Good            |  24 |32.0 |  20 |29.9 |  27 |30.0 |  71 |30.6 |
|----------------+-----+-----+-----+-----+-----+-----+-----+-----|
|Excellent       |   6 | 8.0 |  14 |20.9 |  16 |17.8 |  36 |15.5 |
|----------------+-----+-----+-----+-----+-----+-----+-----+-----|
|Overall Exper:  |     |     |     |     |     |     |     |     |
|----------------|     |     |     |     |     |     |     |     |
|Poor            |  10 |13.3 |   7 |10.4 |  11 |12.2 |  28 |12.1 |
|----------------+-----+-----+-----+-----+-----+-----+-----+-----|
|Fair            |  28 |37.3 |  18 |26.9 |  35 |38.9 |  81 |34.9 |
|----------------+-----+-----+-----+-----+-----+-----+-----+-----|
|Good            |  30 |40.0 |  32 |47.8 |  30 |33.3 |  92 |39.7 |
|----------------+-----+-----+-----+-----+-----+-----+-----+-----|
|Excellent       |   7 | 9.3 |  10 |14.9 |  14 |15.6 |  31 |13.4 |
--------------------------------------------------------------------
```

Percentages Based on Row Totals

With an understanding of how TABULATE computes column percentages, we will now turn to the calculation of row percentages. To define denominator definitions based on *column totals*, as described in the previous section, we must specify the actions taken by SAS to compute a column total: sum column class variable values across rows. Conversely, to create a *row total*, SAS sums across column class variable values. In general, the form for specifying the denominator to compute percentages based on row totals is as follows.

PCTN<*column_variable* ALL>
PCTSUM<*column_variable* ALL>

Note the inclusion of the universal class variable ALL in the denominator definition to represent the column total value.

We will use the survey item shown in **Figure 7-17** to illustrate the computation of percentages based on row totals.

Figure 7-17: Row Percentages Survey Item

9. With how many faculty did you develop a familiar acquaintanceship?

1 None
2 One
3 Two
4 Three or more

In the program to follow note these elements:

- Denominator definitions for both row and row totals are defined as <*column_var* all>.

- The KEEP= data set option has been used to restrict the number of variables included in the DATA step.

- The concatenation function (||) has been used to add **19** to each two-digit year value for the variable COHORT[6].

- The NOSEPS option has been used on the TABULATE statement to suppress horizontal separator lines.

---

6 See Chapters 1 and 3 for more information on variable concatenation.

The results of this program are shown in **Output 7-19**.

SAS Code for Row Percentages

```
libname db 'pb hd:non ret svy';

options ps=65 nodate nonumber ls=70;

data report;
length cohort $4;
 set db.cohort91(keep=q09 cohort)
     db.cohort93(keep=q09 cohort)
     db.cohort95(keep=q09 cohort);
 cohort = '19'||cohort;

proc format;
  value $q09f '1' = 'None'
              '2' = 'One'
              '3' = 'Two'
              '4' = 'Three or More';

proc tabulate data = report noseps;
 class q09 cohort;
 table cohort = ' ' all='All Yrs',
       N*f=5. q09='Number of Faculty'*pctn<q09 all>=
       'Percent'*f=9.1
       all='Yr Total'*pctn<q09 all>='Percent'*f=9.1/
       Box='Entering Cohort' rts=10;
format q09 $q09f. ;
title1
'With How Many Faculty Did You Develop a Familiar
 Acquaintanceship?';
run;
```

Output 7-19: Row Percentages for a Two-dimensional Table

```
With How Many Faculty Did You Develop a Familiar Acquaintanceship?

--------------------------------------------------------------------
|Entering|     |                 Number of Faculty         |        |
|Cohort  |     |    |------------------------------------|        |
|        |     |    |         |         |Three or |        |        |
|        |     | None | One   | Two     | More    |Yr Total |
|        |     |---------+---------+---------+---------+---------|
|        |  N  | Percent | Percent | Percent | Percent | Percent |
|--------+-----+---------+---------+---------+---------+---------|
|1991    |  75 |   24.0  |   26.7  |   21.3  |   28.0  |  100.0  |
|1993    |  68 |   10.3  |   30.9  |   30.9  |   27.9  |  100.0  |
|1995    |  91 |   20.9  |   16.5  |   31.9  |   30.8  |  100.0  |
|All Yrs |  234|   18.8  |   23.9  |   28.2  |   29.1  |  100.0  |
--------------------------------------------------------------------
```

Row Percentages with Subtotals

To illustrate the calculation of percentages based on row totals and subtotals, we will add another variable to the preceding example. It is important to note that even with the addition of another row class variable and a request for subtotals, the denominator definition does not change from the preceding example, since row totals are the function of summing column class variable values. The results of the following program are shown in **Output 7-20**.

SAS Code for Row Percentages and Subtotals

```
libname db 'pb hd:non ret svy';

options ps=65 nodate nonumber ls=80;

data report;
length cohort $4;
 set db.cohort91(keep=q09 cohort sex)
     db.cohort93(keep=q09 cohort sex)
     db.cohort95(keep=q09 cohort sex);
cohort = '19'||cohort;

 proc format;
    value $q09f '1' = 'None'
                '2' = 'One'
                '3' = 'Two'
                '4' = 'Three or More';

 value $sex    'M' = 'Male'
               'F' = 'Female';

proc tabulate data = report;
class q09 cohort sex;
table cohort= ' '*(sex=' ' all='Yr Total') sex='Sex Totals' all='Total',
     N*f=5. q09='Number of Faculty'*pctn<q09 all>='Per cent'*f=9.1
     all='Yr Total'*pctn<q09 all>='Percent'*f=9.1/
Box='Entering Cohort' rts=18;
format q09 $q09f. sex $sex. ;
title1
'With How Many Faculty Did You Develop a Familiar
Acquaintanceship?';
title2 'By Cohort Year and Sex';
run;
```

Output 7-20: Row Percentages with Subgroups

```
        With How Many Faculty Did You Develop a Familiar Acquaintanceship?
                              By Cohort Year and Sex
```

Entering Cohort		N	Number of Faculty				
			None	One	Two	Three or More	Yr Total
		N	Percent	Percent	Percent	Percent	Percent
1991	Female	48	22.9	29.2	29.2	18.8	100.0
	Male	27	25.9	22.2	7.4	44.4	100.0
	Yr Total	75	24.0	26.7	21.3	28.0	100.0
1993	Female	40	10.0	22.5	35.0	32.5	100.0
	Male	28	10.7	42.9	25.0	21.4	100.0
	Yr Total	68	10.3	30.9	30.9	27.9	100.0
1995	Female	55	25.5	10.9	34.5	29.1	100.0
	Male	36	13.9	25.0	27.8	33.3	100.0
	Yr Total	91	20.9	16.5	31.9	30.8	100.0
Sex Totals							
Female		143	20.3	20.3	32.9	26.6	100.0
Male		91	16.5	29.7	20.9	33.0	100.0
Total		234	18.8	23.9	28.2	29.1	100.0

Calculating Percentages with Mean Mathematical Trick

It is sometimes convenient to use a mathematical trick to obtain percentages. We can compute the mean of a variable that has been dichotomized into 100 or 0 values to indicate the presence or absence of some characteristic. For example, if you have a typical "Yes or No" survey question, the percentage of "Yes" observations can be calculated by computing the mean of a new variable PERCENT that has been assigned a value of 100 for all "Yes" values and 0 for all "No" values. You will want to ensure that observations with missing values are not inadvertently assigned a value of 0 for PERCENT. In PROC TABULATE applications, the great advantage of this technique is that you are able to calculate percentages for complicated tables without having to specify a denominator definition. This technique is useful for a second reason as well: if you are reporting the percentage responding "Yes," then it is both redundant and a waste of table space to also report the percentage responding "No." The use of the PCTN or PCTSUM keywords will often force the reporting of percentages of values that could be eliminated from the table.

For Likert-type survey items (1=Poor; 2=Fair; 3=Good; 4=Excellent), a good practice is to collapse the categories and report the percentage "Good/Excellent", "Poor/Fair", etc. Survey results reported in this way are easy to interpret and avoid measurement problems associated with using means on ordinal level data. We will use the survey items shown in **Figure 7-18** to illustrate the reporting of percentages by calculating the means of dummy variables assigned the values of 0 or 100.

Figure 7-18: Calculating Percentages with Means Survey Item

4. (a) If you could begin again, would you choose to attend UNCA?

1   Yes
2   No

(b) Would you choose the same major field of study?

1   Yes
2   No

In the program to follow, the two survey items shown in **Figure 7-18** will be recoded as the variables PERCENT1 and PERCENT2. Respondents who indicated "Yes" to these items will have a PERCENT1/PERCENT2 value of 100 and the "No" responses will have a value of 0. These operations are shown in the highlighted text of the following program. The PROC TABULATE analysis will include academic discipline (DISCIP) and YEAR as class variables or subgroups. The results are shown in **Output 7-21**.

SAS Code for Computing Percentages with Means

```
libname svy 'pb hd:gss';

options ls=70 nodate nonumber ps=65 ;

data report;
 set svy.data95(keep=a4_a a4_b year discip)
     svy.data96(keep=a4_a a4_b year discip);

if a4_a = '1' then percent1 = 100;
else if a4_a = '2' then percent1 = 0;

if a4_b = '1' then percent2 = 100;
else if a4_b = '2' then percent2 = 0;

proc format;
   value $discip 'NS' = 'Natural Sciences'
                 'SS' = 'Social Sciences'
                 'HM' = 'Humanities'
                 'PR' = 'Professional';

   value $year   '95' = '1995'
                 '96' = '1996';

proc tabulate data = report noseps;
   class discip year;
   var percent1 percent2;
   table discip*(Year ALL='Discipline Total') year all='Total',
         N*F=5. percent1 = 'Attend UNCA Again'*mean=
                 'Percent'*F=12.1
                 percent2 = 'Same Major Again' * mean=
                 'Percent'*F=12.1/
rts=23 indent=3;
FORMAT discip $discip. year $year.;
title1 'If You Could Begin Again, Would You Choose To:  ';
title2 '(1) Attend UNCA Or (2) Choose Same Field Of Study?';
run;
```

Output 7-21: Calculating Percentages with Means

```
        If You Could Begin Again, Would You Choose To:
        (1) Attend UNCA Or (2) Choose Same Field Of Study?

     ----------------------------------------------------------
    |                      |     |Attend UNCA | Same Major |
    |                      |     |   Again    |   Again    |
    |                      |     |------------+------------|
    |                      |  N  |  Percent   |  Percent   |
    |----------------------+-----+------------+------------|
    |Humanities            |     |            |            |
    |   1995               |  55 |      85.2  |      90.6  |
    |   1996               |  38 |      94.4  |      88.9  |
    |   Discipline Total   |  93 |      88.9  |      89.9  |
    |Natural Sciences      |     |            |            |
    |   1995               |  75 |      89.7  |      88.9  |
    |   1996               |  59 |      83.1  |      84.7  |
    |   Discipline Total   | 134 |      86.6  |      87.0  |
    |Professional          |     |            |            |
    |   1995               | 122 |      89.1  |      86.8  |
    |   1996               |  90 |      85.2  |      89.9  |
    |   Discipline Total   | 212 |      87.4  |      88.1  |
    |Social Sciences       |     |            |            |
    |   1995               | 117 |      83.3  |      83.0  |
    |   1996               |  92 |      83.0  |      81.9  |
    |   Discipline Total   | 209 |      83.2  |      82.6  |
    |1995                  | 369 |      86.8  |      86.6  |
    |1996                  | 279 |      85.2  |      86.1  |
    |Total                 | 648 |      86.1  |      86.4  |
     ----------------------------------------------------------
```

Analyzing Multiple-Response Items

The use of the phrase *check all that apply* is a widely used survey technique that helps to capture some of the complexity of human behavior. While these items may appear on the survey form as one question, they are electronically stored as a series of dichotomous or dummy-coded variables (1/0, Yes/No, etc.). When reporting dichotomous percentage items (Yes/No, Agree/Disagree, etc.), it is redundant to report percentages for both categories. Moreover, even when variables have four or more responses (e.g., Poor, Fair, Good, Excellent), it is often unnecessary to report percentages for *all* response categories. The reporting of the combined "Good/Excellent" responses will usually meet the information needs of the reader and provide the analyst with more room for creating readable multidimensional tables that provide the most information in the least amount of space.

A potential pitfall in the analysis of multiple-response survey items is the handling of missing data. For these questions phrased *check all that apply*, how do you distinguish between respondents who do not answer any of the optional items (and who should be excluded from the calculation of percentages), and those respondents who selected one or more optional choices? In the analysis of nonmultiple response items, the missing data values will determine this decision, but in this context, depending on how the data were entered, a missing value may be a valid response that should be scored as a 0.

One approach to this problem is to delete observations that have missing values coded for all multiple-response items and then code missing values as a 0 for all respondents who marked at least one category. Note that this logic assumes that there is an "Other" or "None of the above" type response category to ensure that every respondent will be able to mark at least one of the multiple-response items.

There are two basic strategies for working with multiple-response questionnaire items with PROC TABULATE.

- Create a concatenated table with each survey item treated as a row variable.

- Transform the data so that a single new variable is used to represent all the multiple-response items and create new observations to represent each variable value.[7]

We will use the survey item shown in **Figure 7-19** to illustrate the two approaches to the analysis of multiple-response items.

---

[7] This technique of reshaping variables into observations is also covered in Chapter 5, "Data Manipulation" and Chapter 8, "Presenting Survey Graphics."

Figure 7-19: Multiple-Response Survey Item

15. What prevents you from spending more of your leisure time on campus? (*Mark all that apply*)

01   Have to work at a job
02   Activities that interest me occur elsewhere
03   Inconvenience of returning to campus
04   I don't have any more leisure time
05   There is more to do elsewhere
06   Activities are not available at convenient times
07   Cost of additional transportation to/from campus
08   Transportation that I use requires that I leave campus at a certain time
09   Once I've left campus, I am not interested or willing to return
10   Lack of available or convenient child care
11   Other:_____

Method 1: Create Concatenated Tables

The survey question (Q15) shown in **Figure 7-19** has 11 *responses* that are represented as 11 dichotomous character variables (Q15_01 - Q15_11) coded with a "1" to represent positive responses and a "0" to indicate that the respondent did not mark the item. The program to follow will report the percentage of respondents who selected each response category cross-tabulated by residence status (dorm or commuter) in a single table. To use the percentages-with-means trick, use arrays to perform two operations.

- The INPUT function creates a new set of numeric variables PCT01-PCT11 to represent the original Q15_01 - Q15_11 character variables scored as "1" or "0".

- The PCT01 - PCT11 variables are multiplied by 100 so that each variable will have a value of 0 or 100. With this coding scheme, percentages can be obtained by computing the mean for each variable.

SAS Code for Concatenated Multiple-Response Items

```
libname db 'PB HD:stud exp svy';

options ls=85 nodate nonumber ps=65;

data report;
 set db.survey96(keep=q15_01-q15_11 dorm);

 if (q15_01 = ' ' and q15_02 = ' ' and q15_03 = ' ' and q15_04 = ' '
 and q15_05 = ' ' and q15_06 = ' ' and q15_07 = ' ' and q15_08 = ' '
 and q15_09 = ' ' and q15_10 = ' ' and q15_11 = ' ') then delete;

array old $ q15_01-q15_11;
array new pct01-pct11;
do x = 1 to 11;
new{x} = input(old{x},1.);
new{x} = 100*new{x};
end;
if dorm > ' ' then status = 'R';
else status = 'C'
keep status pct01-pct11;

proc format;
   value $status 'C' = 'Commuter'
                 'R' = 'Residence Hall';

proc tabulate data = report noseps;
   class status;
   var pct01-pct11;
   table
        pct01 = 'Have To Work At a Job'
        pct02 = 'Activities Of Interest Occur Elsewhere'
        pct03 = 'Inconvenience Of Returning To Campus'
        pct04 = 'Don't Have Any More Leisure Time'
        pct05 = 'There Is More To Do Elsewhere'
        pct06 = 'Activ Not Available At Convenient Times'
        pct07 = 'Cost of Additional Transp To/From Campus'
        pct08 = 'Must Leave Campus At Certain Time'
        pct09 = 'Not Interested In Returning to Campus'
        pct10 = 'Lack Of Avail/Convenient Child Care'
        pct11 = 'Other',
        status = ' ' *(n*f=3. mean = 'Percent'*f=7.1)
        all='Total'*(n*f=3. mean = 'Percent'*f=7.1)/
box ='Reason' rts=43;
format status $status. ;
title1
'Reasons for Not Spending More Leisure/Discretionary Time
on Campus';
run;
```

Output 7-22: Multiple-Response Table Using Concatenation

```
            Reasons for Not Spending More Leisure/Discretionary Time on Campus


-------------------------------------------------------------------------------
|Reason                                  |            | Residence |           |
|                                        | Commuter   |   Hall    |  Total    |
|                                        |------------+-----------+-----------|
|                                        | N |Percent| N |Percent| N |Percent|
|----------------------------------------+---+-------+---+-------+---+-------|
|Have To Work At a Job                   |142|  62.7|137|  21.2|279|  42.3|
|Activities Of Interest Occur Elsewhere  |142|  48.6|137|  42.3|279|  45.5|
|Inconvenience Of Returning To Campus    |142|  64.1|137|   3.6|279|  34.4|
|Don't Have Any More Leisure Time        |142|  47.9|137|  39.4|279|  43.7|
|There Is More To Do Elsewhere           |142|  23.9|137|  27.7|279|  25.8|
|Activ Not Available At Convenient Times |142|  25.4|137|  25.5|279|  25.4|
|Cost of Additional Transp To/From Campus|142|  14.8|137|   5.8|279|  10.4|
|Must Leave Campus At Certain Time       |142|   3.5|137|   3.6|279|   3.6|
|Not Interested In Returning to Campus   |142|  31.7|137|   5.1|279|  18.6|
|Lack Of Avail/Convenient Child Care     |142|  12.7|137|   0.0|279|   6.5|
|Other                                   |142|  12.0|137|  16.1|279|  14.0|
-------------------------------------------------------------------------------
```

The N statistic is always of interest, but in multiple-response type tables, it will usually have the same value for all rows within a column as shown in **Output 7-22**. This redundancy takes up valuable column space, but yet we need to communicate to readers the sample size for each value of the class variables. One solution to this dilemma is to determine the N for each class variable and then add the N value information to the labels defined in the VALUE statement in PROC FORMAT. The N value information for the universal class variable ALL can be printed as part of the label assigned in the TABLE statement. The program to follow will produce the same table as shown in **Output 7-22** with the N information reported as part of the column headings. The results are shown in **Output 7-23**.

SAS Code for Reporting N as Part of a Column Heading

(The DATA step is the same as the previous program.)

```
proc format;
   value $status 'C' = 'Commuter (n=142)'
                 'R' = 'Residence Hall (n=137)';

proc tabulate data = report noseps;
 class status;
 var pct01-pct11;
 table
      pct01 = 'Have To Work At a Job'
      pct02 = 'Activities Of Interest Occur Elsewhere'
      pct03 = 'Inconvenience Of Returning To Campus'
      pct04 = 'Don''t Have Any More Leisure Time'
      pct05 = 'There Is More To Do Elsewhere'
      pct06 = 'Activ Not Available At Convenient Times'
      pct07 = 'Cost of Additional Transp To/From Campus'
      pct08 = 'Must Leave Campus At Certain Time'
      pct09 = 'Not Interested In Returning to Campus'
      pct10 = 'Lack Of Avail/Convenient Child Care'
      pct11 = 'Other',
      status = ' ' *mean = 'Percent'*f=9.1
      all='Total (n=279)'*mean = 'Percent'*f=9.1/
box ='Reason' rts=43;
format status $status. ;
title1
'Reasons for Not Spending More Leisure/Discretionary
Time on Campus';
run;
```

Output 7-23: Improved Table without N Column

```
  Reasons for Not Spending More Leisure/Discretionary Time on Campus

  -----------------------------------------------------------------------
 |Reason                                  |         |Residence|         |
 |                                        |Commuter |  Hall   |  Total  |
 |                                        | (n=142) | (n=137) | (n=279) |
 |                                        |---------+---------+---------|
 |                                        | Percent | Percent | Percent |
 |----------------------------------------+---------+---------+---------|
 |Have To Work At a Job                   |    62.7 |    21.2 |    42.3 |
 |Activities Of Interest Occur Elsewhere  |    48.6 |    42.3 |    45.5 |
 |Inconvenience Of Returning To Campus    |    64.1 |     3.6 |    34.4 |
 |Don't Have Any More Leisure Time        |    47.9 |    39.4 |    43.7 |
 |There Is More To Do Elsewhere           |    23.9 |    27.7 |    25.8 |
 |Activ Not Available At Convenient Times |    25.4 |    25.5 |    25.4 |
 |Cost of Additional Transp To/From Campus|    14.8 |     5.8 |    10.4 |
 |Must Leave Campus At Certain Time       |     3.5 |     3.6 |     3.6 |
 |Not Interested In Returning to Campus   |    31.7 |     5.1 |    18.6 |
 |Lack Of Avail/Convenient Child Care     |    12.7 |     0.0 |     6.5 |
 |Other                                   |    12.0 |    16.1 |    14.0 |
  -----------------------------------------------------------------------
```

Method 2: Reshape Variables into Observations

Multiple-response tables can also be created by reshaping variables into observations. This technique is based on creating a new variable to represent multiple variables, with a new observation generated for each possible value. An important by-product of this method is that the observation count (N) is based on the number of multiple-response variables and values. This is *not* the same as the number of survey respondents found in the original data set. A limitation of this technique is that it can require a lot of coding although the use of array processing can significantly reduce the amount of code required. To illustrate this technique we will provide two example programs to analyze the survey items shown in **Figure 7-19**. The first program creates a new *single* variable (REASON) to capture responses for each of the Q15_01 - Q15_11 variables. An observation is created for each of the Q15_01 - Q15_11 variables for each respondent. The second version of this program follows the same steps but uses array processing to reduce the amount of SAS code. Arrays are designed to perform the same operations on numerous variables in one step. The first version of this program, without arrays, requires 73 lines of code, while the second version eliminates 28 lines of code for a 38% reduction through the use of array processing. Both of these programs generate the table results shown in **Output 7-24**.

SAS Code for Reshaping Multiple Response Items: Without Array Processing

```
libname db 'pb hd:stud exp svy';

options ls=75 nodate nonumber ps=65;

data report(keep=reason percent status);
length reason $40;
 set db.survey96(keep=q15_01-q15_11 dorm);
 if (q15_01= ' ' and q15_02 = ' ' and q15_03 = ' ' and q15_04 = ' '
 and q15_05 = ' ' and q15_06 = ' ' and q15_07 = ' ' and q15_08 = ' '
 and q15_09 = ' ' and q15_10 = ' ' and q15_11 = ' ') then delete;

if dorm > ' ' then status = 'R';
else status = 'C';

reason = 'Have To Work At a Job';
  if q15_01 = '1' then percent = 100;
  else percent = 0;
  output;
reason = 'Activities Of Interest Occur Elsewhere';
  if q15_02 = '1' then percent = 100;
  else percent = 0;
  output;
reason = 'Inconvenience Of Returning To Campus';
  if q15_03 = '1' then percent = 100;
  else percent = 0;
  output;
reason = 'Don't Have Any More Leisure Time';
  if q15_04 = '1' then percent = 100;
  else percent = 0;
  output;
reason = 'There Is More To Do Elsewhere';
  if q15_05 = '1' then percent = 100;
  else percent = 0;
  output;
reason = 'Activ Not Available At Convenient Times'
  if q15_06 = '1' then percent = 100;
  else percent = 0;
  output;
reason = 'Cost of Additional Transp To/From Campus';
  if q15_07 = '1' then percent = 100;
  else percent = 0;
  output;
```

```
reason = 'Must Leave Campus At Certain Time';
  if q15_08 = '1' then percent = 100;
  else percent = 0;
  output;
reason = 'Not Interested In Returning to Campus';
  if q15_09 = '1' then percent = 100;
  else percent = 0;
  output;
reason = 'Lack Of Avail/Convenient Child Care';
  if q15_10 = '1' then percent = 100;
  else percent = 0;
  output;
reason = 'Other';
  if q15_11 = '1' then percent = 100;
  else percent = 0;
  output;

proc format;
   value $status 'C' = 'Commuter (n=144)'
                 'R' = 'Residence Hall (n=126)';

proc tabulate data = report noseps;
   class reason status;
   var percent;
   table reason= ' ',
         status=' '*percent=' '*mean='Percent'*f=9.1
         all='Total (N=279)'*percent=' '*mean='Percent'*f=9.1/
box ='Reason' rts=43;
format status $status. ;
title1
'Reasons for Not Spending More Leisure/Discretionary
        Time on Campus';
run;
```

SAS Code for Reshaping Multiple-Response Items : With Array Processing

(The DATA step is the same as the previous program.)

```
array q q15_01-q15_11;
do i=1 to 11;
      if i= 1 then reason='Have To Work At a Job';
  else if i= 2 then reason='Activities Of Interest Occur Elsewhere';
  else if i= 3 then reason='Inconvenience Of Returning To Campus';
  else if i= 4 then reason='Don't Have Any More Leisure Time';
  else if i= 5 then reason='There Is More To Do Elsewhere';
  else if i= 6 then reason='Activ Not Available At Convenient Times';
  else if i= 7 then reason='Cost of Additional Transp To/From Campus';
  else if i= 8 then reason='Must Leave Campus At Certain Time';
  else if i= 9 then reason='Not Interested In Returning to Campus';
  else if i=10 then reason='Lack Of Avail/Convenient Child Care';
  else if i=11 then reason='Other';

  if q{i}= '1' then percent=100;
else percent = 0;
  output;
end;

proc format;
   value $status 'C' = 'Commuter (n=142)'
                 'R' = 'Residence Hall (n=137)';

proc tabulate data = report noseps;
   class reason status;
   var percent;
   table reason= ' ',
         status=' '*percent=' '*mean='Percent'*f=9.1
         all='Total (n=279)'*
         percent='
'*mean='Percent'*f=9.1/
box ='Reason' rts=43;
format status $status. ;
title1
'Reasons for Not Spending More Leisure/Discretionary Time
on Campus';
run;
```

Output 7-24: Reshaping Variables into Observations, Multiple-Response Example

```
 Reasons for Not Spending More Leisure/Discretionary Time on Campus

 --------------------------------------------------------------------
|Reason                                 |          |Residence|         |
|                                       |Commuter  |  Hall   | Total   |
|                                       | (n=142)  | (n=137) | (n=279) |
|                                       |---------+---------+---------|
|                                       | Percent | Percent | Percent |
|---------------------------------------+---------+---------+---------|
|Activ Not Available At Convenient Times |    25.4|     25.5|     25.4|
|Activities Of Interest Occur Elsewhere  |    48.6|     42.3|     45.5|
|Cost of Additional Transp To/From Campus|    14.8|      5.8|     10.4|
|Don't Have Any More Leisure Time        |    47.9|     39.4|     43.7|
|Have To Work At a Job                   |    62.7|     21.2|     42.3|
|Inconvenience Of Returning To Campus    |    64.1|      3.6|     34.4|
|Lack Of Avail/Convenient Child Care     |    12.7|      0.0|      6.5|
|Must Leave Campus At Certain Time       |     3.5|      3.6|      3.6|
|Not Interested In Returning to Campus   |    31.7|      5.1|     18.6|
|Other                                   |    12.0|     16.1|     14.0|
|There Is More To Do Elsewhere           |    23.9|     27.7|     25.8|
 --------------------------------------------------------------------
```

The table created by reshaping variables into observations (**Output 7-24**) is essentially the same as the table generated by concatenating row variables (**Output 7-23**). The only difference is in the order of values for the variable REA-SON or the row column headings. With concatenated tables, the order of row variables is based on the order specified in the TABLE statement. In the last example where variables were reshaped into observations, there is only one row variable and the default order is the PROC SORT order: the first character of the values for the variable REASON. Rather than the alphabetic listing of row headings as shown in **Output 7-24**, a more effective table design would be to list the reasons in descending order of the total percentage. This type of ordering would enable read-ers to know at a glance which factors were most and least important. The next section will review techniques for ordering row and column headings.

TIP: Use of LENGTH Statements

LENGTH statements are used to modify the default lengths of character and numeric variables. When creating new character variables, SAS will automatically assign a length value based on the first value defined. In cases where character values are not of consistent length, like the values of REASON in the previous example, values longer than the default or initial length will be truncated. To avoid this problem, use the LENGTH statement to assign a variable length to represent the longest text string. To illustrate, the following statement assigns a length of 40 characters to NEWVAR.

```
length newvar $40 ;
```

Ordering Row and Column Headings

By default, PROC TABULATE will use the logic of PROC SORT to order row and column headings. The principles of effective table design will often require users to alter the default order for these headings. For example, the ordering of class headings by ascending or descending order of an analysis variable is sometimes a more effective tabular presentation than the alphabetic ordering of class headings. There are three options that can be used on the PROC TABULATE statement to override the default ordering system. Recall the general form

PROC TABULATE ORDER = *option*;

Where:

option can be

- DATA (order of class values is based on the order found in a data set).

- FREQ (headings for class values are in descending order of the observation frequency count).

- FORMATTED (class headings are ordered by formatted values as defined by PROC FORMAT and referenced with a FORMAT statement).

We will use the survey item shown in **Figure 7-20** to illustrate the default (or internal), FREQ, and FORMATTED ordering options.

Figure 7-20: Survey Item for PROC TABULATE ORDER= Examples

> 9. Which best describes the area in which you lived during high school?
>
> 1 Rural Area
> 2 Small town (20,000 or less)
> 3 Moderate size city (20,001-60,000)
> 4 Large city (60,001-100,000)
> 5 Urban area (more than 100,000)

The program to follow will generate three separate tables in **Output 7-25** to illustrate the following PROC TABULATE statement ordering options: the default or internal ordering, ORDER=FREQ, and ORDER=FORMATTED. The ORDER=DATA option will be illustrated in the next section.

```
libname library 'pb hd:new student svy';

options nodate nonumber ps=65 ls=80;
proc format;
   value $area '1' = 'Rural Area'
              '2' = 'Small Town (<20,000)'
              '3' = 'Moderate Size City (20,001-60,000)'
              '4' = 'Large City (60,001-100,000)'
              '5' = 'Urban Area (> 100,000)';

proc tabulate data = library.db96 noseps; * default ordering;
   class area;
   table area = ' ' all='Total',
         n*f=5. pctn='Percent'*f=9.1/
rts=36 box='Area Size';
format area $area. ;
title1 'Default Internal Ordering';

proc tabulate data = library.db96 noseps order=freq;
   class area;
   table area = ' ' all='Total',
         n*f=5. pctn='Percent'*f=9.1/
rts=36 box='Area Size';
format area $area. ;
title1 'Order=Freq';
```

```
proc tabulate data = library.db96 noseps order=formatted;
   class area;
   table area = ' ' all='Total',
         n*f=5. pctn='Percent'*f=9.1/
rts=36 box='Area Size';
format area $area. ;
title1 'Order=Formatted';
run;
```

Output 7-25: PROC TABULATE Ordering Options

```
                    Default Internal Ordering

     ---------------------------------------------------------
     |Area Size                             |  N  | Percent |
     |-------------------------------------+-----+---------|
     |Rural Area                            | 114|    18.9 |
     |Small Town (<20,000)                  | 194|    32.2 |
     |Moderate Size City (20,001-60,000)    | 142|    23.6 |
     |Large City (60,001-100,000)           |  65|    10.8 |
     |Urban Area (> 100,000)                |  87|    14.5 |
     |Total                                 | 602|   100.0 |
     ---------------------------------------------------------

                           Order=Freq

     ---------------------------------------------------------
     |Area Size                             |  N  | Percent |
     |-------------------------------------+-----+---------|
     |Small Town (<20,000)                  | 194|    32.2 |
     |Moderate Size City (20,001-60,000)    | 142|    23.6 |
     |Rural Area                            | 114|    18.9 |
     |Urban Area (> 100,000)                |  87|    14.5 |
     |Large City (60,001-100,000)           |  65|    10.8 |
     |Total                                 | 602|   100.0 |
     ---------------------------------------------------------

                         Order=Formatted

     ---------------------------------------------------------
     |Area Size                             |  N  | Percent |
     |-------------------------------------+-----+---------|
     |Large City (60,001-100,000)           |  65|    10.8 |
     |Moderate Size City (20,001-60,000)    | 142|    23.6 |
     |Rural Area                            | 114|    18.9 |
     |Small Town (<20,000)                  | 194|    32.2 |
     |Urban Area (> 100,000)                |  87|    14.5 |
     |Total                                 | 602|   100.0 |
     ---------------------------------------------------------
```

Ordering by the Value of a Statistic

An important element of effective table design is to order row and column head-ings by ascending or descending order based on the values of an *analysis* vari-able. This can be accomplished by using the ORDER = DATA option on the TABULATE statement. To illustrate this technique, we will use the survey question shown in **Figure 7-21** as the analysis variable. The class variable will be academic major.

Figure 7-21: Survey Item for PROC TABULATE ORDER= DATA Example

2. To what extent do you agree with the following statements about your academic major?

    a. Faculty members in the department work together to achieve program goals.

        1 Strongly Disagree
        2 Disagree
        3 Agree
        4 Strongly Agree

In this example, we wish to show by major in descending order the percentage of respondents who indicated "Agree" or "Strongly Agree" in the survey question in **Figure 7-21**. There are five steps in completing this task:

1. Create a new variable PERCENT that is equal to 100 for respondents reporting "Agree" or "Strongly Agree" and 0 for other nonmissing responses.

2. Compute the mean PERCENT score for each major using PROC SUMMARY. The mean PERCENT scores are renamed SORTV and are output to a data set named DUMMY. Note the use of the NWAY option to suppress all but the highest _TYPE_ values. (PROC MEANS could also be used for this step.)

3. Sort by major the DUMMY data and original survey file (REPORT).

4. Merge the DUMMY data set and original survey file (REPORT) to create a new data set called UPDATE. The result of this operation is to add a new variable (SORTV) that indicates the descending sort order for each value of MAJOR.

5. The UPDATE data set is sorted by SORTV, which reorders the file by descend-ing MAJOR PERCENT mean score. The ORDER=DATA option on the PROC TABULATE statement will now produce a table with the desired row-heading order.

The results of this program are shown in **Output 7-26**. It is of interest to note that this approach will continue to produce the desired sort order if data are added or deleted from the original file.

SAS Code for ORDER=DATA Example

```
libname library 'pb hd:prog assess svy';
options nodate ps=65 ls=75;

data report;
set library.progeval(keep=major q21);
if q21 in('3','4') then percent = 100;
else if q21 in('1','2') then percent = 0;
if major in('SPAN','GERM','FREN') then major='FLANG';

proc summary data = report nway;
   class major;
   var percent;
   output out = dummy(keep=major sortv)
   mean = sortv;

proc sort data = dummy; by major;
proc sort data = report; by major;

data update;
   merge dummy report(in=a); by major;
if a;

proc sort data = update; by descending sortv;

proc tabulate data = update noseps order=data;
   class major;
   var percent;
   table major=' ' all='Total',
         N*f=comma7. percent='Percent'*mean= ' '*f=9.1/
         box='Major';
title1 'Faculty Members of This Dept Work Together to
Achieve Program Goals';
title3 'Percent of Students Responding "Agree" or "Strongly Agree"';
format major $major. ;
run;
```

Output 7-26: ORDER=DATA Example

```
      Faculty Members of This Dept Work Together to Achieve Program Goals

         Percent of Students Responding "Agree" or "Strongly Agree"

                     ---------------------------------------
                     |Major              |   N   | Percent |
                     |-------------------+-------+---------|
                     |Classics           |     5|   100.0|
                     |Economics          |    25|   100.0|
                     |Psychology         |    70|    98.5|
                     |Literature         |    50|    95.6|
                     |Art                |    78|    93.2|
                     |Accounting         |    67|    91.9|
                     |Atmospheric Sci    |    54|    88.7|
                     |Biology            |    73|    87.5|
                     |Management         |   137|    86.5|
                     |Physics            |    23|    86.4|
                     |History            |    37|    85.7|
                     |Sociology          |    55|    84.3|
                     |Computer Sci       |    94|    80.0|
                     |Physical Educ      |    46|    73.3|
                     |Architecture       |    11|    72.7|
                     |Forestry           |    22|    71.4|
                     |Area Studies       |    35|    71.0|
                     |Engineering        |    78|    66.7|
                     |Anthropology       |    30|    66.7|
                     |Geology            |   130|    63.1|
                     |Agronomy           |    61|    54.4|
                     |Total              | 1,181|    80.8|
                     ---------------------------------------
```

Ordering by Changing the Internal Mapping of a Variable

There are occasions when none of the PROC TABULATE ORDER= options will produce the desired sort order. For example, consider the following variable named LEVEL with these values:

Code	Value Label
FR	Freshman
SO	Sophomore
JR	Junior
SR	Senior

If you want to produce a report that lists the variable LEVEL in the order shown in the preceding table, neither the default, the FORMATTED, nor the FREQ order options will produce the desired result. The ORDER=DATA option could be used to obtain the desired order of class values, but a more efficient approach would be to remap the internal values of LEVEL to a different coding scheme. For example, consider the following program:

```
data report;
   set survey;
if level = 'FR' then levelx = '1';
else if level = 'SO' then levelx = '2';
else if level = 'JR' then levelx = '3';
else if level = 'SO' then levelx = '4';
```

The default PROC TABULATE order can now be used with the remapped variable LEVELX to obtain the desired order.

TIP: PROC FORMAT Ordering

As an alternative to the internal remapping approach discussed in the previous section, you can modify the sort order of character strings by embedding blanks at the beginning of PROC FORMAT defined value labels. Blanks have a lower sort sequence than the characters A to Z and will not corrupt the appearance of printed labels in PROC TABULATE output. For example, the following PROC FORMAT statement will produce a sort order of "Freshman" -"Sophomore" - "Junior"- "Senior" with the PROC TABULATE ORDER=FORMATTED option. Note the two embedded blanks in the value labels for ' Freshman' and ' Sophomore'.

```
proc format;
     value $class    'FR' = ' Freshman'
                     'SO' = ' Sophomore'
                     'JR' = 'Junior'
                     'SR' = 'Senior';
```

Using PROC TABULATE Supertables

The supertable concept was developed by Tufte (1983) in his classic work *The Visual Display of Quantitative Information*. The basic idea of the supertable is to provide the reader with a comprehensive table of multiple data comparisons clustered around a common dimension. This data-rich unified table is a far better presentation than would be obtained by the tedious repetition of numerous small tables or histograms related to a common dimension. Supertables have a reference-like quality that is based on the amount of information provided in an easy-to-read, attractive format.

The PROC TABULATE supertable is simply a concatenated table with numerous row variables. Since PROC TABULATE, by default, *excludes* all observations with one or more missing class variables, it is important to use the MISSING option on the PROC statement. Given the frequency of missing data in most survey research applications, the MISSING option will prevent the unnecessary loss of observations when respondents provide valid responses to some, but not all, class variables. The program to follow produces a *preliminary* supertable that is shown in **Output 7-27**. A limitation of the MISSING option is that while preserving observations that have missing data for one or more class variables, it also prints the number of missing observations for each class variable. To finalize the preliminary supertable shown in **Output 7-27**, we will need to use a text editor to eliminate the missing row variable counts and to add some separator lines for the optimal presentation.

SAS Code for PROC TABULATE Supertable

```
libname library 'pb hd:gss';

options ls=70 nodate nonumber ps=65;

data supertab;
length year $4;
 set library.data95
     library.data96;
year= '19'||year;
 if a4_a = '1' then percent = 100;
 else if a4_a = '2' then percent = 0;

proc tabulate data = supertab missing noseps;
 var percent;
 class discip admtype cumgpa race sex year;
 table discip='Discipline:'
       admtype = 'Admission's Type:'
       cumgpa = 'Cumulative GPA:'
       race = 'Race:'
       sex = 'Sex:'
       all = 'Total',
       year='Year Graduated'*(n*f=5.0 percent=' '*mean='Pct'*f=5.1)
       all='2-Year Total'*(n*f=5.0 percent=' '*mean='Pct'*f=5.1)/
 rts=23 box='Dimension' ;
format discip $discip. admtype $admtype. cumgpa cumgpa. race $race.
 sex $sex.;
title1 'If You Could Begin Again, Would You Choose to
Attend UNCA';
title2 '(Percent Responding "Yes")';
run;
```

Output 7-27: PROC TABULATE Supertable

```
        If You Could Begin Again, Would You Choose to Attend UNCA
                      (Percent Responding "Yes")


    -----------------------------------------------------------------
    |Dimension                |     Year Graduated      |           |
    |                         |-------------------------|  2-Year   |
    |                         |   1995    |    1996     |  Total    |
    |                         |-----------+-----------+-----------|
    |                         | N  | Pct  | N  | Pct  | N  | Pct  |
    |-------------------------+-----+-----+-----+-----+-----+-----|
    |Discipline:              |    |      |    |      |    |      |
    |                         | 35| 86.2|  14| 63.6|  49| 80.0|
    |Humanities               | 55| 85.2|  38| 94.4|  93| 88.9|
    |Natural Sciences         | 75| 89.7|  59| 83.1| 134| 86.6|
    |Professional             |122| 89.1|  90| 85.2| 212| 87.4|
    |Social Sciences          |117| 83.3|  92| 83.0| 209| 83.2|
    |Admission's Type:        |    |      |    |      |    |      |
    |                         | 37| 87.1|  14| 63.6|  51| 81.0|
    |Freshmen                 |172| 85.7| 130| 88.4| 302| 86.9|
    |Transfer                 |195| 87.6| 149| 82.4| 344| 85.3|
    |Cumulative GPA:          |    |      |    |      |    |      |
    |.                        | 37| 87.1|  14| 63.6|  51| 81.0|
    |2.00-2.49                | 51| 81.6|  34| 53.1|  85| 70.4|
    |2.50-2.99                |110| 85.7|  78| 89.7| 188| 87.4|
    |3.00-3.49                |118| 85.2|  98| 91.5| 216| 88.0|
    |3.50-4.00                | 88| 92.9|  69| 86.6| 157| 90.1|
    |Race:                    |    |      |    |      |    |      |
    |                         | 37| 87.1|  14| 63.6|  51| 81.0|
    |Other                    | 14| 85.7|   8| 87.5|  22| 86.4|
    |Black                    | 12| 95.0|  14| 90.0|  26| 92.3|
    |White                    |341| 87.2| 257| 86.9| 598| 87.0|
    |Sex:                     |    |      |    |      |    |      |
    |                         | 37| 87.1|  14| 63.6|  51| 81.0|
    |Female                   |214| 89.0| 161| 87.4| 375| 88.3|
    |Male                     |153| 83.2| 118| 82.1| 271| 82.7|
    |Total                    |404| 86.7| 293| 84.4| 697| 85.7|
    -----------------------------------------------------------------
```

As shown in **Output 7-27**, the MISSING option generates a missing value row header as the first line for each row variable. This blank header provides little useful information and is likely to confuse readers, but yet the MISSING option is needed to include as many observations as possible in the report. The table shown in **Output 7-27** could be improved by the addition of row separator lines between each new row variable or data "paragraph." The missing data rows can be deleted and the row variable separator lines can be added by using a text editor on the original PROC TABULATE output file. The visual impact of these improvements on the readability of the table is shown in **Output 7-28**. While the use of a text editor may be seem awkward or inconvenient, it is less work than importing the data into a word processor or spreadsheet package.

Output 7-28: Improved Supertable After Editing

```
          If You Could Begin Again, Would You Choose to Attend UNCA
                        (Percent Responding "Yes")


     --------------------------------------------------------------
     |Dimension             |      Year Graduated     |            |
     |                      |-------------------------|  2-Year    |
     |                      |   1995    |   1996      |   Total    |
     |                      |-----------+-----------+-----------|
     |                      |  N  | Pct |  N  | Pct |  N  | Pct  |
     |----------------------+-----+-----+-----+-----+-----+-----|
     |Discipline:           |     |     |     |     |     |      |
     |   Humanities         |  55| 85.2|  38| 94.4|  93| 88.9|
     |   Natural Sciences   |  75| 89.7|  59| 83.1| 134| 86.6|
     |   Professional       | 122| 89.1|  90| 85.2| 212| 87.4|
     |   Social Sciences    | 117| 83.3|  92| 83.0| 209| 83.2|
     |----------------------+-----+-----+-----+-----+-----+-----|
     |Admission's Type:     |     |     |     |     |     |      |
     |   Freshmen           | 172| 85.7| 130| 88.4| 302| 86.9|
     |   Transfer           | 195| 87.6| 149| 82.4| 344| 85.3|
     |----------------------+-----+-----+-----+-----+-----+-----|
     |Cumulative GPA:       |     |     |     |     |     |      |
     |   2.00-2.49          |  51| 81.6|  34| 53.1|  85| 70.4|
     |   2.50-2.99          | 110| 85.7|  78| 89.7| 188| 87.4|
     |   3.00-3.49          | 118| 85.2|  98| 91.5| 216| 88.0|
     |   3.50-4.00          |  88| 92.9|  69| 86.6| 157| 90.1|
     |----------------------+-----+-----+-----+-----+-----+-----|
     |Race:                 |     |     |     |     |     |      |
     |   Other              |  14| 85.7|   8| 87.5|  22| 86.4|
     |   Black              |  12| 95.0|  14| 90.0|  26| 92.3|
     |   White              | 341| 87.2| 257| 86.9| 598| 87.0|
     |----------------------+-----+-----+-----+-----+-----+-----|
     |Sex:                  |     |     |     |     |     |      |
     |   Female             | 214| 89.0| 161| 87.4| 375| 88.3|
     |   Male               | 153| 83.2| 118| 82.1| 271| 82.7|
     |----------------------+-----+-----+-----+-----+-----+-----|
     |Total                 | 404| 86.7| 293| 84.4| 697| 85.7|
     --------------------------------------------------------------
```

Automating Longitudinal Survey Tables with the Macro Language

In the analysis of surveys repeated over time, macro language can save keystrokes and greatly decrease the potential for errors in specifying filenames and permanent data sets as well as title information. The SAS macro facility will enable you to define a macro variable that can be used to replace character strings in repeated sections of a program. Macro variables can be defined for both character or numeric values. The %LET statement is used to define a macro variable as shown in the following example:

```
%let yr = 97;
```

The macro variable YR can now be used anywhere in your SAS job that you would like the value **97** to be represented. To reference and use a macro variable in a SAS statement, specify the macro variable name with an ampersand (&) concatenated to the beginning of the macro variable name, e.g., &YR. SAS does not recognize macro variable names that appear within a character string enclosed within single quotation marks ('). Thus, to reference a macro variable within a TITLE or FOOT-NOTE statement use double quotation marks (") instead of single quotes (') to enclose the character string. Macro variables can also be used as leading or trailing text as part of a SAS statement. For example:

```
proc tabulate data = library.survey&yr;
```

When you are using macro variable references as part of SAS statement text, it is sometimes necessary to use a period (.) to delimit the end of the macro variable name. Note that the period delimiter can always be used, but it is not always required. In the following example, the period delimiter is *not* required:

```
%let yr1 = 90;
%let yr2 = 91;
%let yr3 = 92;

data svy&yr1 svy&yr2 svy&yr3;
    set filename;
```

In cases where a macro variable is used as a prefix to text that begins with a period (e.g., `filename raw sample.dat`), two periods should be used to delimit the macro variable and preserve the original period. In the following table, we will illustrate the specification and result of macro variables using the YR1, YR2, and YR3 variables we have just defined.

Macro Statement	SAS Interpretation
filename raw "survey&yr1..dat";	filename raw "survey90.dat";
set library.data&yr1;	set library.data90;
set db.raw&yr1. db.raw&yr2;	set db.raw90 db.raw91;
if year = &yr2 then delete;	if year = 91 then delete;
title1 "19&yr3 Survey Results";	title1 "1992 Survey Results";

We will now illustrate the use of macro variables in a more complete example where we wish to report income data measured as ten categorical ranges for seven different years, with each year stored as a permanent SAS data set. Since this survey is repeated each year, the analyst has to update only the macro variable values stored in YR1- YR7 to read the most recent seven years of data and have this information correctly reflected in the TITLE statement. The time-saving value of the macro facility is even more pronounced in longer, more complicated programs. The use of macro variables can make the reporting of longitudinal survey data as easy as producing an "off the shelf" standard report.

SAS Code for Macro Example

```
libname library 'pb hd:new student svy';

%let yr1 = 90;
%let yr2 = 91;
%let yr3 = 92;
%let yr4 = 93;
%let yr5 = 94;
%let yr6 = 95;
%let yr7 = 96;
options nodate nonumber ps=65 ls=80;

data report;
set library.db&yr1.(keep=year income)
    library.db&yr2.(keep=year income)
    library.db&yr3.(keep=year income)
    library.db&yr4.(keep=year income)
    library.db&yr5.(keep=year income)
    library.db&yr6.(keep=year income)
    library.db&yr7.(keep=year income);
```

```
proc tabulate data = report noseps;
class year income;
table income =' ' all,
      year = 'P E R C E N T A G E'*(pctn<income all>=' '*F=7.1)/
box='Family Income' rts=19;
keylabel all='Total';
format income income. year $year. ;
Title1 "New Freshmen Family Income: 19&yr1-19&yr7";
run;
```

Output 7-29: Macro Example Results

```
                  New Freshmen Family Income: 1990-1996


------------------------------------------------------------------------
|Family Income      |                 P E R C E N T A G E              |
|                   |--------------------------------------------------|
|                   | 1990 | 1991 | 1992 | 1993 | 1994 | 1995 | 1996 |
|-------------------+------+------+------+------+------+------+------|
|10,000 or Less     |   4.8|   2.3|   3.0|   1.3|   3.9|   2.9|   2.5|
|10,001 - 15,000    |   6.6|   5.6|   3.9|   4.1|   3.6|   5.0|   2.3|
|15,001 - 20,000    |   6.6|   6.6|   5.1|   5.1|   6.1|   5.0|   3.4|
|20,001 - 25,000    |   6.0|   5.6|   7.8|   4.7|   4.4|   5.9|   2.8|
|25,001 - 30,000    |  10.8|   9.6|   9.3|   9.5|   9.2|   4.4|   5.9|
|30,001 - 35,000    |   9.9|   8.6|  10.2|  12.3|   9.2|   6.8|   7.6|
|35,001 - 40,000    |  11.4|  12.9|  10.8|  11.1|  12.2|  10.9|  10.2|
|40,001 - 50,000    |  12.7|  19.9|  14.8|  17.1|  12.5|  10.3|  13.8|
|50,001 - 60,000    |  12.3|  12.9|  14.5|  13.6|  11.7|  14.5|  13.3|
|60,001 or More     |  18.7|  15.9|  20.5|  21.2|  27.2|  34.2|  38.1|
|Total              | 100.0| 100.0| 100.0| 100.0| 100.0| 100.0| 100.0|
------------------------------------------------------------------------
```

TIP: Naming SAS Programs

Give your SAS programs that generate tables the name T01.SAS-TXX.SAS and your SAS/GRAPH programs the name G01.SAS-GXX.SAS, or use some other naming convention that uses a minimal number of characters and distinguishes between tables and figures. This will make it easier to manage your files and save you keystrokes. We are all candidates for carpal tunnel syndrome. For surveys repeated over time, it's also helpful to have a table of contents file to show a description for each T01.SAS-TXX.SAS program.

Chapter

8

Presenting Survey Graphics

"... clarity and excellence in thinking is very much like clarity and excellence in the display of data. When principles of design replicate principles of thought, the act of arranging information becomes an act of insight."

Edward R. Tufte
Visual Explanations

Introduction

The SAS System provides two levels of graphics presentation. The base product can produce plots and histograms with PROC PLOT and PROC CHART. These base product procedures are designed to provide the analyst with quick and easy-to-use graphics tools for understanding data structures and relationships. PROC PLOT and PROC CHART have limited customization features and do not provide presentation-quality graphics output. The use of PROC PLOT and PROC CHART as analysis tools is discussed in Chapter 6, "Analyzing Survey Data." This chapter will focus on SAS/GRAPH software, which is designed to develop presentation-quality graphics.

The power and flexibility of computer software is usually reflected in the size and complexity of its documentation. There are many computer graphics "point-and-click" software products that are probably easier to use than SAS/GRAPH, but none can match its comprehensiveness and capacity for users to control all aspects of their graphical presentation. This chapter will reduce the complexity of the 1,500-page *SAS/GRAPH Software: Reference, Volume 1* and *Volume 2* to the essential elements needed by researchers to display survey data in customized plots and histograms that exemplify the principles of graphical excellence.

Tufte's Principles of Graphical Excellence

The graphical display of survey data is an essential tool for communicating key findings to readers and policy makers. Mahon (1977) makes the interesting point that misusing or overusing graphics is worse than neglecting them. Tufte's (1983, p. 51) landmark work on the presentation of quantitative information provides a compelling set of principles to define graphical excellence:

> Graphical excellence is the well-designed presentation of interesting data–a matter of *substance*, of *statistics*, and of *design*.

> Graphical excellence consists of complex ideas communicated with clarity, precision, and efficiency.

> Graphical excellence is that which gives to the viewer the greatest number of ideas in the shortest time with the least ink in the smallest space.

> Graphical excellence is nearly always multivariate.

> And graphical excellence requires telling the truth about the data.

Avoid Chartjunk and Graphical Decoration

It is an unfortunate fact that ugly, vibrating statistical graphics are all too common in the popular press, professional literature, and unpublished research reports. Tufte coined the word *chartjunk* to describe poorly designed graphics that have the following characteristics (1983, p. 107). The graphics

- use an overwhelming amount of ink to describe a few numbers

- print label information vertically

- use cross-hatching patterns that vibrate (e.g. , see **Figure 8-6**)

- attempt to describe differences with indecipherable graphical elements (e.g., pie charts, block charts, star charts).

Tufte makes the humorous point that chartjunk is often a form of "unintentional optical art." Many chartjunk applications arise from their creator's naive "look-what-I-did-with-a-computer" syndrome rather than from a well-thought-out concept of the data presentation. Without exception, the designers of graphical and presentation

---

1 Tufte (1983, p. 112) reports that 68% of the graphical examples shown in the 1980 SAS/GRAPH Users Guide had these "vibrating" patterns.

2 Three-dimensional graphics that provide the reader with a multivariate three-dimensional relationship are not chartjunk, but most three-dimensional graphics are simply decoration used to describe a thin two-dimensional data set.

software have made it very easy for unwary users to produce chartjunk based on program defaults (e.g. , cross-hatched patterns)[1] or easy-to-use procedures (e.g., pie charts, three-dimensional charts[2], block charts, bubble charts, etc.) that exemplify bad graphical design.

Create User-Friendly Graphics

Based on the principles of graphical excellence, Tufte (1983) provides us with the following comparison of *friendly* and *unfriendly* graphics.

Figure 8-1: Characteristics of User Friendly vs. Unfriendly Graphics

Friendly	Unfriendly
Spelled out words - no cryptic labels.	Many abbreviations - unnecessary reader effort is necessary to understand the intended message.
Labels are printed left to right.	Vertical labels - words in several directions.
Messages help reader understand data.	Cryptic graphics information.
Labels appear on the graphic so the reader can instantly understand graphics elements.	Reader must go back and forth between legend and graphic. Graphic uses cross-hatching and garish colors.
Graphic entices reader.	Graphic is chartjunk.
If colors are used they are chosen to help color-blind readers, most of whom can distinguish blue from almost all other colors.	Graphic uses red and green for side-by-side contrasts
Type is easily readable and not overbearing.	Type is "clotted and overbearing."
Type is serif, a mix of capital letters and lowercase.	Type is sans serif, all uppercase.

Getting Started with SAS/GRAPH

The first step in working with SAS/GRAPH is to define the graphics environment with the GOPTIONS statement. The GOPTIONS statement is similar in function but more comprehensive than the OPTIONS statement used in the base product. Graphics options and parameters are used to specify graphical display and output devices, and to define size, appearance, and the destination of graphical output.

There are approximately 150 options that can be specified on the GOPTIONS statement. A list of some of the most commonly used follows. Consult Chapter 5 of *SAS/GRAPH Software: Reference* for more information.

Figure 8-2: Commonly Used Options for the GOPTIONS Statement

Function	Option	Description
Define Output	DEVICE=	Device-driver name
	TARGETDEVICE=	Device-driver name - preview output for one device on another device
	GSFNAME=	Used when creating a graphics stream output file
Size/Shape	ROTATE=	Used to specify portrait or landscape print mode
	HPOS=	Number of column positions
	VPOS=	Number of row positions
	VSIZE=	Vertical size of graphics output
Color/Fonts	HSIZE=	Horizontal size of graphics output
	COLORS=	Used to specify color order - important for pen plotters
	CBACK=	Background color
	CTEXT=	Default color for all text and borders
	FTEXT=	Default font
Global Options	RESET=	ALL and GLOBAL values reset graphics options and cancel global statements to default values

Viewing SAS/GRAPH Output

The DEVICE = *name* option is used to specify the type of device used to view SAS/GRAPH output. If you are viewing output on one device and printing on another device, the TARGETDEVICE = *name* option will enable you view output on the first device as it will appear on the second device. For example, the SAS/GRAPH applications used in this book are generated on a Macintosh computer and printed on an Apple laser writer printer. This combination of display and output devices is specified as follows:

```
goptions device=maccolor targetdevice=aplplus;
```

This GOPTIONS statement will enable you to view SAS/GRAPH output on a Macintosh color monitor (MACCOLOR) as it would appear on the printed laser writer (APLPLUS) page.

New SAS/GRAPH users need to become familiar with the characteristics and device-driver names of their graphical display and output devices. A list of all graphical display devices supported by SAS/GRAPH can be generated with PROC GDEVICE as shown by the following SAS code.

```
proc gdevice;
run;
```

Once you have determined the appropriate device-driver name for your device(s) using the GDEVICE procedure, it is useful to know the default page size height, width, orientation, and number of rows and columns for your device(s). This information can be obtained by running PROC GTESTIT. We will illustrate this procedure by using SAS/GRAPH on a Macintosh computer. The program shown in the following log will print the log shown in **Figure 8-3** and also the test pattern shown in **Output 8-1**.

Figure 8-3: PROC GTESTIT Log

```
1      proc gtestit pic=1;
2      run;

D=MACCOLOR B=1200    R= 24 C= 75 P=256
H= 16 W= 7 MAX=***   D=C000000000000000
RF=8000800000000000 S=0000000000000000
OPTS=D592244058280000 NCOLORS= 11
Background color = WHITE
Color 1 = BLACK
Color 2 = RED
Color 3 = GREEN
Color 4 = BLUE
Color 5 = CYAN
Color 6 = MAGENTA
Color 7 = GRAY
Color 8 = PINK
Color 9 = ORANGE
Color 10 = BROWN
Color 11 = YELLOW
Ratio = 0.72316
Hsize = 7.37501
Vsize = 5.33334
F=1
```

The most important device parameter information in the GTESTIT log (**Figure 8-3**) is highlighted. The values R = 24 and C = 75 represent the default number of row (R) and column (C) positions for the graphics device. These values also equate to the VPOS (Rows) and HPOS (columns) graphics options, which will be discussed later in this section. Knowledge of these default values is very important when resizing the length and width of the graphics output. The values HSIZE = 7.37501 and VSIZE = 5.33334 are the default width and height dimensions of the graphics output page.

Output 8-1: PROC GTESTIT Test Pattern

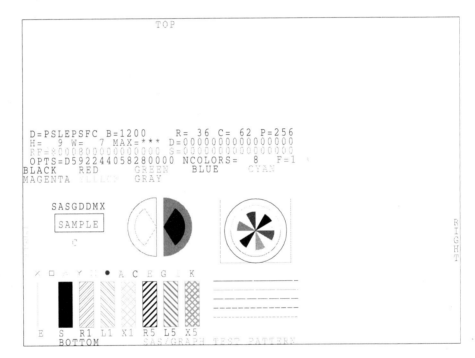

Customization Techniques

In developing graphical presentations of quantitative data, Bertin (1981) notes that we have eight visual variables for describing relationships or variation that the eye can perceive

- X Y - two dimensions of the plane

- Size

- Value

- Texture

- Color

- Orientation

- Shape.

The principles of graphical excellence are achieved through the manipulation of these visual variables. The effective visual display of quantitative information with SAS/GRAPH (or any other graphics software) will almost always require users to modify program defaults to include axis scaling, plot symbols, patterns, line characteristics, and legends. Customized graphics also require informed user control over graphics labeling, size, font, and color. This section will illustrate the use of TITLE, FOOTNOTE, AXIS, PATTERN, SYMBOL, and NOTE statements to customize the appearance of SAS/GRAPH output.

Using Titles and Footnotes

The TITLE and FOOTNOTE statements in SAS/GRAPH are functionally equivalent to these statements in base SAS software. The major difference is that with SAS/GRAPH, users are able to control graphics height (HEIGHT=), color (COLOR=), justification (JUSTIFY=), and font (FONT=) in each TITLE and FOOTNOTE statement. PROC GSLIDE is used to create text slides and will be used to illustrate the use of color, font, height, justification, and box options in the program to follow.

SAS Code for Title and Footnote Example

```
proc gslide;

title;
title1 c=gray01 'Output 8-2: Title and Footnote Example';
title3 h=1.5 c=black      'Default Justification is Centered';
title4 h=1.3 j=r c=gray90  'Title Number 3 is Right Justified';
title5 h=1.0 j=l c=grayaa  'Title Number 4 is Left Justified';
title6 c=gray01 h=1.5 'You Can'
                h=1.4 ' Change Text'
                h=1.3 ' in the'
                h=1.2 ' Middle of a'
                h= .8 r=45 ' Title';
footnote1 h=1 c=gray01 box=2 ' Boxes Work with Titles and Footnotes ';
run;
quit;
```

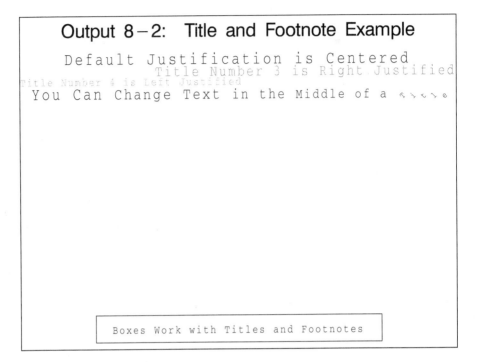

Output 8–2: Title and Footnote Example

Controlling the Appearance of Axes

The creation of information-rich, yet user-friendly, graphics will almost always require users to modify the scaling, tick marks, and labeling of axes for plots and histograms. Tight user control over axis scaling and appearance is a critical step in creating plots and histograms that are based on the principles of graphical excellence. SAS/GRAPH provides two mechanisms for controlling the appearance of axes in PROC GPLOT and PROC GCHART.

Both procedures have built-in options for controlling some aspects of axis appearance and scaling. Full user control of axis definitions is achieved through use of the AXIS statement. Both of these methods for specifying axis appearance provide the ability to control value ordering, axis color, and the number of minor tick marks. It is important to note that you can use LABEL statements (as discussed in Chapter 4) with PROC GPLOT and PROC GCHART to label axes, but this procedure will not allow you to control color, font, size, and text angle.

However, *all* aspects of axis appearance can be controlled by using the AXIS statement, whose definitions can then be referenced in the PROC GPLOT or PROC GCHART procedure. The process of defining AXIS statements and referencing them with a PROC GPLOT or PROC GCHART option is analogous to defining value labels with PROC FORMAT and then assigning them to a variable with a FORMAT statement.

PROC GPLOT and PROC GCHART Axis Options

A list of the options that provide axis control without using the AXIS statement follows in **Figure 8-4**.

Figure 8-4: PROC GCHART and PROC GPLOT Axis Options

Dimension	PROC GCHART	PROC GPLOT
Scale Ordering	RAXIS=*value-list* MAXIS=*value-list*	HAXIS=*value-list* VAXIS=*value-list* VZERO HZERO VREVERSE HREVERSE
Minor Tick Marks	MINOR=*n*	HMINOR=*n* VMINOR=*n*
Color	CTEXT=*color* CAXIS=*color*	CTEXT=*color* CAXIS=*color*

AXIS Statement

The AXIS statement provides full user control over all dimensions of vertical and horizontal axes for graphics output that is generated with PROC GPLOT and PROC GCHART. The general form of the AXIS statement and its most commonly used options follows:

AXIS<1...99>
    <scale-options>
    <appearance-options>
    <tick-mark-options>
    <text-options>;

Selected Scale and Tick Mark Options

  ORDER=(*value-list*)
  MAJOR=(*description*)|NONE
  MINOR=(*description*)|NONE

Where:

description can include the following elements:

    COLOR=*tick-mark-color*
    HEIGHT=*n <units>*
        where *n* is number of units

    NUMBER=*n*
        where *n* is number of tick marks
    WIDTH=*n*
        where *n* is width of line

<u>Selected Axis Appearance Options</u>

COLOR=*axis-color*
WIDTH=*n*

<u>Selected Axis Labeling Options</u>

LABEL=(*text-description* | 'text')
VALUE=(*text-description* | 'text')

Where:

text-description can include the following elements:

ANGLE=*degrees*
COLOR=*text-color*
FONT=*font-name*
HEIGHT=*n* <*units*>
JUSTIFY=LEFT | CENTER | RIGHT
ROTATE=*degrees*

A complete description of all AXIS statement options is provided in *SAS/GRAPH Software: Reference*. The use of the AXIS statement will be illustrated in the examples to follow.

Using Colors

The use of colors in SAS/GRAPH software is limited only by the capabilities of your graphics display device. Colors can be specified globally in the GOPTIONS statement or as part of individual SAS statements (e.g., TITLE, FOOTNOTE, AXIS, etc.). Colors are specified as follows:

COLOR=*color*

With the GOPTIONS statement, the following options are often useful for defining the color scheme of a graph.

Graphics Option	Description
CBACK=	Background color
CPATTERN=	Pattern color
CSYMBOL=	Symbol color
CTEXT=	Text color
CTITLE=	Title color

These global color options can be selectively overridden with the specification of a color in a procedure statement. For example, the following SAS code assigns black as the global default color and uses blue in the graphics title.

```
goptions device=maccolor ctext=black;
title1 c=blue 'Change color to blue for this title only';
```

Using Gray Scales

Although color output devices have become affordable and commonplace in many organizations, it is still not practical for most users to produce hardcopy color graphics in more than a limited quantity. The use of gray scale gradations to represent variation is an excellent alternative to color. It is far superior to assorted black-and-white pattern schemes that rely on optically painful vibrating cross-hatching to distinguish graphics elements from one another. SAS/GRAPH provides 256 levels of gray ranging from GRAY00 (black) to GRAYFF (white). A sample of gray scale colors is illustrated with the following program, which produces **Figure 8-5**.

SAS Code for Sample Gray Scales

```
data test;
input shade $;
cards;
gray00
gray30
gray45
gray60
gray75
gray90
gray99
grayaa
graybb
graycc
graydd
grayee
grayff
;
pattern01 c=gray00 v=s;
pattern02 c=gray30 v=s;
pattern03 c=gray45 v=s;
pattern04 c=gray60 v=s;
pattern05 c=gray75 v=s;
pattern06 c=gray90 v=s;
pattern07 c=gray99 v=s;
pattern08 c=grayaa v=s;
```

```
pattern09 c=graybb v=s;
pattern10 c=graycc v=s;
pattern11 c=graydd v=s;
pattern12 c=grayee v=s;
pattern13 c=grayff v=s;

 proc gchart;
   axis1 value=none c=grayff;
   hbar shade/nostats patternid=midpoint raxis=axis1;
   title1 'Figure 8-5: SAS/GRAPH Grayscales: Selected Shades';
 run;
 quit;
```

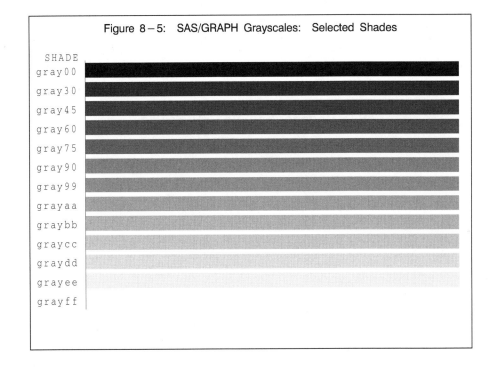

Figure 8–5: SAS/GRAPH Grayscales: Selected Shades

Fonts

The process for specifying fonts in SAS/GRAPH is very similar to the designation of colors. SAS/GRAPH will allow you to specify the following types of fonts:

- SAS/GRAPH software fonts

- Device-specific hardware fonts

- User-created fonts.

A full description of SAS/GRAPH fonts is provided in *SAS/GRAPH Software: Reference*. If a font is not specified, SAS will use your device's default hardware font. Fonts can be specified globally in the GOPTIONS statement or as part of individual SAS statements (e.g. TITLE, FOOTNOTE, AXIS, etc.). Fonts are specified as follows:

FONT=*font*

With the GOPTIONS statement the following options are often useful for defining the color scheme of a graph:

FTEXT   (specifies font for all text)
FTITLE   (specifies font for first title only)

Using Patterns

PATTERN statements and definitions are used with PROC GCHART to define bar color and fill design. The general form of the PATTERN statement follows:

PATTERN*n*

COLOR=*pattern-color*
VALUE=*bar-pattern*

where:

bar-pattern can be

EMPTY
SOLID

style<density>

where:

style can be L | R | X (left|right|crosshatch)
density can be 1...5

A sampling of patterns that can be used with PROC GCHART is shown in **Figure 8-6**. Consult *SAS/GRAPH Software: Reference* for a complete description of the PATTERN statement.

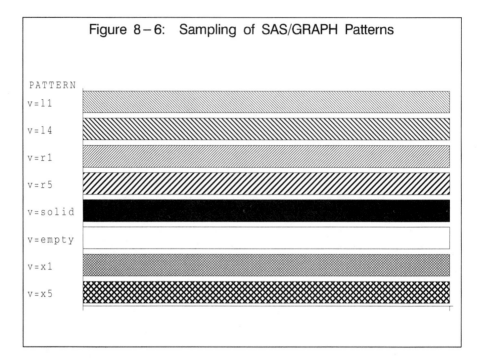

Figure 8 – 6:   Sampling of SAS/GRAPH Patterns

Using Symbols

SYMBOL statements are used to control the following characteristics of PROC GPLOT output.

- Plot symbol appearance, color, and size

- Plot lines - type, thickness, and color

- Method of interpolation.

The general form of the SYMBOL statement is

SYMBOL*n options*

Selected SYMBOL Options		
Plot Symbol	**Plot Line**	**Interpolation**
CV=*value-color*	CI=*line-color*	INTERPOL=JOIN (connect points - with straight lines)
FONT=*font*	CO=*confidence limit line color*	INTERPOL=BOX (box and whisker plot)
HEIGHT=*n*	CV=*value-color*	INTERPOL=R L (linear regression)
VALUE=*special-symbol* (see **Figure 8-7**)	LINE=*line-type* (1-46 with 1=solid)	INTERPOL=RQ (quadratic regression)
	WIDTH=*n* (>*n* = increasing thickness)	INTERPOL=RC (cubic regression)
		INTERPOL=SPLINE (smoothed line)

A complete list of SYMBOL definitions is provided in *SAS/GRAPH Software: Reference.* Several commonly used plotting symbols are shown in **Figure 8-7**.

Figure 8 – 7: Sampling of Special Plot Symbols

Value=	Plot Symbol
=	☆
DIAMOND	◇
CIRCLE	○
+	⊕
SQUARE	□

Writing Text in the Graphics Area with Notes

Providing readers with helpful label information is an important step in creating well-designed, user-friendly graphics. TITLE and FOOTNOTE statements provide header information, but they do not allow you to write text in the graphics output area. As a principle of graphical excellence, the use of legends to identify plot lines is to be *avoided* as it makes the reader work harder than necessary to understand the most important dimensions of the graph. The NOTE statement provides an easy-to-use means of writing text directly in the graphics area with full user control over font, size, color, and angle. The ability to use NOTE statements to control the placement and appearance of text is a prerequisite for achieving graphical excellence with SAS/GRAPH. NOTE statements can be used in both PROC GCHART and PROC GPLOT. The form of the NOTE statement is as follows:

NOTE <*options*> '*text*';

Selected Appearance Options

COLOR=*color*
FONT=*font*
HEIGHT=*n<units>*

where:

      units can be IN|CELLS|CM|PCT

Selected Placement Options

JUSTIFY=LEFT|CENTER|RIGHT (default is LEFT)
MOVE=(*x <units>, y <units>*)

where:
      x = horizontal position
      y = vertical position

      units can be IN|CELL|PCT

Angling and Character Rotation

ANGLE=*degrees* (angle of baseline of entire text string)
ROTATE=*degrees* (angle at which each character is rotated)

The primary difference between the NOTE statement and TITLE and FOOTNOTE statements is the power of the MOVE=(x,y) option on the NOTE statement to position text anywhere in the graphics output area. TITLE and FOOTNOTE statements can write text at the top and bottom of the graphics output area, respectively. However, to position text with the MOVE= option, you must specify *x* (horizontal) and *y* (vertical) coordinates. The coordinates for notes can be expressed as cells (CELLS), percentages (PCT), inches (IN) or centimeters (CM). The value for the units used by the *x* and *y* coordinates is determined by the value of the GUNIT= option. The default value for GUNIT= is CELLS, and the size of the cells is determined by the values of the HOPS and VPOS graphics options. The CELL coordinate system is based on the VPOS and HPOS values for your device type. For example, if your device has a VPOS of 40 (rows) and an HPOS of 100 (columns), then the vertical CELL range of your graphics area is 1-40, and the horizontal range is 1-100. Thus, with this cell-based coordinate system, the exact center of the graphics output would be MOVE=(20,50). You may find it easier to work with a percentage-based coordinate system or to use a combination: cells for titles and footnotes and percentages for notes. You can override the specified GUNIT= option value or the cell default inside the MOVE= option by specifying the desired measurement unit beside the values *x* and *y*.

The specification of text labels positioned with coordinates may seem tedious, but with a little practice, this important task can be accomplished relatively quickly with only a couple of trial-and-error attempts.[3] In assigning MOVE=(*x,y*) coordinates, it is helpful to understand that MOVE=(50 PCT, 50 PCT) will always represent the *exact center* of your graph and you can mentally adjust initial values from this reference point. The example to follow is designed to illustrate the use of the MOVE= option to position text at various points in the graphics output area. The text labels written on the graph indicate the actual x, y values used to write the text. Both CELL and PCT coordinate systems are used in the example.

SAS Code for Note Example

```
data test;
input x y;
cards;
1  1
2  2
3  3
4  4
5  5
6  6
7  7
8  8
9  9
10  10
;
symbol1 c=grayff;

proc gplot;
    axis1 order = (1 to 10 by 1) minor=none color=gray99
          value=(color=gray99);
plot x*y/vaxis=axis1 haxis=axis1;
title1 h=1.5 'Output 8-3: Note Statement Move Commands';
  note h=1 c=gray00 move=(1,1)    '(1,1)'
                    move=(15,15)  '(15,15)'
                    move=(10,29)  '(10,29)'
                    move=(50,10)  '(50,10)'
                    move=(30,25)  '(30,25)'
          c=gray45  move=(75 pct, 75 pct) '(75 pct, 75 pct)'
                    move=(25 pct, 25 pct) '(25 pct, 25 pct)'
                    move=(50 pct, 50 pct) '(50 pct, 50 pct)'
                    move=(75 pct, 15 pct) '(75 pct, 15 pct)';
    run;
    quit;
```

---

3 Text labels in the graphics output area can also be assigned using the SAS/GRAPH Graphics Editor. The Graphics Editor allows you to use point-and-click commands to write and position text, but this work is not retained if the original source code is reexecuted.

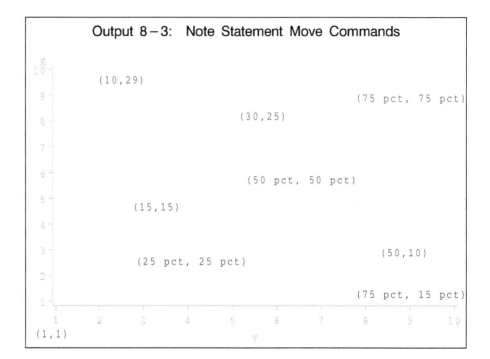

Output 8 – 3: Note Statement Move Commands

Histograms

PROC GCHART is used to create vertical and horizontal histograms or bar charts, pie charts, block charts, and star charts. Histograms are useful for showing group differences and frequency distributions. Based on the principles of graphical excellence, pie charts, block charts, and star charts are not recommended for presenting quantitative data. Bertin (1981) and Tufte (1983) argue convincingly that tables are far superior to *dumb* pie charts and that the only thing worse than a single pie chart is a group of pie charts because in that case

> ... the viewer is asked to compare quantities located in spatial disarray both within and between pies.... Given their low data-density and failure to order numbers along a visual dimension, pie charts should never be used.[4]

PROC GCHART can be used to graph both numeric and character variables to show frequency counts, percentages, sums, and means. The bars can be arranged in groups and individual bars can also be segmented to represent group information. As a general rule, horizontal histograms are easier to read than vertical bar charts for the following reasons.

---

4 Tufte, E. R., *The Visual Display of Quantitative Information* (Cheshire, Conn., 1983, p. 178).

- It is easier for the eye to read down than to scan across.

- Horizontal bar charts have more room for label information than vertical bar charts.

Furthermore, SAS/GRAPH, by default, provides a statistical table for horizontal bar charts to report frequencies, cumulative frequencies, percentages, and cumulative percentages.

The general form of the GCHART procedure for producing horizontal (HBAR) and vertical (VBAR) charts follows.

PROC GCHART DATA = *name*;

VBAR|HBAR *chart-variable/ options*;

where:
　　chart-variable represents each bar

Selected Appearance Options

CAXIS=*color*　　(axis color)
COUTLINE=*color* (bar outline color)
CTEXT=*color*　　(text color)

PATTERNID=GROUP|MIDPOINT|SUBGROUP (specifies when to change
　　　　　　　　　　　　　　　　　　　　　　　　pattern definition)
CFRAME=color　　(background color)
FRAME　　　　　　(draw frame around graphics output area

Selected Statistical Calculation Options

FREQ=*numeric-variable*　　(identifies variable used to weight each observation)
G100　　　　　　　　　　　　(calculates percentages separately for each group value)
SUMVAR=*numeric-variable* (identifies analysis variable)
TYPE=*statistic*

where:

　　statistic is one of the following:
　　CFREQ
　　CPERCENT
　　FREQ
　　MEAN
　　PERCENT
　　SUM

Selected Statistical Display Options

CFREQ
CPERCENT
FREQ
MEAN
NOSTATS   (does not print default statistical table - HBAR only)
PERCENT SUM

Selected Midpoint Options

DISCRETE   (treats numeric variables as discrete values for defining
                            bar midpoints
MIDPOINTS=*value-list*   (orders bars based on specified values)

Selected Grouping Options

GROUP=*variable*   (groups bars according to variable specified)
SUBGROUP=*variable*   (divides bars into segments)

Selected Axes Options

GAXIS=AXIS*n*   (assigns AXIS*n* definition to GROUP axis)
MAXIS=AXIS*n*   (assigns AXIS*n* definition to bar midpoint axis)
RAXIS=AXIS*n*   (assigns AXIS*n* definition to response variable axis)

MINOR=*n*   (signifies the number of minor tick marks between
                            major tick marks on response axis)

ASCENDING   (positions bars in ascending order of chart statistic)
DESCENDING   (positions bars in descending order of chart statistic)

In the sections to follow, we will present examples of horizontal and vertical bar charts that are commonly used in reporting survey research findings. Consult *SAS/GRAPH Software: Reference* for a full description of all PROC GCHART options and capabilities. Our approach will be to illustrate the fundamentals of PROC GCHART and then to extend the basic example by customizing the output based on the principles of graphical excellence.

Basic Horizontal Histogram

We will illustrate the use of PROC GCHART to generate a basic horizontal histogram or bar chart to show frequency counts and percentages with the following survey question.

Figure 8-8: Survey Example for Bar Charts

14. How important is it to you to take part in college life beyond attending class?

> 1 Not Important
> 2 Somewhat Important
> 3 Important
> 4 Very Important

In the program to follow note that the HBAR statement is used to request a horizontal bar chart and identify the variable for which bars are created to represent each value. For example, the statement **HBAR SEX** would create a bar chart with two bars, one for males and one for females. By default, SAS will create a histogram to show a frequency distribution of the variables specified on the HBAR or VBAR statement.

SAS Code for Basic Horizontal Bar Chart

```
libname db 'PB HD:stud exp svy';

proc format;
   value $q14f '1' = 'Not Impt.'
               '2' = 'Somewhat Impt.'
               '3' = 'Important'
               '4' = 'Very Impt.';

proc gchart data =db.survey96;
hbar q14;
label q14 = 'Level Impt.';
format q14 $q14f. ;
title1 'Output 8-4: Default Horizontal Bar Chart';
title3
'How Important is it to you to Take Part in College Social Life?';
run;
quit;
```

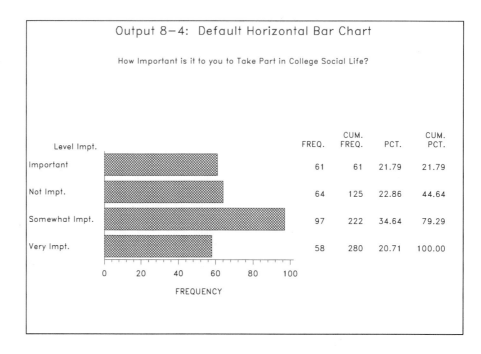

Output 8−4: Default Horizontal Bar Chart

How Important is it to you to Take Part in College Social Life?

Level Impt.		FREQ.	CUM. FREQ.	PCT.	CUM. PCT.
Important		61	61	21.79	21.79
Not Impt.		64	125	22.86	44.64
Somewhat Impt.		97	222	34.64	79.29
Very Impt.		58	280	20.71	100.00

FREQUENCY

The basic horizontal bar chart shown in **Output 8-4** is easy to generate as it requires only two PROC GCHART statements. The PROC GCHART defaults, however, do not produce an aesthetically pleasing graph that exemplifies principles of graphical excellence. The histogram shown in **Output 8-4** would be improved by

- Eliminating the vibrating cross-hatching patterns used with each bar

- Reducing the unnecessary detail on the horizontal response axis

- Ordering the bars by level of importance rather by the default alphabetic order of the bar labels.

The deficiencies noted in **Output 8-4** will be remedied in the program to follow. The PATTERN statement will be used to override the default black and white cross-hatching with a solid gray color. In addition, the COUTLINE = BLACK option defines the color outline of the gray bars. By default, SAS will order bar charts according to the alphabetic order in which PROC FORMAT assigned labels or data values if a format was not specified. Bars can also be ordered with the ASCENDING or DESCENDING option on the HBAR or VBAR statement. In this case, none of these three ordering options will provide the desired bar order. The MIDPOINTS = label option is used on the HBAR statement to order the bars in the desired sequence. Note that the label values are the value labels specified by PROC FORMAT. The horizontal response axis values can be controlled with the

RAXIS= options on the HBAR or VBAR statement. We can also control the number of minor tick marks with the MINOR=*number* option. Lastly, we can specify the size of text in TITLE statements with the HEIGHT= parameter.

SAS Code for Enhanced Basic Horizontal Bar Chart

```
pattern1 c=grayaa v=s;

proc gchart data =db.survey96;
hbar q14/midpoints='Not Impt.' 'Somewhat Impt.' 'Important'
              'Very Impt.' coutline=black
                    raxis=0 to 100 by 10 minor=0;
label q14 = 'Level Impt.' ;
format q14 $q14f. ;
title1 h=2 'Output 8-5: Customized Basic Horizontal Bar Chart';
title3 h=1
'How Important is it to you to Take Part in College Social Life?';
run;
quit;
```

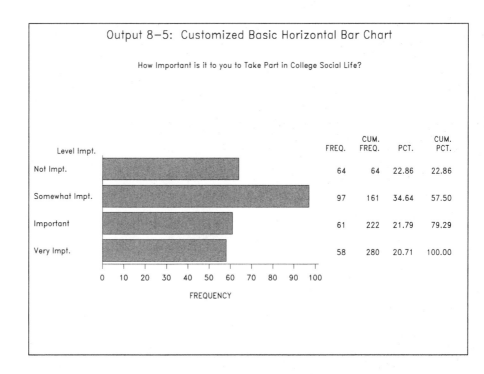

Output 8–5: Customized Basic Horizontal Bar Chart

How Important is it to you to Take Part in College Social Life?

Level Impt.	FREQ.	CUM. FREQ.	PCT.	CUM. PCT.
Not Impt.	64	64	22.86	22.86
Somewhat Impt.	97	161	34.64	57.50
Important	61	222	21.79	79.29
Very Impt.	58	280	20.71	100.00

Bar Chart of Groups

It is often interesting to generate a set of bars for two or more classification groups (race, sex, team, etc.) on the same graph. Bar charts are grouped using the GROUP= option on the VBAR or HBAR statement as shown in next example. It is important to note that by default SAS calculates percentages and cumulative frequency statistics for all groups combined rather than for each group individually. Users will almost always want these statistics to be calculated for each group *separately*, and this is accomplished with the G100 option. With the G100 option, percentages will total 100% for each group separately. The PATTERNID = option is used to control the assignment of patterns to individual bars or groups. The PATTERNID = MIDPOINT option instructs SAS to change patterns for every bar. The PATTERNID = GROUP option value will change the pattern value when group values change. To illustrate a bar chart with grouped data, we will graph separately for two values of AGEGRP the survey question shown in **Figure 8-8.** The results are shown in **Output 8-6**.

SAS Code for Bar Chart of Groups

```
libname db 'PB HD:stud exp svy';

 proc format;
  value $q14f '1' = 'Not Impt.'
              '2' = 'Somewhat Impt.'
              '3' = 'Important'
              '4' = 'Very Impt.';

  value agegrp 16-25  = '16-25'
               26-high = '26-Up';

pattern1 c=grayff v=s;
pattern2 c=grayaa v=r3;
pattern3 c=grayaa v=s;
pattern4 c=gray22 v=s;

proc gchart data =db.survey96; where age > .;
hbar q14/group=age g100
        midpoints='Not Impt.' 'Somewhat Impt.' 'Important'
                  'Very Impt.'
          coutline=black raxis=0 to 100 by 10 minor=0
                  patternid=midpoint;
label q14 = 'Level Impt.'
      age = 'Age';
format q14 $q14f. age agegrp. ;
title1 h=2 'Output 8-6: Horizontal Bar Chart With Group Dimension';
title3 h=1.75
'How Important is it to you to Take Part in College Social Life?';
title4 h=1 'by Age Group';
run;
quit;
```

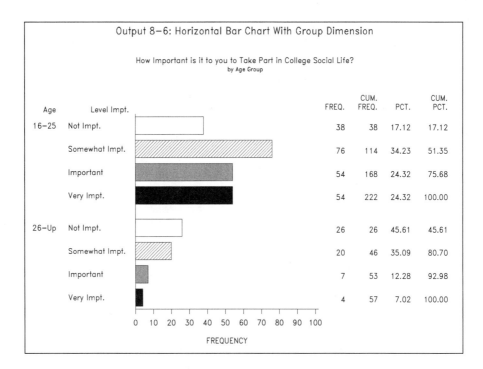

Output 8–6: Horizontal Bar Chart With Group Dimension

How Important is it to you to Take Part in College Social Life?
by Age Group

Age	Level Impt.		FREQ.	CUM. FREQ.	PCT.	CUM. PCT.
16–25	Not Impt.		38	38	17.12	17.12
	Somewhat Impt.		76	114	34.23	51.35
	Important		54	168	24.32	75.68
	Very Impt.		54	222	24.32	100.00
26–Up	Not Impt.		26	26	45.61	45.61
	Somewhat Impt.		20	46	35.09	80.70
	Important		7	53	12.28	92.98
	Very Impt.		4	57	7.02	100.00

FREQUENCY

TIP: Selecting Graphics Color Schemes

It is always desirable to use color schemes that have intuitive appeal to readers. With black and white graphics, gray scale patterns are preferable to stark black and white cross-hatching. In the preceding example, we used increasing levels of gray scale darkness to represent increasing levels of importance.

Horizontal Bar Chart of Means

In addition to histograms of frequency counts and percentages, PROC GCHART can produce charts to show sums and means. This type of bar chart requires the specification of an analysis variable with the SUMVAR=*variable* option on the VBAR or HBAR statement. The type of statistic (SUM, MEAN, FREQ, PERCENT) is also specified on the VBAR or HBAR statement. The default statistic is FREQ. The next program will continue to use the survey question shown in **Figure 8-8,** and we will create a chart to show mean hours of employment (WRKHRS) for each value of Q14 (importance of social life).

SAS Code for Horizontal Bar Chart of Means

```
libname db 'PB HD:stud exp svy';

 proc format;
  value $q14f '1' = 'Not Impt.'
              '2' = 'Somewhat Impt.'
              '3' = 'Important'
              '4' = 'Very Impt.';

pattern1 c=grayaa v=s;

proc gchart data =db.survey96;
hbar q14/sumvar=wrkhrs type=mean
        midpoints='Not Impt.' 'Somewhat Impt.' 'Important' 'Very Impt.'
        coutline=black ;
label q14 = 'Level Impt.'
      wrkhrs = 'Hrs Wrk';

format q14 $q14f. ;
title1 h=1.75 'Output 8-7: Horizontal Bar Chart of Means';
title3 h=1.5
'How Important is it to you to Take Part in College Social Life?';
title4 h=1 'by Hours of Employment';
run;
quit;
```

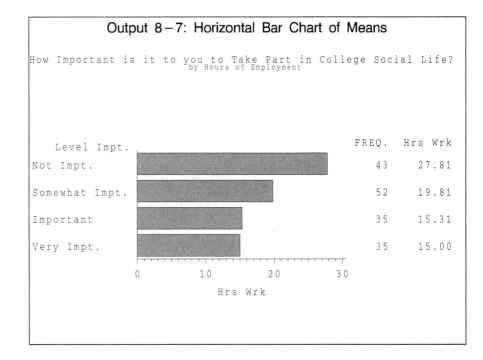

Vertical Bar Chart of Means

Vertical histograms are created with the VBAR statement. A nice feature of the VBAR statement is that it can print the results of the summary statistic at the top of each bar. This action is accomplished by specifying the name of the statistic (SUM, MEAN, PERCENT, and FREQ) on the VBAR statement. Note that this specification is in addition to the TYPE= *statistic*. The program to follow illustrates this procedure with the results shown in **Output 8-8.**

SAS Code for Vertical Bar Chart of Means

```
proc gchart data =survey;
vbar q14/sumvar=hrswrk type=mean mean
        midpoints='Not Impt.' 'Somewhat Impt.' 'Important' 'Very Impt.'
        coutline=black raxis= 0 to 30 by 5 minor=4;
label q14 = 'Level Impt.'
      hrswrk = 'Hrs Wrk';
format q14 $q14f. hrswrk 4.1;
title1 h=1.75 'Output 8-8: Vertical Bar Chart of Means';
title3 h=1.5
'How Important is it to you to Take Part in College Social Life?';
title4 h=1 'by Hours of Employment';
run;
quit;
```

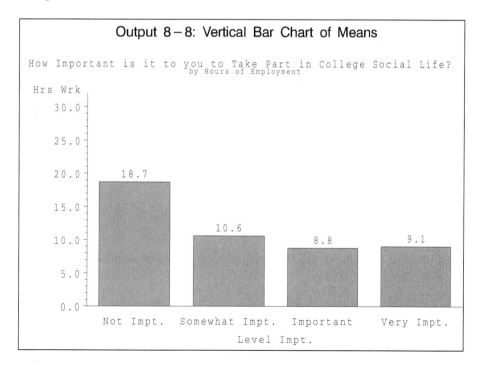

Output 8 – 8: Vertical Bar Chart of Means

Charting Multiple Response Items

PROC GCHART is designed to create histograms in which the bars represent the values of a *single* variable. When reporting survey data for numerous items related to a common dimension, the use of multiple bar charts to report each item separately not only wearies the reader, but may also obscure important relationships. A good technique for presenting this type of data is to transform the data so that multiple response variables can be captured as one variable and then displayed on a single graphic. This type of data manipulation involves reshaping variables into observations.[5] To illustrate this process, we will reshape the four survey items shown in **Figure 8-9** and report them as a single dimension.[6] The results are shown in **Output 8-9**.

Figure 8-9: Survey Items for Reshaping Data Example

19. How would you rate each of the following at UNCA?	Poor	Fair	Good	Excellent
a. Your academic experience	1	2	3	4
b. Your out-of-class experience	1	2	3	4
c. Your overall experience	1	2	3	4
d. The quality of undergraduate students	1	2	3	4

In the following program, the four variables Q19A-Q19D will be represented by a single variable named DIM that will be assigned *values* to capture the original Q19A-Q19D *variable* names. A second new variable (PERCENT) will be created to report the percentage of respondents providing the response "Good" or "Excellent" to each of the four dimensions. PERCENT will be dichotomously scored (100/0) to compute this percentage by using the mean statistic. Note the use of the OUTPUT and KEEP statements to reshape the data set.

---

5 This technique is also described in Chapter 5, "Data Manipulation," and Chapter 7, "Creating Custom Tables with PROC TABULATE."

6 A similar example that uses array processing to reduce coding is shown in Chapter 7. See Output 7-24 and its source code.

SAS Code for Reshaping Multiple Response Items

```
libname db 'PB HD:stud exp svy';

pattern1 c=grayaa v=s;

 data survey(keep=percent dim);
length dim $18;
   set db.survey96(keep=q19a q19b q19c q19d);
dim = 'Academics';
if q19a in ('4','3') then percent = 100;
else if q19a in ('1','2') then percent = 0;
else percent = . ;
output;

dim = 'Out-of-Class Exper';
if q19b in ('4','3') then percent = 100;
else if q19b in ('1','2') then percent = 0;
else percent = . ;
output;

dim = 'Overall Exper';
if q19c in ('4','3') then percent = 100;
else if q19c in ('1','2') then percent = 0;
else percent = . ;
output;

dim = 'Student Quality';
if q19d in ('4','3') then percent = 100;
else if q19d in ('1','2') then percent = 0;
else percent = . ;
output;

proc gchart data =survey;
hbar dim/sumvar=percent type=mean descending nostats coutline=black
        frame raxis=0 to 100 by 10 minor=1;
label   DIM = 'Dimension'
      PERCENT = 'Percent';
title1 h=1.7 'Output 8-9: Reshaping Data to Graph Multiple Variables';
title3 h=1.5 'Student Rating of College Experience';
title4 h=1.3 'Percent Reporting "Good" or "Excellent"';
run;
quit;
```

TIP: OUTPUT Statement and Missing Data Caution

When using the OUTPUT statement to transform multiple variables into multiple observations with a new common variable, one must be very careful with missing data. If any of the original variables have missing data, the most recent value of the new *common* variable will be retained and output. In the preceding program, note how the new common variable PERCENT was set to missing prior to each new OUTPUT statement. Without this action, the values of PERCENT for records with missing values for Q19A-Q19D would continue to retain the last value of PERCENT rather than to take a missing value. The reinitialization of PERCENT to missing before each OUTPUT statement ensures that missing data are properly handled. A second technique for handling missing data is to eliminate all records with missing data in the original variables. This was the approach used in the Chapter 7 reshaping examples, but it may not always be a good strategy, depending upon the question structure.

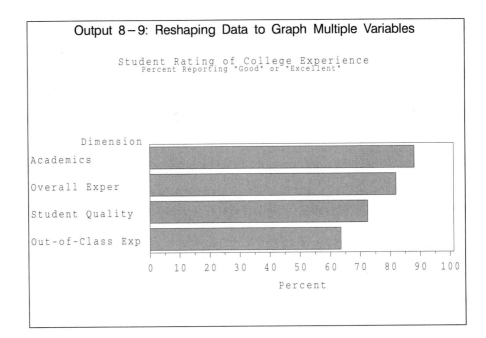

Output 8–9: Reshaping Data to Graph Multiple Variables

Subdivided Bar Charts

Subdivided bar charts allow you to subgroup *individual* bars into two or more segments to show group differences. As a graphics presentation device, the subdivision of bars with more than *two* segments is generally a bad idea as it is very difficult to interpret the spatial representation of three or more subgroups. However, in survey research applications, employing segmented bar charts can be a useful technique under two conditions.

* The variables can be grouped into two categories.

* Interpretation of individual bar segments is of secondary importance to the total bar length.

Using these guidelines, you can describe differences among numerous groups, each represented by a single bar arranged in descending or ascending order. Vertical or horizontal reference lines can also be added to help the reader understand at a glance which groups are above or below the sample average. In previous chapters, we have discussed the advantages of reporting four- or five-point Likert-type items as a combined "good/excellent" or "agree/strongly agree" single percentage measure rather than as mean scores or percentages for all scale values. With subdivided bars, the percentage of "good" and percentage of "excellent" can be reported separately within each bar with the total bar length representing the combined "good/excellent" percentage statistic.

Subdivided bar charts are created with the SUBGROUP=*variable* option on the HBAR or VBAR statement. We will demonstrate this procedure with the survey question shown in **Figure 8-10**.

Figure 8-10: Survey Example for Subdivided Bar Chart

B01. How would you rate advising in your major?

1 Poor
2 Fair
3 Good
4 Excellent

As shown in the previous example, we will need to reshape the survey data into two new variables. The original "Excellent" or "Good" values will be transformed into a new variable called RESPONSE that has values of **G** or **E**. This RESPONSE variable will be used as the subgroup variable for segmenting the bars. We will compute the percentage of observations responding "good" or "excellent" by calculating the mean of a dummy coded (0/100) variable PERCENT. The values of PER-CENT will be calculated and output separately for each value of RESPONSE **G** or **E**. Since we are using the mean trick[7] to calculate percentages, it is necessary to calculate these statistics prior to the PROC GCHART step and then to use the SUM statistic in PROC GCHART to display the results. By using the SUM statistic on a single summary measure for each bar, we are able to "trick" SAS into producing the desired table.

The program to follow will perform these operations with the resulting histogram shown in **Output 8-10**.

SAS Code for Subdividing Bars

```
libname library 'pb hd':prog assess svy';

data survey;
set library.progeval(keep=major qb01);
if qb01 = ' ' then delete;
if qb01 = '3' then percent= 100;
else if qb01 in ('1','2','4') then percent = 0;
response = 'G';
output;
if qb01 = '4' then percent= 100;
else if qb01 in ('1','2','3') then percent = 0;
response = 'E';
output;

proc summary data = survey nway;
  class major response;
  var percent;
  output out = stats
  mean = ;

pattern1 c=gray99 v=s;
pattern2 c=grayff v=e;
```

---

[7] This technique is also discussed in Chapters 5, 6, and 7.

```
proc gchart data = stats;
axis1 order = (0 to 90 by 10)
      minor = (n=1)
      label = ('Percent');
hbar major/sumvar=percent subgroup=response type=sum nostats
          descending vref=59 coutline=black frame raxis=axis1
          nolegend;
note h=.9  move=(15,22) c=gray99 'Excellent'
           move=(50,22) c=black  'Good'
           move=(60,9)  c=black  'Univ Average';
title1 h=1.5 'Output 8-10: Segmented Bar Chart';
title2;
title3 h=1 'Student Rating of Advising by Major';
title4 h=.75 '(Percent Responding "Excellent" or "Good")';
run;
quit;
```

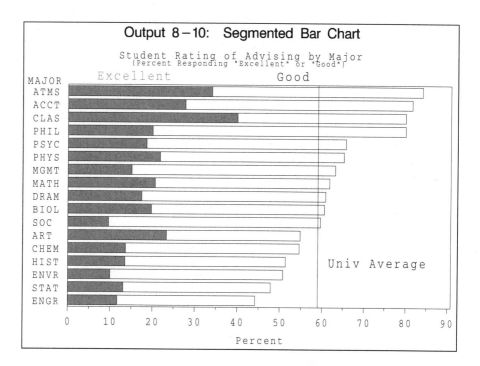

Note the use of the FRAME and NOSTAT options to frame the graphics area and to suppress the default statistical table respectively. For this type of graph, the frequency and percentage statistics would take a lot of room and add little useful information. The FRAME option has the useful effect of keeping the reader's eye focused on the graphics space. We also chose to suppress the default legend as it tends to make the reader work harder than necessary to understand the graph. NOTE statements are used to label the segments above of the first bar.

Plots

PROC GPLOT is used to create two-dimensional scatter and line plots with SAS/GRAPH. PROC GPLOT has two major advantages over commonly used point-and-click spreadsheet or graphical software packages:

- PROC GPLOT can easily create a second right-hand vertical axis.

- SAS/GRAPH will automatically update the graphical display with new data by simply adding fresh observations to the data source file and reexecuting the program.

PROC GPLOT is an easy-to-use procedure for generating basic plots, but it takes knowledge of SYMBOL, NOTE, and AXIS statements to create user-friendly output that embodies the principles of graphical excellence. We will illustrate the use of PROC GPLOT to create three types of plots.

- Scatter plots (data points not connected)

- Single-line plots (data points connected with a line)

- Multiple-line plots (data points connected for more than one data series or group value).

The basic form of PROC GPLOT and its commonly used options follows.

PROC GPLOT DATA = *name*;

To set the left vertical axis and horizontal axis

    PLOT *vertical_var*horizontal_var/options*;

To plot two variables by the values of a third group variable

    PLOT *vertical_var*horizontal_var=group_var/options*;

To add right vertical axis

    PLOT2 *vertical_var*horizontal_var/options*;

Appearance Options

AREAS=*n*	(fills area below plot line *n* with a pattern)
NOLEGEND	(suppresses printing of default legend)
OVERLAY	(places two or more plot requests on same axes)

Reference lines

AUTOHREF	(draws reference lines at all major horizontal tick marks)
AUTOVREF	(draws reference lines at all major vertical marks)
CHREF=*color*	(color of horizontal reference line)
CVREF=*color*	(color of vertical reference line)
GRID	(draws reference lines at all major tick marks for both axes)
HREF=*value-list*	(horizontal scale values for drawing reference lines)
VREF=*value-list*	(vertical scale values for drawing reference lines)
LHREF=*line-type*	(horizontal line type: solid, dotted, etc.: values 1-46)
LVREF=*line-type*	(vertical line type: solid, dotted, etc.: values are 1- 46)

Axes Options

HAXIS=*value-list*	(specifies major tick marks for horizontal axis)
VAXIS=*value-list*	(specifies major tick marks for vertical axis)
HAXIS=AXIS*n*	(assigns AXISn statement to HAXIS)
VAXIS=AXIS*n*	(assigns AXISn statement to VAXIS)
HMINOR=*n*	(n is number of minor tick marks for horizontal axis)
VMINOR=*n*	(n is number of minor tick marks for vertical axis)
HZERO	(horizontal axis scaling begins at 0)
VZERO	(vertical axis scaling begins at 0)
CAXIS=*color*	(specifies color for horizontal and vertical axes)
CFRAME=*color*	(background color for axes area)
CTEXT=*color*	(specifies color for all axis text color)
FRAME	(draws frame around axes area)

Consult *SAS/GRAPH Software: Reference* for a full description of the GPLOT procedure.

Basic Scatter Plot

To illustrate the creation of a basic scatter plot using the PROC GPLOT defaults, we will plot the frequency distribution of employment hours (HOURS) for college students enrolled full-time (CREDHRLD >= 12). Before we can plot this distribution, we must first calculate the frequencies by summing the number of observations for each value of the variable CREDHRLD. In this example, we will accomplish this task by creating a counter variable N with a value of 1 for each observation. PROC SUMMARY[8] will then be used to sum N for each value of CREDHRLD. The last step will be to use PROC GPLOT to graph the SUMMARY output data set to produce the desired graph. The plot results are shown in **Output 8-11**.

---

8 PROC MEANS could also be used to perform these calculations.

SAS Code for Basic Scatter Plot

```
libname library 'pb hd:new student svy';

data newsvy;
   set library.DB96(keep=hours credhrld);
if credhrld >= 12;
n = 1;

proc summary data = newsvy nway;
   class hours;
   var n;
   output out = stats
   sum = ;

proc gplot data = stats;
plot n*hours;
title1 'Output 8-11: Basic Scatterplot';
title2 'How Many Hours Per Week Will You be Employed on Average?';
title3 '(Full-Time Students Employed One or More Hrs Per Week)';
run;
quit;
```

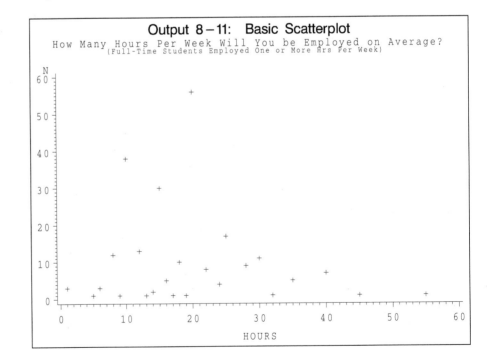

Enhanced Scatter Plot

To illustrate the power of SAS/GRAPH to achieve principles of graphical excellence, we will enhance the basic scatter plot shown in Output 8-11 by customizing the following:

- Plot symbol (SYMBOL statement)

- Vertical and horizontal axis scaling (AXIS statement)

- Axis labeling (AXIS statement)

- Horizontal reference line (HREF= option)

- Placement of explanatory text in graphics output area (NOTE statement)

- Right-hand vertical axis (PLOT2 statement)

- Framing of graphics output area (FRAME option).

These customization features are illustrated using the program for the previous example. The DATA step is the same, but the SAS/GRAPH enhancements are highlighted. The improved scatter plot is shown in **Output 8-12**.

SAS Code for Enhanced Scatter Plot

```
symbol1 c=gray00 v=diamond;

proc gplot data = stats;
axis1 order=(0 to 60 by 5) minor=(number=1)
      label=('Employment Hours');
axis2 order=(0 to 60 by 10) minor=(number=1);
plot n*hours/frame href=18.4 haxis=axis1 vaxis=axis2;
plot2 n*hours/vaxis=axis2;
note h= 1.2 move=(32,10) langle=90 'Mean Hours';
title;
title1 'Output 8-12: Improved Scatter Plot';
title2 'How Many Hours Per Week Will You be Employed on Average?';
title3 '(Full-Time Students Employed One or More Hrs Per Week)';
run;
quit;
```

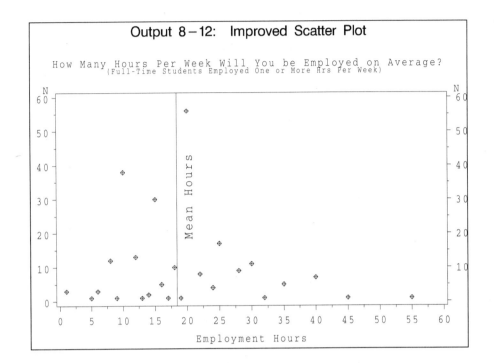

Output 8–12: Improved Scatter Plot

Line Plots

GPLOT line graphs are very useful for displaying group differences on a time-series dimension. This type of graph can also be used to plot the frequency distributions for multiple samples or groups. Data points are connected with the SYMBOL INTERPOL= option. The INTERPOL option has 16 different interpolation values. The most commonly used are shown in the following table.

INTERPOL=	Description
JOIN	Connects data points with straight lines
BOX	Creates box-and-whisker plot
R	Fits linear regression line
RCLM	Fits regression line and confidence limits for mean predicted values
RCLI	Fits regression line with individual predicted values
SPLINE	Connects data points with a smoothed line using a spline routine

The first line plot example is based on the same survey project that was used in the preceding PROC GPLOT examples. We now wish to show the trend in mean employment hours over time. This survey has been repeated annually and the data are stored in separate SAS data sets for each year. For convenience, a variable YEAR is included in each data set. This example will illustrate the use of the SYMBOL statement to connect the data points with a solid gray straight line. We will also illustrate the PROC GPLOT GRID option to draw reference lines automatically at every horizontal and vertical axis major tick mark. The results are shown in **Output 8-13**.

SAS Code for Simple Line Plot with Grid Marks

```
libname library 'pb hd: new student svy';

data newsvy;
  set library.db90(keep=hours year credhrld)
      library.db91(keep=hours year credhrld)
      library.db92(keep=hours year credhrld)
      library.db93(keep=hours year credhrld)
      library.db94(keep=hours year credhrld)
      library.db95(keep=hours year credhrld)
      library.db96(keep=hours year credhrld);
if credhrld >= 12;

proc summary data = newsvy nway;
  class year;
  var hours;
  output out = stats
  mean = ;

symbol1 v=square c=gray00 i=join line=1 w=2;

proc gplot data = stats;
axis1 order=(0 to 25 by 5) minor=(number=1) label=('Hrs Wrk');
 plot hours*year/frame grid vaxis=axis1;
 plot2 hours*year/vaxis=axis1;
title1 'Output 8-13: Line Plot With Grid';
title2 'New Student Employment Hours by Year';
run;
quit;
```

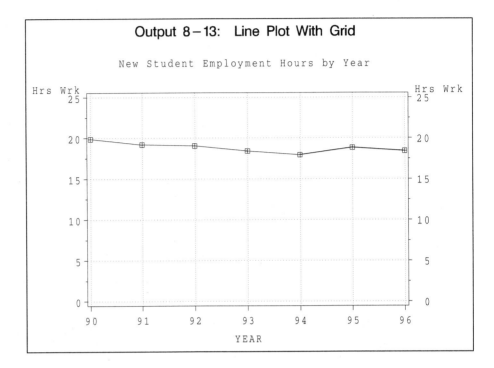

Output 8−13: Line Plot With Grid

Line Plots with Fill Pattern

Fill patterns are used to assign a pattern design and to color the graphics space below the plot line. Three steps are required to create this type of graph.

- Use the INTERPOL= option on the SYMBOL statement to connect the data points.

- Assign a PATTERN*n* statement to describe the fill area design (solid, vertical lines, etc.) and color.

- Use the AREAS=*n* option to designate which line values are to be used for a given PATTERN statement.

Although this type of plot is easy enough to generate with SAS/GRAPH, it has a very low data-to-ink ratio and probably should be used only sparingly, if at all, in written publications. This principle of graphical excellence can probably be relaxed for graphics used in oral presentations since the audience typically has only a short period of time to view any particular graphic before the speaker moves on to the next point. The use of color in this type of area plot may be an effective device for focusing the attention of the audience on the data presentation.

The following example is based on the same survey variables used in the preceding examples and illustrates the use of the AREAS= option and PATTERN statement to create a fill pattern beneath the GPLOT line. The DATA step is not shown. The results are shown in **Output 8-14**.

SAS Code for Line Plot with Fill Pattern

```
symbol1 v=none i=spline c=gray00;
pattern1 v=s c=grayff;

proc gplot data = stats;
axis1 order=(0 to 25 by 5) minor=(number=1) label=('Hrs Wrk');
  plot hours*year/frame vaxis=axis1 areas=1;
  plot2 hours*year/vaxis=axis1;
title1 'Output 8-14: Line Plot With Fill Pattern';
title2 'New Student Employment Hours by Year';
run;
quit;
```

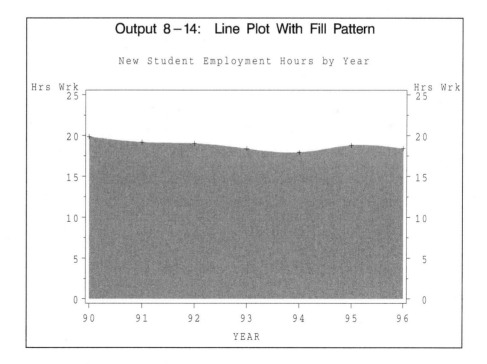

Output 8-14: Line Plot With Fill Pattern

New Student Employment Hours by Year

Multiple-Line Plot

Separate plot lines can be generated for each value of a group variable on the same graph by using the following form:

PLOT *vertical-var*horizontal-var=group-var;*

To distinguish among the different group variable values, we need separate SYM-BOL statements to define plot symbols, color, and line characteristics. We will build on the previous example by adding a new variable (TSTUDENT) to illustrate this process. TSTUDENT has two values (**transfer** and **freshmen**) and the program to follow will generate a separate line plot to show mean hours of employment over time for each TSTUDENT category. Note the inclusion of TSTUDENT on the CLASS statement to calculate the summary plot variables.

As a principle of graphical excellence, we never use legends to identify for the reader which plot lines represent each group value. The problem with using legends is that it makes the reader work harder than necessary to understand the most important elements of the graph. The NOLEGEND option is used on both the PLOT and the PLOT2 statements to suppress the printing of a default legend.[9] The NOTE statement is used to write text on the graphic to label each plot line with the proper group label. The NOTE statement provides us with full control over the placement, color, font, angle, and size of text labels needed to make user-friendly graphics. NOTE statements are discussed in more detail in the next section.

SAS Code for Multiple Line Plot

```
libname library 'pb hd:new student svy';

data newsvy;
  set library.db90(keep=hours tstudent year credhrld)
      library.db91(keep=hours tstudent year credhrld)
      library.db92(keep=hours tstudent year credhrld)
      library.db93(keep=hours tstudent year credhrld)
      library.db94(keep=hours tstudent year credhrld)
      library.db95(keep=hours tstudent year credhrld)
      library.db96(keep=hours tstudent year credhrld);
if credhrld >= 12;
```

---

[9] We suggest using the default legend in early runs of your graph to make sure you label each line correctly when you are using NOTE statements.

```
proc summary data = newsvy nway;
  class year tstudent;
  var hours;
  output out = stats
  mean = ;

symbol1 v=diamond c=gray00 i=join line=2 w=4;
symbol2 v=circle  c=gray00 i=join line=1 w=4;

proc gplot data = stats;
axis1 order=(0 to 25 by 5) minor=(number=1) label=('Hrs Wrk');
  plot hours*year=tstudent/frame vaxis=axis1 nolegend;
  plot2 hours*year=tstudent/   vaxis=axis1 nolegend;
  note move = (40,19) c=gray00 h=1.2 'Transfer'
       move = (40,13) c=gray00 h=1.2 'Freshmen';
title1 'Output 8-15: Multiple Line Plot';
title2 'New Student Employment Hours by Type and Year';
run;
quit;
```

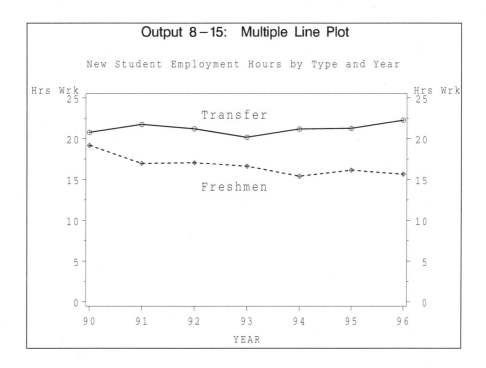

Labeling Data Points with Notes

The ability to use NOTE statements to write text in the graphics output area is a critical skill for achieving graphical excellence with SAS/GRAPH. In the graphical display of summary measures, a powerful two-dimensional visual presentation can often be made by providing text labels beside each data point. This type of graphic is especially useful when each data point represents an organizational entity known to the reader (e.g., department, college, state, sales region). To illustrate this process of labeling data points with NOTE statements, we will use the survey question shown in **Figure 8-11**, a two-part item that is designed to measure both student *use* and perceived *quality* of campus programs and services.

Figure 8-11: Survey Question for Labeling Data Points

22. We would like to ask you a few questions about general University programs and services. Please indicate how frequently you have used each service and the quality of the service you received.

	a. How often have you used this service?				b. How would you rate the quality of the service you received?				
	Never	Seldom	Occationally	Frequently	Poor	Fair	Good	Excellent	Not Applic
a. Library	1	2	3	4	1	2	3	4	5
b. Career Planning	1	2	3	4	1	2	3	4	5
c. Counseling Ctr	1	2	3	4	1	2	3	4	5
d. Outdoor Recreation	1	2	3	4	1	2	3	4	5
e. Health Service	1	2	3	4	1	2	3	4	5
f. Reading Lab	1	2	3	4	1	2	3	4	5
g. Writing Lab	1	2	3	4	1	2	3	4	5
h. Math Lab	1	2	3	4	1	2	3	4	5
i. Dining Hall	1	2	3	4	1	2	3	4	5
j. Snack Bar	1	2	3	4	1	2	3	4	5
k. Cafe Ramsey	1	2	3	4	1	2	3	4	5
l. Bookstore	1	2	3	4	1	2	3	4	5

To create a two-dimensional graph of use and perceived quality for each of the 12 campus services, it will be necessary to transform these 24 variables into 3 variables to represent: SERVICE, USE, and RATING. After using PROC SUMMARY to compute mean scores, each observation will represent one of the campus service units with a measure of USE and RATING on the same record. This process of handling multiple response items is also discussed in Chapters 5 and 7.

SAS code for Labeling Data Points

```
libname db 'PB HD:stud exp svy';

data survey(keep=service use rating);
length service $30 rating 4 use 4 ;
  set db.survey96(keep= q22a_a q22a_b q22a_c q22a_d q22a_e q22a_f
                        q22a_g q22a_h q22a_i q22a_j q22a_k q22a_l
                        q22b_a q22b_b q22b_c q22b_d q22b_e q22b_f
                        q22b_g q22b_h q22b_i q22b_j q22b_k q22b_l);

service = 'Library';
use  = q22a_a;
rating = q22b_a;
output;

service = 'Career planning/placement';
use  = q22a_b;
rating = q22b_b;
output;

service = 'Counseling center';
use  = q22a_c;
rating = q22b_c;
output;

service = 'Outdoor recreation activities';
use  = q22a_d;
rating = q22b_d;
output;

service = 'Health service';
use  = q22a_e;
rating = q22b_e;
output;

service = 'Reading lab';
use  = q22a_f;
rating = q22b_f;
output;
```

```
service = 'Writing lab';
use   = q22a_g;
rating = q22b_g;
output;

service = 'Math lab';
use   = q22a_h;
rating = q22b_h;
output;

service = 'Dining hall';
use   = q22a_i;
rating = q22b_i;
output;

service = 'Dante''s snack bar';
use   = q22a_j;
rating = q22b_j;
output;

service = 'Cafe ramsey';
use   = q22a_k;
rating = q22b_k;
output;

service = 'Bookstore';
use   = q22a_l;
rating = q22b_l;
output;

data final;
   set survey;
if rating = 5 then rating = . ;

proc summary nway data = final;
   class service;
   var use rating;
   output out = stats(drop=_type_ _freq_)
   mean = ;

symbol1 c=gray00 h=1.0 v=diamond;
```

```
proc gplot data = stats;
axis1 label=('Frequency of use') w=2 order=(1 to 4 by .5) minor=none;
axis2 label=('Rating') w=2 order=(1 to 4 by .5) minor=none;
plot rating*use/haxis=axis1 vaxis=axis2 vref=3.0 cvref=grayaa href=3.0
            chref=grayaa nolegend;
plot2 rating*use/nolegend vaxis=axis2;
note h=.75 c=gray00 move=(45,12)                'Dining Hall'
                    move=(22,15) langle=340     'Career Planning'
                    move=(16,17) langle= 45     'Counseling Ctr'
                    move=(36,15) langle=0        'Snack Bar'
                    move=(41,17)                 'Health Service'
                    move=(65,19)                 'Library'
                    move=(28,18) langle= 45     'Math Lab'
                    move=(22,16) langle=350     'Outdoor Rec'
                    move=(10,14) langle=340     'Reading Lab'
                    move=(21,17) langle= 45     'Writing Lab'
                    move=(32,17) langle= 45     'Cafe Ramsey'
                    move=(59,15) langle=0        'Bookstore'
         h=1. c=grayaa move=(17,23)   'Lower Use/Higher Quality'
                    move=(60,23)                 'Higher Use/'
                    move=(60,22)                 'Higher Quality'
                    move=(60,7)                  'Higher Use/'
                    move=(60,6)                  'Lower Quality'
                    move=(17,7)      'Lower Use/Lower Quality'
         h=.75      move=(7,2)                   'Never'
                    move=(29,2)  'Seldom' move=(50,2) 'Occasionally'
                    move=(75,2)                  'Frequently'
                    move=(2,4)                   'Poor'
                    move=(2,9)                   'Fair'
                    move=(2,15)                  'Good'
                    move=(2,21)                  'Excel-'
                    move=(2,20)                  'lent' ;

title1 h=1 'Output 8-14: Labeling Data Points';
title2 H=1
'Use of Programs and Services by Perceived Quality of Service';
run;
quit;
```

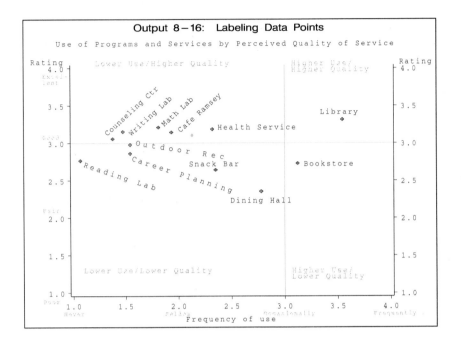

Output 8–16: Labeling Data Points

Resizing Graphics Output

A primary distinction between the proper use of tables and graphs is the concept that tables outperform graphs in reporting *exact numbers* while graphs are best suited for showing *relationships* among variables. Based on the default page-size dimensions of most output devices, there is a natural tendency for users to create graphics images that are *larger* than necessary to communicate relationships among variables. In reporting survey data, it is often interesting to incorporate graphics output into word processing text files or presentation software such as PowerPoint or Persuasion. Both of these applications usually require modifying the default page-size height and width to avoid distortion or truncation of the original graphical image. To properly resize SAS/GRAPH output we must control the following dimensions:

- Vertical size (VSIZE=*n*)

- Horizontal size (HSIZE=*n*)

- Number of vertical cell positions (VPOS=*n*)

- Number of horizontal cell positions (HPOS=*n*)

The physical height and width of the graphics output area as measured in cells (CELLS), inches (IN), or centimeters (CM) is defined by the VSIZE and HSIZE parameters. The first step in resizing SAS/GRAPH output is to determine the default VSIZE or HSIZE and VPOS or HPOS values for your particular graphics output device. This information can be obtained by executing the GTESTIT procedure (see **Figure 8-3**). While the graphics output page size is determined by the HSIZE or VSIZE parameters, it is important to proportionally adjust the VPOS or HPOS values to avoid distortion in the graphical image. As you *decrease* the physical vertical or horizontal page size, you should proportionately *increase* the number of VPOS or HPOS values to create a larger number of cells that are smaller in size.

To illustrate this process, we will use the MACCOLOR device shown in **Figure 8- 3**. Assume that we want to reduce the size of the graphic by 15% on both vertical and horizontal dimensions. From the PROC GTESTIT log shown in **Figure 8-3** we can determine the default page size and the VPOS or HPOS specifications. The calculations used to reduce the graphic by 15% are shown in the table below.

Parameter	Default	Ratio	Resized Value
HSIZE	7.37	.85	6.26
VSIZE	5.30	.85	4.51
VPOS	24	1.15	28
HPOS	75	1.15	86

The following GOPTIONS statement will decrease the default MACCOLOR horizontal and vertical page size by 15% and increase the number of vertical or horizontal cells by 15% to minimize any distortion that might occur as a result of resizing the graph.

```
goptions device=maccolor hsize=6.26 vsize=4.51
         vpos=28 hpos=86
```

Afterword The Practice of Survey Research: Concluding Remarks

"Better information is worthless; only better decisions are worth anything."
B. H. Mahon

As modes of intellectual inquiry, survey research and statistical analysis are tools for seeking truth. The design, execution, analysis, and presentation of survey projects is an exciting field of endeavor on two dimensions. On a *personal* level, survey research provides the analyst with the intellectual joy of being able to constantly test his or her notions of how social forces interact and affect the world in which we live. *Organizationally*, survey results can provide the impetus for structural change, as well as influence policy and redirect the allocation of resources.

This book has concentrated on the use of SAS software to accomplish the technical aspects of survey implementation, data analysis, and the presentation of survey findings in well-designed tables and graphs. However, the development of a quality information product does not in itself ensure that it will be used in appropriate ways. The effective use of the survey product may depend on the ability of the researcher to communicate with the recipients of the information. B. H. Mahon, (1977, p.299) in a speech to the Royal Statistical Society nearly a quarter of a century ago, articulated five experience-based rules for communicating the results of statistical analysis that are still imperative today. (Recipients of survey information are referred to as *customers*.)

1. Put yourself in the customers' shoes. Tell them only what is of interest to them and say it in language they understand.

2. Respect the customers. Listen to them, even if they seem to hold some absurd views; there is always something to be learned. Remember that a man may have six crackpot ideas and one very good one.

3. Indulge the customers' irrationalities if it costs nothing. If they will adopt a method you propose provided some useless (but harmless) modification is made, give way.

4. Be persistent. But do not expect a medal when, after a long struggle, everyone comes round to your view. The speed of metamorphosis from contentious point to "well known fact" is amazing; suddenly everyone really knew it all along.

5. Spare no trouble with presentation. Concentrate on communicating a few essential points.

The continual expansion of the Internet and the World Wide Web provides survey researchers with powerful new tools of the trade that have an *unknown* social psychology. Surveys conducted through electronic mail and Web sites have the great advantage of getting respondents to perform their own data entry. Electronic surveys provide enormous cost savings in postage, printing, labor, and materials, and they make it possible for researchers to provide data daily to policy makers as the survey is being conducted. As with any new technology, there are a number of problems that have yet to be resolved in conducting surveys through the World Wide Web: access, security, and communications with respondents to name a few. As a dissemination device, the Web offers a great cost savings in making the survey results available to a large number of people. We have found it effective to use electronic mail to send executive summaries of survey projects to a large number of people and to provide recipients with the opportunity to request a hard copy of the full report or to point them to a World Wide Web URL where they can view the detailed findings of the survey report online.

The production of formalized research papers and studies is a sometimes necessary but often insufficient method of putting survey results to use. The formal report is useful to document the project for future reference and to establish the credibility of the study. It is through letters, memos, "hallway" and group conversations, however, that users of survey data are most likely to internalize the meaning of the results and make decisions that lead to actions. The development of multimedia and presentation software provides researchers with powerful tools for presenting survey results to both large and small groups. The combination of interesting, revealing data with well-designed color graphics and text slides creates a compelling presentation that engages and focuses the attention of the audience.

Appendix A

A Beginner's Guide to SAS-L

Want to know how you can tap into a wealth of SAS knowledge that's shared by SAS users all over the world? NESUG[1] offers you an electronic mail conversation between NESUG founding member Ray Pass and Mike Davis.

Ray: A BIG Hearty Welcome to SAS-L, Mike! But why'd you wait so long to join?

Mike: I thought you had to be part of a university to join. I also thought that you had to open a subscription to a commercial timesharing service that charged you by the minute, like a cab.

Ray: Nah, SAS-L is just a list of e-mail IDs of persons who are SASaholics like us. If your corporate e-mail system has gateways to X.400 e-mail systems, you can join in. MCIMail, Compuserve, or other commercial subscription service account and a modem work just fine for getting onto SAS-L. If you can tie into something whose name contains NET, MAIL, or 400, you probably have all you need to subscribe to SAS-L. Besides timesharing services, you can also join via the Internet or Usenet.

Mike: The other reason why I took so long to subscribe was that I thought SAS-L was just a glorified CB radio.

Ray: Glad you wised up, Mike. SAS-L is a forum for SAS users to communicate on a variety of SAS topics. The most common form of communication is Q&A. Someone posts a question like:

I'm having trouble getting SAS/GRAPH to print to my Smith-Corona typewriter using SAS Release 1.26 on my VIC-20 with 8K of memory, and Toyota jumper cables. The only output I get is in inverse obverse reverse converse mode. Has anyone solved this problem?

Then a dozen users post their solution. Some always ask questions. Others always seem to find time to supply answers.

---

[1] NorthEast SAS Users Group.

Another valuable use for SAS-L is "code swapping" or "codefilching" as the case may be. I've gotten quite a few invaluable tidbits from the list, and hope that I've contributed a few. Archives of SAS-L messages are kept which can be queried by date, time period, or literal text string, and there is also an archive of valuable sections of SAS code maintained at the University of Illinois at Chicago that SAS-L'ers routinely contribute to, and extract from. Other types of messages on SAS-L are announcements on various topics including regular postings by those who get and share the SAS Institute press releases. Often SAS-L breaks into a high-spirited "debate" on topics ranging from SAS fee structures, to the elusive "best" platform, to the color of the SUGI SAS-L BOF T-shirt.

Bylaws do exist governing the use of the different networks, but there are no stringent rules other than courtesy and common sense. Mike, why don't you tell our NESUG buddies how to sign up for SAS-L.

Mike: One way to subscribe to SAS-L is to put the request in the body of an e-mail message and send it to one of the following addresses:

listserv@vm.marist.edu	Marist University
listserv@vtvm1.cc.vt.edu	Virginia Tech
listserv@uga.cc.uga.edu	University of Georgia
listserv@AKH-WIEN.AC.AT	University of Vienna

The message should include the following line ONLY:

SUBSCRIBE SAS-L *your name*

You'll soon receive confirmation of your subscription. Then just sit back and read. To post a message to SAS-L, send mail to one of the following addresses:

sas-l@vm.marist.edu	Marist University
sas-l@vtvm1.cc.vt.edu	Virginia Tech
sas-l@uga.cc.uga.edu	University of Georgia
sas-l@AKH-WIEN.AC.AT	University of Vienna

Use a subject line. If your subject line is "No Subject" many people will ignore your message.

Note: SAS-L is also available on Usenet. See comp.soft-sys.sas

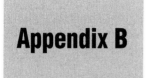

Appendix B

SAS® Resources on the Web

- SAS Institute maintains a Web site at
  http://www.sas.com/

- The SAS Web site includes technical support FAQ pages
  http://www.sas.com/service/techsup/faq/index.html

- Don Cram has notes on converting between Excel spreadsheets and SAS
  (both ways) at
  http://www-leland.stanford.edu/class/gsb/excel2sas.html

- Arnold Schick maintains libraries of SAS macros at
  http://members.tripod.com/~schick/m-index.html
  http://members.tripod.com/~schick/p-index.html

- The Claremont Graduate University maintains a beginner's guide to SAS at
  http://www.cgs.edu/acit/help/sas.html

Source: Tim Berryhill, SAS-L FAQ

Glossary

ANOVA

analysis of variance, a statistical method of breaking down variance into components. ANOVA is commonly used to investigate group differences and is related to multiple regression.

ASCIII

American Standard Code for Information Interchange, also used to describe text files that can be processed by almost all computer software.

Bar chart

also known as a histogram. A graphical display of quantitative information that uses rectangular figures with lengths proportional to the variable measured.

Chartjunk

term coined by Edward R. Tufte to describe poorly designed graphics that have one or more of the following characteristics: they use too much ink to describe a few numbers, they are reader unfriendly, or they attempt to describe differences with indecipherable graphical elements. Chartjunk is often a form of *unintentional* optical art.

Chi-square test

a statistical test for comparing frequency distributions.

Comma delimited

refers to a data file in which variables are separated by a comma. This type of file is a convenient way of importing and exporting data between SAS and spreadsheets or other types of programs.

Concatenate

the process of combining two or more items. In the analysis of survey data, one often needs to concatenate or append both variables and files. The concatenation function symbol (||) is used to combine two or more variables, as in `name=lasname||', '||firname`. Files are concatenated with the SET statement in a new DATA step. In the following example, the data set COMBINE is created by concatenating or appending the YEAR1, YEAR2, and YEAR3 data sets.

```
data combine;
    set year1  year2  year3;
```

Dillman Survey Process

refers to Don A. Dillman's classic work *Mail and Telephone Surveys: The Total Design Method*, which provides a widely used system for obtaining high response rates to mail surveys.

Dummy coding

a method of dichotomous coding that assigns a 1 or 0 to a variable to indicate the presence or absence of some characteristic. In this way, a demographic characteristic like sex can be treated as a numeric variable by creating a new variable FEMALE with values 1 and 0.

Histogram

See bar chart.

Independent *t*-test

a statistical procedure to compare the means of two independent samples. For example, a comparison of mean starting salaries for men and women could be analyzed with an independent *t*-test procedure (PROC TTEST).

Interval measurement (scales)

These scales have the qualities of nominal and ordinal scales with the additional feature of numerically equal scale value distances or intervals that reflect equal distances in the variable being measured.

Likert scale

a type of questionnaire attitude scale in which subjects indicate their level of agreement or disagreement with some dimension. Usually these scales have five, seven, or nine response categories.

Mean

usually refers to the arithmetic mean that is the commonly known average or mathematical center of the data.

Median

a type of average that represents the midpoint of the data in which one-half of the observations are below the median, and one-half are above the median.

Measures of central tendency

refers to the three types of *averages*: mean, median, and mode that provide a measure of central tendency.

Mode

an average that is defined as the value with the highest frequency of response. The mode is used mostly for descriptive purposes rather than for statistical tests.

Multiple regression

a statistical technique for analyzing the contributions of two or more dependent variables toward predicting or explaining variation in a single dependent variable.

Multiple-response item

a type of survey question in which respondents are asked to *mark all that apply*. While this question appears as a single item on the survey form, it is really a series of *dummy-coded* variables.

Nominal measurement: (scales)

the lowest level of measurement in which numbers are placed to distinguish objects, but do not themselves have inherent meaning. For example, various religious denominations could be coded on a survey form as (1,2,3 ...N).

Open-ended survey item

a type of survey question in which respondents are asked to write qualitative comments. This type of information, while tedious to process, often helps to explain the numerical results and is of interest to readers.

Ordinal measurement (scales)

assumes that the values of a scale can be rank ordered, but that the numbers neither represent absolute quantities nor have equal distance between values. For example, a scale with values 1=Poor 2=Fair 3=Good 4=Excellent is ranked ordered, but the difference between "Poor" and "Fair" may not be the same as the difference between "Good" and "Excellent."

Paired comparisons *t*-test

a statistical procedure to compare means of two dependent samples. For example, comparison of pre- and post- scores for each subject are dependent samples. In SAS, this type of test is done with PROC MEANS and not with PROC TTEST.

Random digit dialing

a telephone survey research technique that uses the computer to randomly generate the last four digits of phone numbers. The area codes and prefixes are selected based on the geographical area of the study. This technique is quick and easy, and it has great advantage of including unlisted and new numbers that may not be listed in published sources.

Random sample

a method of selecting a sample in which every unit of the population has an equal chance of being selected.

Response rate

the percentage of completed surveys returned for a mail survey project (n returned/n mailed)* 100. It is usually appropriate to adjust the value of n mailed for the number of respondents who did not have valid addresses.

Sampling error

the discrepancy between the observed sample estimates and the true population values.

SAS automatic variables

variables that are created by SAS and can be used in the DATA step to control which observations are output. Examples are IF FIRST.*varname* and IF LAST.*varname*, _N_, _TYPE_, and _FREQ_.

SAS Type I SS

Type I Sums of Squares (SS), also known as sequential sums of squares, are computed based on the order of class variables entered into the model. For balanced designs (equal classification group sizes), Type I SS and Type III SS are equal. Type III SS should be used for unbalanced designs.

SAS Type III SS

Type III Sums of Squares (SS) are part of the default PROC GLM output. In the computation of Type III SS, every class variable is treated as if it were entered last; thus the specification order on the MODEL statement does not affect the SS calculations. Type III SS should be used with unbalanced designs that have an unequal number of observations in class groupings.

Scale reliability

the accuracy or precision of a measuring instrument. Note that this is not the same as *validity*, which speaks to the nature and meaning of variables. With the SAS System, reliability can be estimated with Cronbach's coefficient alpha, which is a PROC CORR option (ALPHA).

Scatter plot

a graphical representation of data points to show relationships between two variables represented by horizontal and vertical axes.

Simple random sample

the most basic sampling design in which every element of the population has an equal chance of being selected into the sample.

Stratified random sample

a method of sampling in which the population can be subdivided into two or more mutually exclusive groups from which simple random samples are taken.

Standard deviation

a statistical measure of variability about a mean.

Summated scale

usually designed to measure an attitude dimension by asking respondents to indicate the extent to which they agree or disagree with a series of questionnaire items. The responses can be summed or averaged to yield a total summated scale score.

Supertable

term coined by Edward R. Tufte to describe a statistical table that provides the reader with a set of multiple data comparisons for a single dimension. Supertables have a reference-like quality based on the amount of information provided in an easy-to-read, attractive format.

References

Bertin, Jacques (1981), *Graphics and Graphic Information Processing*, Hawthorne, NY: Walter De Gruyter Inc.

Carpenter, Arthur L. and Charles E. Shipp (1995), *Quick Results with SAS/GRAPH Software*, Cary, NC: SAS Institute Inc.

Cody, Ronald P. and Jeffrey K. Smith (1991), *Applied Statistics and the SAS Programming Language, Third Edition*, Englewood Cliffs, N.J.: Prentice Hall, Inc.

Corning, Betsy (1994), "Designing and Producing Effective Graphs with SAS/GRAPH Software: Using Graphic Elements Effectively," *Observations*, Vol. 3, No. 2, 73-86.

Corning, Betsy (1994), "Designing and Producing Effective Graphs with SAS/GRAPH Software: Making Graphs Informative," *Observations*, Vol. 3, No. 3, 3-17.

Corning, Betsy (1994), "Designing and Producing Effective Graphs with SAS/GRAPH Software: Presenting Data Effectively," *Observations*, Vol. 3, No. 4, 4-20.

Dillman, Don A. (1978), *Mail and Telephone Surveys: The Total Design Method*, New York: John Wiley & Sons, Inc.

Ehrenberg, A.S.C. (1977), "Rudiments of Numeracy," *Journal of the Royal Statistical Society* (A), 140, 277-297.

Hatcher, Larry and Edward J. Stepanski (1994), *A Step-by-Step Approach to Using the SAS System for Univariate and Multivariate Statistics*, Cary, NC: SAS Institute Inc.

Keene, Tina (1991), "Computing Percentages with the TABULATE Procedure," *Observations*, Vol. 1, No. 1, 5-17

Littell, Ramon C., Rudolf J. Freund, and Philip C. Spector (1991), *SAS System for Linear Models, Third Edition*, Cary, NC: SAS Institute Inc.

Mahon, B.H. (1977), "Statistics and Decisions: The Importance of Communication and the Power of Graphical Presentation," *Journal of the Royal Statistical Society (A)*, 140, 298-323.

Salant, Priscilla and Don A. Dillman (1994), *How to Conduct Your Own Survey*, New York: John Wiley & Sons, Inc.

SAS Institute Inc. (1989), *SAS/STAT User's Guide, Version 6, Fourth Edition, Volume 1* and *Volume 2*, Cary, NC: SAS Institute Inc.

SAS Institute Inc. (1990), *SAS Guide to TABULATE Processing, Second Edition*, Cary, NC: SAS Institute Inc.

SAS Institute Inc. (1990), *SAS Language: Reference, Version 6, First Edition*, Cary, NC: SAS Institute Inc.

SAS Institute Inc. (1990), *SAS Procedures Guide, Version 6, First Edition*, Cary, NC: SAS Institute Inc.

SAS Institute Inc. (1990), *SAS/GRAPH Software: Reference, Version 6, First Edition, Volume 1* and *Volume 2*, Cary, NC: SAS Institute Inc.

SAS Institute Inc. (1994), *Introduction to Market Research Using the SAS System*, Cary, NC: SAS Institute Inc.

SAS Institute Inc. (1997), *SAS Macro Language: Reference, First Edition*, Cary, NC: SAS Institute Inc.

Scheaffer, Richard L., William Mendenhall, and Lyman Ott (1979), *Elementary Survey Sampling*, 2nd Edition, North Scituate, MA: Duxbury Press.

Sharpe, Jason R. (1994), "Ordering Data Values: Dummy Data and Mapping Techniques," *Observations*, Vol. 3, No. 2, 61-72.

Spector, Paul E. (1993), *SAS Programming for Researchers and Social Scientists*, Newbury Park, CA: Sage Publications.

Tufte, Edward R. (1983), *The Visual Display of Quantitative Information*, Cheshire, Conn.: Graphics Press.

Tufte, Edward R. (1997), *Visual Explanations: Images and Quantities, Evidence and Narrative*, Cheshire, Conn.: Graphics Press.

About the Author

Archer R. Gravely is Director of Institutional Research and University Planning Officer at The University of North Carolina at Asheville. He has conducted nearly 100 survey research projects since 1981 using the SAS System. *Your Guide to Survey Research Using the SAS® System* is the product of extensive survey research experience combined with nearly ten years of teaching workshops on the topic and a strong interest in the principles of graphical excellence and table design.

Index

*Welcome * Bienvenue *Willkommen *Yohkoso * Bienvenido*

SAS® Publications Is Easy to Reach

Visit our SAS Publications Web page located at www.sas.com/pubs/

You will find product and service details, including

- **sample chapters**
- **tables of contents**
- **author biographies**
- **book reviews**

Learn about

- **regional user groups conferences**
- **trade show sites and dates**
- **authoring opportunities**
- **custom textbooks**
- **FREE Desk copies**

Order books with ease at our secured Web page!

Explore all the services that Publications has to offer!

Your Listserv Subscription Brings the News to You Automatically

Do you want to be among the first to learn about the latest books and services available from SAS Publications? Subscribe to our listserv **newdocnews-l** and automatically receive the following once each month: a description of the new titles, the applicable environments or operating systems, and the applicable SAS release(s). To subscribe:

1. Send an e-mail message to **listserv@vm.sas.com**

2. Leave the "Subject" line blank

3. Use the following text for your message:

  subscribe newdocnews-l *your-first-name your-last-name*

  For example: subscribe newdocnews-l John Doe

  Please note: newdocnews-l ◄——— that's the letter "l" not the number "1".

For customers outside the U.S., contact your local SAS office for listserv information.

Create Customized Textbooks Quickly, Easily, and Affordably

SelecText™ offers instructors at U.S. colleges and universities a way to create custom textbooks for courses that teach students how to use SAS software.

For more information, see our Web page at **www.sas.com/selectext/**, or contact our SelecText coordinators by sending e-mail to **selectext@sas.com**.

You're Invited to Publish with SAS Institute's User Publishing Program

If you enjoy writing about SAS software and how to use it, the User Publishing Program at SAS Institute Inc. offers a variety of publishing options. We are actively recruiting authors to publish books, articles, and sample code. Do you find the idea of writing a book or an article by yourself a little intimidating? Consider writing with a co-author. Keep in mind that you will receive complete editorial and publishing support, access to our users, technical advice and assistance, and competitive royalties. Please contact us for an author packet. E-mail us at **sasbbu@sas.com** or call 919-677-8000, then press 1-6479. See the SAS Publications Web page at **www.sas.com/pubs/** for complete information.

Read All about It in *Authorline*®!

Our User Publishing newsletter, *Authorline*, features author interviews, conference news, and informational updates and highlights from our User Publishing Program. Published quarterly, *Authorline* is available free of charge. To subscribe, send e-mail to **sasbbu@sas.com** or call 919-677-8000, then press 1-6479.

See *Observations*®, Our Online Technical Journal

Feature articles from *Observations*®: *The Technical Journal for SAS*® *Software Users* are now available online at **www.sas.com/obs/**. Take a look at what your fellow SAS software users and SAS Institute experts have to tell you. You may decide that you, too, have information to share. If you are interested in writing for *Observations*, send e-mail to **sasbbu@sas.com** or call 919-677-8000, then press 1-6479.

Book Discount Offered at SAS Public Training Courses!

When you attend one of our SAS Public Training Courses at any of our regional Training Centers in the U.S., you will receive a 15% discount on any book orders placed during the course. Each course has a list of recommended books to choose from, and the books are displayed for you to see. Take advantage of this offer at the next course you attend!

SAS Institute Inc.
SAS Campus Drive
Cary, NC 27513-2414
Fax 919-677-4444

E-mail: sasbook@sas.com
Web page: www.sas.com/pubs/
To order books, call Book Sales at 800-727-3228*
For other SAS Institute business, call 919-677-8000*

* **Note:** Customers outside the U.S. should contact their local SAS office.